M000307744

GOVERNING SPIRITS

GOVERNING SPIRITS

Religion, Miracles, and Spectacles
in Cuba and Puerto Rico, 1898–1956

᠅ REINALDO L. ROMÁN ᠅

The University of North Carolina Press
Chapel Hill

© 2007 The University of North Carolina Press
All rights reserved
Manufactured in the United States of America

Designed by Heidi Perov
Set in Electra and Bureau Empire

The paper in this book meets the guidelines for permanence and
durability of the Committee on Production Guidelines for
Book Longevity of the Council on Library Resources.

Library of Congress Cataloging-in-Publication Data

Román, Reinaldo L., 1970–
Governing spirits : religion, miracles, and spectacles in
Cuba and Puerto Rico, 1898–1956 / Reinaldo L. Román.
p. cm.
Includes bibliographical references and index.
ISBN 978-0-8078-3141-0 (cloth : alk. paper)
ISBN 978-0-8078-5836-3 (pbk. : alk. paper)
1. Cuba—Religion. 2. Cuba—Religious life and customs.
3. Puerto Rico—Religion.
4. Puerto Rico—Religious life and customs.
I. Title. BL2566.C9R66 2007
200.97291'09041—dc22
2007023195

cloth   11 10 09 08 07   5 4 3 2 1
paper   11 10 09 08 07   5 4 3 2 1

for Alexa and Lucía,
who have shared the joys and afflictions

CONTENTS

ILLUSTRATIONS

ACKNOWLEDGMENTS

In writing this book, I incurred debts in several countries. (The total varies depending on how one negotiates the count). Although the account I offer draws principally from archival and periodical sources, I am deeply grateful to the Cubans and Puerto Ricans who spoke to me about intimate matters of faith and healing. Without their insights, candor, and aid, mine would be a poorer story. Yolanda Trull and her husband, Juan, put me up in Santiago de Cuba on more than one occasion. They arranged for my introduction to palo and espiritismo de cordón, and tracked down documents on my behalf. In Puerto Rico, my debts run deep and wide. I am particularly grateful to Vuestra Madre's followers in San Lorenzo, Cayey, Yabucoa, and surrounding towns who spoke to me about Elenita's ministry and the sanctuary in Montaña Santa. If these people remain anonymous, it is out of regard for their privacy. As I note in the text, Elenita's identity remains disputed. The faithful must negotiate a difficult transaction between obedience to the church and the conviction that the Virgin has graced barrio Espino with her presence since 1899. Finally, I must thank Carmen Julia Vázquez, who granted me several interviews to speak about her aunt "La Samaritana" and who shared with me her own manuscript papers.

I owe debts of gratitude to researchers and archivists at a variety of institutions. I am especially grateful to Ernesto Chávez Alvarez, Tomás Fernández Robaina, Amparo Hernández Denis, Fe Iglesias, Olga Portuondo Zúñiga, Belkis Quesada, Isabel Reyes, María Antonia Reynosa, and the staff members of the Archivo Nacional de Cuba, Archivo Provincial de Santiago de Cuba, Biblioteca Nacional José Martí, Centro de Antropología de Cuba, Instituto de Literatura y Lingüística, and Instituto de Historia de Cuba. In Puerto Rico, I depended on the generosity of Javier Almeyda Loucil, Else Zayas León, and the librarians and archivists at the Archivo General de Puerto Rico, Archivo Diocesano de la Arquidiócesis de San Juan, Centro de Estudios Avanzados del Caribe, and the Centro de Investigaciones Sociales and Colección Puertorriqueña of the Universidad de Puerto Rico.

In completing the book manuscript, I had the assistance of numerous scholars who guided my investigations, commented on drafts, and honed my thinking. At the University of California in Los Angeles, I had the unstinting encouragement of José C. Moya, Robert Hill, and Vinay Lal. In subsequent years, I have depended on the counsel of Dain Borges, Arcadio Díaz-Quiñones, Fernando Picó, and especially Stephan Palmié. I also want to thank Rosanne Adderley, Robin Derby, Juan José Baldrich, Humberto García Muñiz, Alejandro de la Fuente, David Sartorius, Jalane Schmidt, Xavier Totti, and Kevin Yelvington, who commented on chapters of this book when they were in nascent form.

Among my colleagues in the Department of History at the University of Georgia, I owe special thanks to Kathleen Clark, Claudio Saunt, and Pamela Voekel, who have heard more about this project than collegiality could ever require. I also want to acknowledge my intellectual and personal debts to a group of scholars who are now scattered in universities across North America, Europe, and the Caribbean: Manuel Barcia, Alejandra Bronfman, Susan Gantt, Jorge Giovanetti, Marial Iglesias, Adrián López Denis, Mark Mairot, Marc McLeod, José Ortega, and Rebecca J. Scott. Besides offering ideas, suggestions, and research materials, they have sustained me in ways that I shall not detail, lest the recitation become confessional.

I am grateful to the Ford Foundation, the Social Science Research Council, the Institute for Latin American Studies at the University of North Carolina in Chapel Hill, and the History Department and Willson Center for Humanities and Arts at the University of Georgia for the financial support and leave time that made my work possible. I must thank also UNC Press senior editor Elaine Maisner; were it not for her direction and patience, I could not have written this book. Finally, I want to thank UNC Press editor Mary Caviness and Carol White and Kathy Gilbreath for sorting out my lapses and formatting errors in spite of pressing deadlines.

GOVERNING SPIRITS

INTRODUCTION

"Tú sabes cómo es la gente aquí." In the last months of 1995, my mother, Ana Isabel García, repeated that sentence nearly every time we talked on the telephone. Her bemused "you know how people are here" punctuated the conversation whenever we spoke of the *chupacabras* or the rumors surrounding the latest animal killings. She offered the refrain as a sociological truism, a knowing echo of the often-heard assertions linking the depredations of the "goatsucker" to the proclivities of Puerto Rico's people. Puerto Ricans, she reminded no one in particular, were as given to overindulgence in supernaturalism as they were susceptible to fads. A monstrous celebrity like the chupacabras exploited both weaknesses. The truism was more camouflage than self-contempt, however; it provided cover for the white lies we traded. The introductory "you know" was a discreetly reassuring fib aimed at placating my immigrant's yearning for enduring insights into the island's affairs. The lilting "aquí" (literally, here), that shibboleth of Puerto Rico's cultural nationalists, validated our nativist claim to the chupacabras despite emerging evidence of its itinerant disposition.

My mother did not dismiss the news of mysterious animal deaths. Unlike other critics, she never referred to the reports as fantasies. But she saw the media's sensational coverage and the appetites it whetted as symptoms of excesses that afflicted and defined the island. Even as it drew precious fluids, from backyard animals no less, the chupacabras revealed Puerto Ricans' prodigality. Opportunism, credulity, and disbelief spilled over with every turn of the narrative. She assured me that she was not surprised when politicians and pundits and *desordenados* (literally, disorderly but also disrespectful people) began to appear wherever the chupacabras was spotted, looking to conjure opportunities amid the din. Political stalemate, a stifling water shortage, and crime's rising tide were suffocating the island. The chupacabras offered a respite. Surely, elected officials were grateful for headlines that drew attention away from their failings. Newspaper editors had reasons to rejoice, too. The mysterious attacks were doing more for circulation figures than another exposé of corruption or scandalous politicking ever could. At least that is what our long-distance accounting suggested.

The evidence of collusion between the press and politicians may have been circumstantial, but it was abundant. The first paper to offer daily coverage of the chupacabras was *El Vocero*, a San Juan tabloid that still prints its headlines in blood-red lettering. *El Vocero's* reputation for yellow journalism gave us pause, even if we, like most other readers, did not know of the events of 1975. That was the year when the Association of Journalists reprimanded *El Vocero* reporter Augusto R. Vale Salinas for his lurid stories concerning the first of the island's twentieth-century bloodsuckers. Association president Tomás Stella charged that Vale's coverage of the "vampire" that "terrorized" the western town of Moca "harked back" to an unspecified time when "falsehood and obscurantism" went uncontested. The editors of *El Vocero* denied the charges: sensational or not, the reports met a public need, and they urged the authorities to find answers. The editors conceded, however, that the stories had helped the daily reach a circulation of nearly 90,000 copies during its first year of publication.[1]

If the throngs of reporters that covered the chupacabras in the 1990s recalled *el Vampiro de Moca* and the censures that followed it, they cast their recollections aside to tend to the business at hand. After the mayor of Canóvanas began organizing safaris, even the editors of the *San Juan Star*, who had largely refused to join the fray, ran several pieces on the subject. These ranged from glib op-ed columns to historically minded news analyses; the latter cited experts such as the founding director of the Institute of Puerto Rican Culture, archaeologist Ricardo Alegría. Alegría reportedly contended that the sightings had an ancestry "that [stemmed] back to the beginnings of Puerto Rican society and the cultures from which modern Puerto Rican [sic] was formed."[2] In the next months, the chupacabras made appearances in all Puerto Rican dailies and the *New York Times*, the *Washington Post*, *El Fígaro*, and the *Herald Tribune*, to name only a few notable newspapers.

Mayor José Ramón "Chemo" Soto announced on 25 October 1995 that he intended to take the chupacabras alive. He would use nets, tranquilizer darts, and a large cage adorned with steel scrolls, evidently the handiwork of a burglar-bars shop. Initially, Soto explained his extraordinary undertaking in the usual fashion: the people of Canóvanas, a northeastern municipality located a short distance from the jagged edge of the capital's sprawl, had suffered significant material losses and incalculable anxieties. As first executive, Soto was duty-bound to protect the citizenry. Canóvanas's residents deserved answers. In addition, Soto noted, an expedition could yield invaluable scientific data. Rumor had it that unseen scientists working for an agency of the U.S. government had engineered the predator in a genetics laboratory. Extraterrestrial origins were alleged, too. According to Mayor Soto, as unlikely an advocate of the Enlightenment as has been seen in recent years, such contentions required investigation.

Soto's plan called for the deployment of a small force of twenty off-duty police officers supplemented with personnel from the Civil Defense and Natural Resources Department. On the designated evening, however, self-appointed volunteers outnumbered the mayor's men ten to one. More than 200 citizens, many of them carrying sticks, machetes, and firearms, scattered to search for the chupacabras as journalists watched over the scene. As many had hoped, a group of hunters caught a glimpse of the chupacabras near a creek in barrio Campo Rico. Contrary to the mayor's wishes, they did not attempt to capture the predator. Instead, they fired their weapons at once. *El Vocero*, writing in a strained law-and-order register, censured the volunteers for endangering nearby residents. (Soto claimed later that area residents were responsible for the shots.) As luck would have it, the volley missed neighbors and chupacabras alike. The shooters, a group that did not include Soto or his subalterns, saw a shadowy figure slip into a large drainage pipe. The evasive maneuver was a credit to the predator's well-publicized agility. The flight also called attention, albeit indirectly, to the water shortage that afflicted Canóvanas and that Soto had denounced days earlier. The chupacabras had escaped through a dry sewerage line.[3]

In the months and years that followed, the hunt for the mysterious killer revealed grievances of other sorts. Melba Rivera, Soto's political rival, condemned the expedition as a publicity stunt. She called for an investigation to determine if the mayor had misused public funds to finance what she described as a staged act resembling "an old episode of Fantasy Island."[4] But the denunciation did not have the desired effects. No such inquest was carried out, and the voters reelected Soto in 1996, 2000, and 2004. Meanwhile, the chupacabras went on a killing spree that left behind thousands of carcasses with telltale puncture wounds at the neck and occasional signs of mutilations. Attacks were reported in every one of Puerto Rico's municipalities, including the islands of Vieques and Culebra. By May 1996, the international press and Spanish-language television networks based in the United States were reporting sightings in Costa Rica, the Dominican Republic, Mexico, and the United States.[5]

To describe the profusion of chupacabras sightings, commentators employed metaphors of contagion. A chupacabras "fever" was said to be spreading, presumably among consumers of the media's tainted products. Others, writing in the editorial pages of newspapers and electronic bulletin boards, suggested that panic had seized hold of people predisposed by history to maladies of ratiocination. In Puerto Rico, however, the hunt for the chupacabras gave rise to satirical performances that respectable newscasters portrayed as inconsequential sideshows. In these episodes, witnesses and bystanders did more than read and watch; they lampooned the mechanisms through which their demands—for explanations, protection, and government transparency—were transformed into news items, turned into cause for fruitless inquiries by committee, and transmogrified into the stuff of partisan jockeying. One might argue, as I do in the epilogue, that through their participation in safaris, broadcasts, and the circulation of rumors, citizens ensnared government officials and engaged each other in open-ended dialogues about the political order. These conversations differed from others that broached such topics. Among other things, they could not be brought to a close with sound bites and partisan formulae.

Although oppositional notes were discernible in the citizens' satire, the chupacabras stories did more than voice critiques of "millennial capitalism" and Puerto Rico's enduring subjection to neocolonial rule.[6] The rumors surrounding Puerto Rico's bloodsuckers pointed at occult economies and the history of imperial designs, as Robin Derby has shown.[7] But they also spoke crassly in a tongue that scholarly translations have muffled. The dominant interpretation describes Puerto Rico's bloodsuckers in a neofunctionalist idiom that limits expressive possibilities. The chupacabras is said to be one more monster in the bestiary that latter-day capitalism has roused around the globe.

Governments, Citizens, and Superstitions

Although this is not a book about the chupacabras, the analyses that follow betray its passage through Puerto Rico and its far-flung networks. It was in talking and musing about the elusive killer that I came to the central concern of this account. Put plainly, these pages deal with the government of so-called superstitions in Puerto Rico and Cuba during the first half of the twentieth century. In the episodes discussed below, all of them media events in some fashion, journalists, politicians, intellectuals, and the public—a corporate actor that the various parties invoked to tendentious ends—engaged in complex exchanges over matters of belief. As in the case of the chupacabras, issues of citizenship and governance were implicated. In these instances, however, direct linkages were forged between mis-belief, fantasy, and religious forms that authorities found objectionable. African-derived "witchcraft," Spiritism, popular Catholicism, and the alleged jumble of fraudulent healing practices going by the catchall *curanderismo* fell under re-newed suspicion in the early twentieth century shortly after the formal declara-tion of religious freedom and the expansion of citizenship rights.

Citizenship claims, the flash point of bloody struggles and protracted socio-political impasses in nineteenth-century Cuba and Puerto Rico, remained con-tentious long after the end of slavery and Spanish colonialism. To understand the urgency that surrounded such conflicts, one must consider that questions about who counted as a fully recognized member of society implied the inter-rogation of race-making practices, nation-building ideologies, and the prospects for "progress."[8]

At the turn of the century, progress was a commodious term; it implied infra-structural development, technological innovation, and liberal political reforms. But progress also meant moral uplift; to seek it was to call for the "regeneration" of societies that observers denounced as morally corrupt. In Cuba and Puerto Rico, critics presented wizards, healers, visionaries, and saints as obstacles to re-generation and potential threats to public order. Suspicion that superstitious men and women could embrace misguided agendas gave rise to anxieties about the governments' capacity to keep moral and political order. The overriding con-cerns, however, had as much to do with the meanings attached to superstition as they did with fear of what misbelievers could attempt: what did the persistence of superstitions at the dawn of the twentieth century *say* about the country, its citi-zens, and their future? Ironically, many of those accused of retarding progress saw themselves as agents of moral advancement. Cuban and Puerto Rican Spiritists, for example, included reformists who campaigned against slavery and Spanish colonialism and clamored for scientific education, the separation of church and state, freedom of worship, penal reforms, and the end of capital punishment.[9]

Far from settling questions about the status of nonwhites, suffrage rights, and the extent of individual freedoms, the occupations of Cuba and Puerto Rico by the United States after the campaign known in North America as the Spanish-American War aggravated old wounds and introduced new uncertainties. The military intervention of the United States hastened the demise of Spanish colo-nialism but left Spain's last American colonies in disarray.

The American occupation threw Cuba's political future into question. After fighting three wars in the name of emancipation and independence, Cubans had to ponder under what terms the United States would countenance the establishment of their republic. Moreover, the arrival of American troops exacerbated tensions that had been mounting for years along the racial fault lines of the revolutionary coalition. Even before the U.S. intervention, a conservative faction in the patriots' camp had sought to marginalize "rustic" blacks and mulattoes who had risen to positions of authority in the Liberation Army. As a result, men like Quintín Bandera, an enormously popular black general whom many regarded as a hero, were stripped of command for transgressions that underscored their alleged lack of culture and moral judgment. Maneuvers of this sort ensured the primacy of "civilized" and mostly white men in postwar politics without appearing to invalidate the claims that held the insurgency together. Cuban patriots maintained that through their multiracial struggles they had transcended the racism of the colonial era.[10]

After 1898, influential American actors encouraged a politicized and racialized reexamination of Cuban culture and legitimated the further devaluation of purportedly primitive, African-derived ways.[11] Maj. Gen. Leonard Wood, the island's military governor, opposed Cuba's immediate independence. Instead, he favored a period of tutelage that would end when Cubans had demonstrated their fitness for self-rule, preferably by demanding annexation to the United States.[12] In such a context, "superstitions" could and were construed as obstacles to republican ambitions since they could be counted as evidence that Cubans were unprepared for the responsibilities of citizenship. Moreover, those who opposed universal (male) suffrage could cite alleged connections between blackness and "African" superstition in making a case against black and mulatto voters.

In Puerto Rico, where anticolonial uprisings had not unleashed revolutionary upheavals, the arrival of American troops led to the establishment of a regime that left the island's political status ill-defined. Puerto Rico was neither annexed as a state of the union nor declared an independent country. The Organic Act of 1900, known as the Foraker Law after its congressional sponsor, formalized many of the measures that the island's military governors imposed during a two-year period of rule by decree, but it failed to articulate a clear vision for the future. Article 2 placed the "citizens of Puerto Rico," an entity with no international juridical standing, "under the protection" of the United States. The formula signaled the primacy of American authority in the island but was otherwise short on specifics. Like Cubans, Puerto Ricans were given to understand that a long-term political resolution would require a period of tutelage during which their culture and competence would be assessed.

The provisions of the Foraker Law left few doubts that the new colonial officials regarded Puerto Ricans as a people unfit for self-rule. The law placed Puerto Rico under the direct authority of the Congress of the United States and granted the federal executive ample powers. The act provided for the president to appoint the island's governor and executive council. Thirty-five members of the House of Representatives were to be elected through a suffrage restricted to literate, propertied males.[13] Overall, Puerto Ricans lost rights they had secured from Spain under the terms of the 1897 Autonomic Charter.

Some of the issues that the American occupations raised were addressed in subsequent legislation that recognized new prerogatives while creating novel ways of regulating citizens' engagements in politics and civil society. Cuba became a republic in 1902 following the ratification of a constitution that recognized the suffrage rights of all men. Puerto Ricans attained similar voting rights in 1904. And after two decades of uncertainty, the Jones Act of 1917 extended statutory U.S. citizenship to all Puerto Ricans, albeit without resolving the political status of the island. But even these measures did not settle the social and political unrest surrounding citizenship. Contests over political participation and individual rights and day-to-day demands for equality persisted, often erupting far from the halls in which laws were signed.

Recent studies of the republic have shown that Cubans' understandings of citizenship and race were renegotiated during the first decades of the twentieth century amid scandals involving African-derived religious practices. In 1904, only two years after the inauguration of a racially inclusive republic, newspaper headlines decried the abduction and murder of a girl named Zoila. It was alleged that a group of *negros brujos* (black wizards) with connections to a *cabildo* (social and religious institutions that housed ethnically identified Afro-Cuban communities) had sacrificed the child, who was white, in order to extract her organs for use in a cure. Aline Helg has interpreted the rise of child-murder rumors and the anti-witchcraft scares they engendered as attempts by a white ruling class to justify the continued exclusion of newly empowered black and mulatto citizens. In addition, Helg has proposed that allegations of *brujería* (witchcraft) were intended to hobble Afro-Cuban political mobilizations, driving a wedge between working-class and rural Afro-Cubans with continued attachments to African-derived religions and a black and mulatto petite bourgeoisie that sought recognition as modern and civilized. And indeed rumors about crimes connected to witchcraft resulted in lynchings and other bursts of violence that must have had chilling effects on Cubans of color.[14]

But one need not characterize the dominant political dynamic of the republic as one of black and mulatto exclusion to accord the emergence of cannibalistic wizards and witches a profound significance. Alejandra Bronfman has argued that brujería charges emerged in a republican context in which political integration was in fact predominant. In spite of the virulence of the anti-witchcraft campaigns, Afro-Cubans made steady gains, securing representation quotas within mainstream political parties and extracting concessions from patronage networks. What journalistic, legal, and social-scientific attention to child-murder stories did in Bronfman's view was to crystallize "amorphous anxieties about race defined as Latin, African, or Anglo-Saxon, pure or mixed, degenerating or regenerating, into the figure of the black criminal."[15] Bronfman concedes that the mainstream consensus consigned brujos to a sphere beyond the pale where they were stripped of all entitlements. But the debates surrounding witchcraft had unexpected outcomes, too. Although brujería linked blackness to criminality, notions of black primitivism did not suffice to prosecute alleged perpetrators in court. More surprising still, the scientific study of witchcraft, a distinctly republican pursuit as Bronfman and Stephan Palmié have shown, renewed the intelligentsia's confidence in the viability of an inclusive Cuban democracy.

Fernando Ortiz, a criminologist and ethnographer who would become Cuba's most influential social scientist of the twentieth century, transformed brujos into signs of Cuba's progress. Rather than denounce the persistent primitiveness of Cuban society, Ortiz interpreted witchcraft as an evolutionary dislocation. If the brujos appeared savage, he argued, it was only because they had been relocated forcibly from African locales of scant civilizational attainments to a modern society where rationality and a superior morality prevailed. Practices that appeared eminently reasonable and even well-intentioned in their original contexts turned into horrendous crimes when they reappeared in republican Cuba.[16]

The dynamics that surrounded superstition in Puerto Rico were not entirely dissimilar. Scrutiny of healers and other religious leaders precipitated debates regarding the state of civilization and the place of racially marked populations within the polity. Though the campaigns against superstition did not target citizens of color in the same manner, officials and cultural critics in Puerto Rico turned their attention to the rural poor and found them generally unfit to assume their responsibilities as citizens. In twentieth-century Puerto Rico, however, violent, antisuperstition scares were exceedingly rare. Government officials arrested religious leaders when their activities disrupted rural labor, or when their mobilizations became public enough to be construed as disturbing the peace. Ordinarily, the authorities tried to influence conditions from afar, altering the environments that gave rise to superstition but leaving targeted campaigning to established churches and the pressures that "public opinion" could exert upon miscreants. Puerto Rico's social scientists, however, did not offer the sort of re-assurances that Ortiz was able to extract from Cuba's negros brujos.

Those who called for the extirpation of superstition in the early 1900s feared that objectionable practices, especially those that appeared African-derived, could give rise to "unorthodox versions of citizenship."[17] As Bronfman has underscored, the establishment of the Cuban republic was marked with public celebrations and several rounds of arrests. On the day of the republic's inauguration, the police disbanded two gatherings of suspected *ñáñigos*. This derogatory name designated members of the all-male Abakuá societies, an African-derived system of lodges that had been subject to intense prosecution since the nineteenth century. Abakuá had been linked to acts of allegedly superstitious savagery since at least the 1880s, when Spanish authorities declared members enemies of the state.[18] Unsurprisingly, those arrested on 2 May 1902 denied involvement in *ñañiguismo*. They claimed that they were celebrating the island's independence. Opportune as these assertions of patriotism may have been, they cannot be discounted as mere pretexts. During the raids, police confiscated drums and dozens of other objects that would prove incriminating when placed under new forms of criminological examination. They also found a Cuban flag, an object that suggested the imbrication of nationalism and superstition.

The authorities in Puerto Rico were evidently less concerned with the possibility that superstitious practices could result in heterodox assertions of citizenship. Nevertheless, there is some evidence that unsanctioned religious practices could have (or could be seen to have) unwelcome political effects there, too. José de los Santos Morales, a preacher (*inspirado*) who spoke under the protection of Saint John the Baptist, once dreamed of a guerrilla army of faithful Catholics who would repel the Protestant proselytizers who arrived in Puerto Rico shortly after Gen. Nelson Miles and his troops. By 1904, Morales and his associates had abandoned that bellicose vision. Instead, Morales joined forces with other preachers to found a corps of itinerant *misioneros* — self-appointed lay preachers — known as the Hermanos Cheos. The Cheos were tenacious in the defense of Catholicism, its sacraments, and the saints. Still, priests kept a weary eye on Cheo-led initiatives, which included the establishment of chapels throughout the countryside.[19] To some clergymen, the Cheos posed troubling ambiguities. Though they professed obedience to the church, their practices reminded some priests of Spiritism and others of Protestantism. And there were also those who objected to the Cheos as dubious "miracle-makers." Cheos became known by the names of the saints who "inspired" them, but the precise nature of the connection between saint and misionero remained open to multiple interpretations.

Little is known about the animus behind the Cheos's politics.[20] William A. Jones, Puerto Rico's bishop from 1907 to 1921, believed, however, that the Cheos promoted the Unión Party. The *unionistas* represented the interests of hacienda owners and their former dependents and opposed the "Americanization" of the island. The institutional church, for its part, had been integrated into the United States and was under the direction of a hierarchy that was largely committed to the pursuit of neocolonial policies. For this reason and the suspicions listed above, Jones bristled when he learned that the parish priest of San Lorenzo had published a letter lauding the labors of a Cheo known as Brother Pancho. The priest, Pedro Puras, denied taking part in missions. He also rejected allegations that he had promoted the ministry of a recently deceased *misionera* known as Vuestra Madre whom some had come to regard as the Virgin Mary incarnate. As for the politics, Father Puras said only that he was not to blame if "the country-side [was] all unionist."[21]

Perplexing as it may appear, the ability of government officials to confront superstition diminished precisely as the preoccupation with the meanings of religious deviance increased. Shortly after the war, Cuba and Puerto Rico witnessed the establishment of new police forces and the passage of laws and measures intended to reestablish order after decades of unrest. The new regimes, however, made it difficult for the judiciary to dispose of all who were now thought to promote backwardness. The provisions of the Treaty of Paris called for freedom of worship in Cuba and Puerto Rico. Subsequent pronouncements made it clear that the American occupation would entail the immediate separation of church and state, another measure that reformists and advocates of independence had sought.

Puerto Rico's Organic Acts (1900 and 1917) and the constitution of the Cuban republic (1902) ratified these measures. Article 26 of the Cuban charter established that "all religions may be freely practiced, as well as the exercise of all sects, with no other limitation than respect of Christian morals and public order. The Church shall be separate from the State, which may not subsidize any religious group." The language left republican extirpators some room to maneuver —"Christian morals" and "public order" were open to interpretation, after all— but the article enshrined the notion that all religions were permissible unless they were otherwise disqualified. The Jones Act left an arguably narrower opening for regulation. Article 2 stated that no law would be passed "relative to the establishment of any religion or that forbids its free exercise."[22]

Under these conditions, police officers and prosecutors who wanted to put an end to allegedly atavistic practices relied on contortions, subterfuges, and procedural technicalities. In Cuba, where the political economy of the republic made the suppression of superstition more pressing than in Puerto Rico, politicians and police officers resurrected decades-old provisions, many of them put in place under Spain, in an attempt to curb the new century's misbelievers. Religious organizations were disbanded for failure to comply with the Spanish law of associations (1880–82); gatherings were dissolved for failure to secure permits from the municipal authorities; Spiritist societies were closed for noncompliance with registration and record-keeping requirements; and healers were prosecuted for practicing medicine illegally.

Useful as Spain's tool kit could be, court officers, social scientists, and journalists recognized that they lacked the knowledge necessary to mount successful campaigns of moral sanitation in Cuba's postcolonial context. The Spanish legal apparatus had been geared primarily to contend with the political consequences of "fanaticism." That regulatory perspective left a good deal of the religious landscape uncharted and failed to address the most immediate concerns: what did superstition intimate about the state of civilization in Cuba and Puerto Rico?

Although Spanish military officers had put suspected miscreants under surveillance and had taken measures to limit the diffusion of "fanaticism," they possessed a limited ability to read the religious terrain. In Cuba, fear of another insurgency had led to an intensification of surveillance efforts in the 1880s. But the authorities focused on groups that agitated against Spanish colonialism, or that were deemed capable of unleashing a "race war." The police investigated Abakuá societies in Havana and Regla for fear that the crimes of the ñáñigos would escalate into civil unrest. Military agents spied on Spiritists, many of whom espoused anticlerical and anticolonial sentiments. Finally, the authorities mandated the registration and reorganization of Cuba's famed *cabildos de nación*. These organizations anchored Cuba's neo-African ethnicities and gave African-derived religious practices the institutional conditions that ensured their reproduction. The authorities came to believe, however, that cabildos could become hotbeds of dissent.[23] Although these efforts covered a lot of ground, a good deal remained uncharted. Spanish law might do to contend with ñáñigos and cabildos but did little to address diffused and sinister practices such as brujería. In fact, Spanish law did not recognize brujería's rituals as crimes.

Spain's knowledge of Puerto Rico's nineteenth-century religious landscape was even less precise. Although some memoirs refer to instances of harassment and note that soldiers were posted at the doors when Spiritist associations met, few surveillance reports comparable to those produced in Cuba in the 1880s have been located in Puerto Rico.[24] One finds little concrete information regarding

African-derived religious practices in the nineteenth century, a circumstance that is surely related to the absence of legally recognized institutions like cabildos. Judging by the evidence that is presently available, the task of investigating suspect religious practices fell largely upon the Catholic Church. Bishops conducted pastoral visits and required priests to report on the activities of masons, freethinkers, and Spiritists. Ecclesiastical knowledge, however, was distant from the realities on the ground. Throughout much of the nineteenth century, Puerto Rico's countryside was in dire need of pastoral attention. Those conditions contributed to widening the gap between popular practices and the church's norms and also resulted in the rise of self-appointed leaders who functioned as religious intermediaries. The latter included prayer specialists, unofficial catechists, healers, midwives, Spiritists, and misioneros similar to the Cheos.[25]

The American occupation renewed official interest in unsanctioned religious practice, but the surveillance efforts undertaken under the new dispensation also left much to be desired. The first attempts undertaken in Cuba during the first American occupation (1898–1902) relied on legal-administrative mechanisms similar to those that Spain had used to regulate associations.[26] On 2 December 1900, General Wood ordered the Department of Justice to create and maintain a registry of religions that would include a list of all authorized ministers.[27] The language of Military Order No. 487 justified the measure as an attempt to simplify state functions involving the clergy; the text specified that the "sole purpose" of the catalog was to determine "what priests, clergymen or ministers [would] be authorized to perform the marriage ceremony." It did not take an astute critic, however, to see that a registry of this sort would have broader implications. Officials expected the registry to impose order on the thickets of Cuban faith; that is, to produce what James Scott might call a "thin" or "simplified" version of reality.[28] Practices omitted from the official list would not be recognized as religions for any licit purpose. Finer distinctions between ill-advised and criminal pursuits would be left to the police and the courts. Though only the latter practices would be subject to criminal prosecution, practitioners of nonreligions would be denied some basic rights.

The effort to make religions legible through good administration fell short of the mark. Protestant ministers complied with the registration requirement, as did Catholic priests. By early 1902, however, it had become apparent that the registry would create difficulties of its own. Confronted with an application from a man who claimed to be a minister of the "Iglesia Evolucionista de Cuba," Secretary of Justice José Varela balked. There was "nothing to show," he argued, that the Evolutionist Church was "a branch of a duly established religion," or that it possessed a following extensive enough to warrant "the privilege of performing marriage ceremonies." If such a group were registered under the law, any association with a religious "coloring" would have to be recognized as a church.[29]

To deal with the problem of objectionable practices that were illegible as religions and as crimes, the authorities turned to police officers. In December of 1900, the Havana Detectives Bureau filed a report with the headquarters of the military government. The document summarized the findings of an undercover investigation conducted in the eastern court district in response to the notion that "witchcraft" was practiced there under a variety of guises. The report offered a street-level accounting of the trickeries of fortune-tellers, healers, and mediums, but it failed to resolve some of the fundamental questions. "African" brujos were grouped alongside "gypsies" and Spiritist "wizards," a label applied to solo practitioners but apparently not to those who met in registered Spiritist societies that did not serve paying clients.[30] In the end, the report made witchcraft legible only as a confidence game. The model did not capture all suspicious practices, nor would it work reliably at trial unless it could be shown that payments had changed hands.

From Government to Management

The chapters that follow are largely self-contained. Each deals with religious practitioners who found themselves at the center of heated disputes in newspapers, learned journals, and courthouses. These episodes, dispersed over time and geography, may be viewed as scattered data points. Plotting a figurative line through them, it is possible to trace the rise, though not precisely the triumph, of a managerial approach to the regulation and disciplining of religious deviants.

The early 1900s witnessed government officials and their allies seeking to banish "superstitions" from public life so as to uplift newly constituted citizenries in Cuba and Puerto Rico. The quest for reformed citizens and the commitment to the rule of law were predicated, however, on the possibility of violence at the hands of state officials and incensed publics. The dynamic became especially evident in Cuba: after Zoila's alleged murder in 1904, Cubans charged with brujería were as likely to stand trial as they were to face lynch mobs. The liberal application of the *ley de fugas*, which authorized state agents to kill prisoners who attempted to escape, was another grim possibility.

By the 1950s, official agendas had shed some of their most ambitious items. While some columnists, politicians, and social scientists continued to write of the need to forge moral political actors, many midcentury officials were content to extract proper public conduct from Cubans and Puerto Ricans. Healers, seers, and even a stigmatic gathered sizable followings without inciting hostile responses from the authorities. In instances that appeared to involve "traditional" and "Catholic" practices, government functionaries took supporting roles, stage-managing pilgrimages, escorting religious figures, and providing emergency services at shrines. In such cases, state officials usually remained noncommittal about religious claims so long as these did not challenge interests under government protection, such as the prerogatives of health professionals.

The managerial approach did not represent the unalloyed triumph of freedom of religion, nor were its measures as laissez-faire as they might appear. As a governing strategy, the management of suspect religious forms relied on decades of developments that made official interventions more effective than they had been at the turn of the century. By the 1950s, officials possessed a longer administrative reach and they were armed with specialized knowledge of religious deviance. Several generations of journalistic observations and social-scientific inquiry had produced classification schemes that officials could employ to distinguish between religion and hazardous superstitious practices. The growth of the state and its bureaucracy gave officials the capacity to intervene in remote corners. But by the 1950s, the need for repression had abated, too. Cubans and Puerto Ricans were no longer as vulnerable to neocolonial assessments of their cultural states. Rather than speak to debased states of civilization, some formerly devalued "traditions" had begun a process of rehabilitation and institutionalization as folklore. This allowed Cuban and Puerto Rican observers to deploy suspect practices in the service of nation-building projects. Finally, the rise of populist leaders also contributed to a shift in governing strategies. Though they differed dramatically in many respects, the governments of Fulgencio Batista and Luis Muñoz Marín both reached understandings with voters whose religious practices had inspired suspicion in the past.

The contrasts between what one might call governmental and managerial approaches become clearer if one examines specific careers. Between 1901 and 1902, Cuban authorities did their best to discourage gatherings around the home of a black healer that some called San Hilarión; others declared him a "new god," a weighty title given to the leaders of several nineteenth-century "drums of affliction" in eastern Cuba.[31] Hilario Mustelier Garzón, a veteran of the War of Independence (1895–98), had established a Spiritist healing complex in Alto Songo, a municipality located twenty-four kilometers north of Santiago de Cuba. At first, Songo's mayor tried to intimidate the healer to dissuade him from hosting large gatherings of Spiritists at his home. But Mustelier remained undaunted; he continued ministering to all callers for several months.

The healer's good fortune held until the press began to demand his arrest. Havana's *El Fígaro* expressed consternation upon learning that a dangerous "messiah" was operating with impunity. Following the denunciations, which journalists characterized as a public outcry, local officials resolved to act forcefully. They detained Mustelier and sent him to Santiago's Hospital Civil for a psychiatric evaluation, a procedure that could require a month-long confinement to a cell. Although the measure was not punitive in the strictest sense, it mollified critics. More importantly, it allowed officials to intervene without violating laws that guaranteed freedom of religion. In September of 1902, less than a year after the hospitalization, the Rural Guard arrested Mustelier. This time the prosecution charged him with impersonating a clergyman and practicing medicine illegally.[32]

The manner in which Mustelier's prosecution was handled revealed the broad aims of a governmental approach. Rather than disposing of the healer through extralegal violence—a distinct possibility for those who were accused of brujería between 1904 and the early 1930s—judges and government officials, especially the governor of the province of Oriente, were determined to deal with Mustelier through proper channels. They hoped that such a course of action would dispel the air of sanctity that enveloped the healer and preclude the reproduction of further superstitions. The government's intent, then, was to ameliorate Alto Songo's soil so that the seeds of regeneration could thrive.

For purposes of illustration, one might contrast the treatment Mustelier received with the manner in which Cuban officials dealt with La Estigmatizada. In 1956, Irma Izquierdo, a young woman from Güira de Melena (Havana province) whom journalists described as a country girl, or *guajira*, attained island-wide notoriety shortly after news of her Christlike suffering began to circulate. Nearly all major publications covered the stigmatic's brief career, but the most comprehensive accounts appeared in Havana's illustrated journals. *Carteles*, one of the capital's most popular magazines, offered thoroughgoing descriptions of Izquierdo's body, along with titillating documentary photographs. The journal also provided narrations of Izquierdo's visions and a day-to-day account of her pilgrimage, a mission she undertook after repeated questioning from reporters regarding the purpose of her ministry.

Izquierdo left the province of Havana on foot early in the summer of 1956. She was bound for El Cobre, the eastern town renowned for its miraculous image of Cuba's patroness, Our Lady of Charity. Thousands of Cubans greeted Izquierdo along a pilgrimage route. Throngs gathered on the outskirts of the towns she passed, and some joined her for stretches of the journey hoping that in sharing the stigmatic's penance, they might gain a blessing and aid her cause: "To go to El Cobre walking, so that peace might reign in the world."

Popular as she became, Izquierdo did not fulfill all expectations. She had intimated that a miracle might occur in El Cobre when she arrived, but, according to the news, nothing of the sort took place. Some pilgrims were reportedly disappointed to learn that the stigmatic did not heal the sick. Others wondered if her polished fingernails and cigarette smoking could be reconciled with the emulation of Christ's passion. There were questions about Izquierdo's mental health, the extent of her stigmata, which appeared to be shallow, self-inflicted lacerations, and her asceticism. *Bohemia*, one of Latin America's most popular magazines, described Izquierdo as a "merry pilgrim," noting that her daily routines combined piety with tourism.

Far from discouraging a suspect pilgrimage, the Cuban government underwrote it, albeit without disclosing the extent of its support. Wherever suitable accommodations were unavailable, Izquierdo spent the night at the police headquarters. A government-supplied ambulance and an army escort trailed her, accompanying her on the road to El Cobre and wherever else she went. Soldiers and police officers were seen carrying the cross that Izquierdo took up at the outset of the journey.

Evidently, the government's stage-management efforts did not meet with the approval of the press. In 1950s Cuba, a managerial intervention of this sort could be interpreted as a cynical attempt to manipulate public sentiment. *Carteles* correspondent Oscar Pino Santos was not alone when he intimated that the government's involvement reflected Batista's desire to curry favor with the citizenry at a moment of profound political crisis. Other reports, including some that appeared in *Bohemia*, suggested that Batista had created the conditions that made Izquierdo a celebrity. Batista had suspended the constitution and had imposed a media blackout. Those measures had forced journalists to fill their publications with innocuous features that were sure to meet with the approval of censors.[33]

Transparent as it may have appeared, political opportunism of this sort was not a distinctive feature of a managerial approach. As Alejandro de la Fuente has observed, politicians denounced brujería routinely during the first decades of Cuba's republican life. But they did not forget that blacks and mulattoes constituted crucial voting blocks. Liberals in particular were accused repeatedly of courting brujos and ñáñigos.[34] Critics charged that witchcraft persisted in the plenitude of the twentieth century precisely because perpetrators enjoyed political patronage.

In Puerto Rico, where the commonwealth system had just been inaugurated in July of 1952, the press celebrated the government's efforts to manage religious conduct. When the Virgin Mary appeared in the western Puerto Rican town of Sabana Grande in 1953, government officials in San Juan mobilized a contingent of police officers. Rather than disperse the tens of thousands of pilgrims who congregated in barrio Rincón, the police were instructed to direct the stream of traffic that arrived from every corner of the island. Other officers were assigned to an escort detail charged with protecting the children who had witnessed the Virgin's apparition. As the crowds swelled, the authorities dispatched personnel from all branches of the government bureaucracy. Electricians and technicians installed a public address system that the police used to control the crowds and to deliver entreaties that took on religious overtones. Sanitation specialists were sent to test the quality of spring waters that the Virgin had blessed and that pilgrims procured only after waiting in penitential lines. Finally, physicians and nurses from the Department of Health opened a field clinic that handled exhaustion, heatstroke, and the death of an undernourished infant who perished after several days at the shrine.

Journalists, though divided when it came to the visionaries and the marvels they described, were unanimous in their assessments of the government's measures. Even *El Mundo*, a newspaper whose editors advised readers to heed the church and avoid barrio Rincón, pointed at the behavior of the multitudes, which reportedly reached 150,000, as evidence of the government's hard-earned success. Rather than denounce officials for opportunistic involvement in the apparitions, Puerto Rican journalists transformed the site where the Virgin had appeared into a shrine to good administration; Sabana Grande was hallowed ground where state officials had delivered the miracle of order.[35]

Ruling Knowledge, Journalistic Knowledge

In the early 1900s, Cuban and Puerto Rican officials had to contend with the "illegibility" of religious landscapes of evident complexity amid an apparent recrudescence of superstition. Under conditions of de jure religious freedom, corrective interventions demanded precise mappings. Officials had to determine when and where to intervene, distinguishing between those religions that were entitled to legal protection and those practices that should or could be suppressed. But the regulators' problems went beyond what one might call target acquisition. Even when suppression was deemed practicable, judicial actions could be hampered by imprecise intelligence. When Cuban authorities charged Mustelier with masquerading as a minister, the prosecution was hard-pressed to specify whose religious authority the healer had "usurped." Faced with these challenges, government officials turned to those who could spot superstition when they saw it; that is to say, journalists and social scientists.

The Cuban press proved especially adept at producing knowledge that could be applied to regulatory effects. Government officials and politicians did not welcome interventions in every instance, as the meandering path to Mustelier's prosecution revealed. Journalists, however, embraced their responsibilities with surprising vehemence. Manuel Márquez Sterling, a man with unassailable revolutionary credentials known as the dean of Cuban journalism, celebrated the founding of Cuba's Press Association in April of 1904. In his exultant commentary, Márquez Sterling proposed that the creation of the association, to whose board he was elected, signaled that journalists were poised to assume new roles. An organized press would strengthen civil society, curb the excesses of morally crippled politicians, and guard against the spread of ignorance. Eight months later, the association's first vice president, Eduardo Varela Zequeira, was leading a campaign against Zoila's alleged killers. Besides generating good copy for *El Mundo*, the reporter's undertaking highlighted the moralizing functions that the profession had embraced.[36]

As journalists saw it, they had multiple roles to play in the struggle for regeneration. They would represent civil society, speaking with the authority of public opinion to demand government actions. If those measures proved insufficient, they would exhort citizens to protect the good name of the country by taking matters into their own hands. Meanwhile, journalists would do their best to even the odds in the contest between the agents of order, who were more or less bound by the law, and the agents of backwardness. It was precisely to improve the government's chances of eradicating brujería that Varela Zequeira identified suspects, guided police officers to their haunts, and collected evidence that prosecutors used to secure death sentences for Zoila's killers.

Journalistic accounts of superstitious practices functioned as alternatives to the government's flawed instruments. Reporters like Varela Zequeira crafted narrative grids that could render criminal misbelief more legible than a government-operated registry. In what was surely his most influential intervention, Varela Zequeira helped to transform Zoila's case into a template for understanding and prosecuting brujería. After the conviction of Zoila's alleged killers, newspaper and judicial accounts of kidnappings acquired generic qualities. A stock narrative filled evidentiary gaps and helped to transform republican witchcraft into a "moral artifact" that others could wield.[37]

Between 1904 and the 1940s, brujos were accused of kidnapping or attempting to abduct no fewer than thirty-six children. Convention assigned the role of victim to young white children and identified blacks, usually males, as the perpetrators. Unless the authorities intervened, the stories were expected to climax with a ritual murder followed by cannibalism—a new charge of distinctly republican vintage. The motives adduced typically had to do with nefarious healing procedures. It was assumed that these crimes were the result of collusion and that the conspirators included members of Afro-Cuban cabildos, or people linked to Santería house-temples. Helg and others have noted that some of the genre's particulars changed noticeably over time. Though early on, the prototypical brujo was African-born, by the late 1910s and 1920s many were identified as Haitian and Jamaican migrants. This was not the case, however, in the most notorious of anti-witchcraft scares. In 1919, the city of Matanzas was placed under martial law following a round of brujería-related violence that left several black Cuban men—and two would-be lynchers—dead.

Although no one individual or agency was capable of controlling the entire spectrum of discourses associated with brujería, generic stories of ritual murder were deployed to regulatory ends. In 1910, a twenty-five-year-old black man named Desiderio Padrón was charged with the attempted kidnapping of a girl named Esperanza. Although there was no evidence linking Padrón to the child's disappearance from El Gabriel, Zoila's case allowed an officer of the Rural Guard to conjure an incriminating scenario. The officer noted that Padrón was married but childless. On the strength of that finding, he concluded that Padrón had probably kidnapped Esperanza to cure his wife's infertility, as brujos were known to do.[38]

Superstition and the Ecology of Representations

Most who have commented on the connection between journalism and so-called superstitions in Cuba and Puerto Rico have identified the press as a vehicle for the propagation of fantasies and misguided practices. With the exception of those scholars who have examined the involvement of the media in Cuba's anti-witchcraft scares, few have noted that journalists and their accounts had regulatory effects on religious conduct that merit examination. Though journalistic characterizations have certainly changed since the days when reporters saw themselves as agents of regeneration, the revaluation of objectionable practices and cultures—by means of a process that some scholars call "folklorization"—has not resulted in the abandonment of efforts to manage superstition and control its meanings. Recent studies of the nationalization of ethnically marked cultural practices in Cuba and Puerto Rico have shown that the government's redeployment of aestheticized "traditions" was accompanied by the rise of new regulatory mechanisms. Folklore, after all, is also the purview of state-run institutions that specialize in its preservation, promotion, and public presentation.[39]

In the 1950s, scholars, clergymen, and a few editors denounced newspapers like Puerto Rico's *El Imparcial* for their coverage of Marian apparitions in Sabana Grande. Those reports and others dealing with weeping statues and sightings of unidentified flying objects were said to undermine government efforts to curtail superstition through the outreach branch of the Department of Education (DIVEDCO). In a newspaper column published in 1975, Fernando Picó, a preeminent historian of Puerto Rico, called *El Vocero's* reporters to task for their sensationalistic coverage of Moca's vampire, a figure that he likened to "subversives," "communists," and "imperialist ogres." In Picó's estimation, these were all bogeymen that the press put forth to the detriment of political dialogue. Picó charged that Puerto Rico's newspapers had begun to cultivate a "taste for the occult and the lurid" in the 1960s when they began to compete with television newscasts.[40]

Cuban journalism has been characterized in a similar fashion. The press of the "pseudorepublic" is cited frequently for its pecuniary motives and its complicity with illegitimate political interests. There, however, sensationalism is said to have appeared earlier in the twentieth century. Most observers cite the violent anti-witchcraft campaigns of 1919 and Batista's dictatorship as particularly low points. Many recall that it was in the 1950s that print media and the radio made celebrities of such personages as Irma Izquierdo and the healer-entertainer Clavelito.[41]

For a time in the 1940s and 1950s, *Bohemia* revisited the ways of brujería in articles bearing such titles as "On Santería's Dark Trail" and "The Strange Cults of Today's Mankind."[42] A closer reading reveals, however, that midcentury sorties differed in tone from earlier forays into superstition. In these accounts, brujería was largely an object of curiosity, often a dreadful human-interest story in which the brujos figured primarily as tragic, delusional characters.[43] Superstition no longer spoke of obstacles to the entire nation's regeneration. Instead, it said that some practices that had been slated for elimination had survived the twentieth century. And such survivals were not to be regretted in every instance. By then, some formerly suspect practices were being declared embodiments of popular piety and other virtues.

The tendency to redeploy devalued practices and peoples, often for nationalistic purposes, has been observed in many Latin American societies, including Puerto Rico. Patricia Pessar has shown that Brazilian *santos* who were condemned as "fanatics" in the first decades of the twentieth century are presented today as symbols of the nation itself. Even millenarian communities that were once regarded as menacing are now recommended destinations for those interested in Brazilian folkways.[44] A similar shift has taken place in Puerto Rico. Raquel Romberg has argued that in the island former "charlatans" have been cast in the role of "saviors." According to Romberg, this transformation followed the government's turn toward multiculturalism in the early 1980s. Under the new representational regime, spaces that were once teeming with superstitions have been reimagined as "havens" in which Puerto Rico's cultural heritage has been preserved.[45]

Romberg, however, may have been too quick to link this shift to the inauguration of a governance regime she dubs "spiritual laissez-faire."[46] While it is true enough that for the last three decades even self-proclaimed practitioners of brujería have been allowed to go about their business with rare intrusions from state agents, it is no less true that the marketplace in which witchcraft enterprises operate is a regulated one. Beyond the imposition of incorporation requirements, taxation, and other routinized articulations of state power, the characterization of brujería as folklore has influenced what the enduring presence of brujos may say about contemporary Puerto Rico.

In my view, the exchanges and representations surrounding the chupacabras suggest that the regime that currently governs superstition has not granted full autonomy to allegedly superstitious citizens. While the depredations of the chupacabras have not resulted in prosecutions, the discursive climate in which the predator appears limits what the bloodsucker is heard to say. Frequent allusions to the chupacabras as folklore have tended to estrange the creature from the present, relocating it to an unspecifiable historical past or to an unrealized future.[47] The chupacabras, after all, has been characterized as a revenant form of misbelief and also as the "folklore of the future." One curious consequence of many such characterizations is that they purport to uncover what the chupacabras is "really" about, often without referring to those who experience the depredations except as victims of history or carriers of cultural legacies. Once represented as folklore, the possibility that the chupacabras may allow speakers to initiate new, politically significant dialogues, regarding citizenship, for instance, can be set aside.

It is not my purpose to offer an apologia for invidious journalistic practices or to account for folklorization as such. Instead, the aim of this book is to historicize the relationship between journalists, state officials, and practitioners of suspect traditions to offer a more precise accounting of its shifting dynamics. Journalists, I propose, played important roles in the government and management of religion and in the transition between those regimes. Rather than discount midcentury journalistic portraits of miscreants as manifestations of commercial interests alone, I maintain that journalistic representations changed in character during the first decades of the century. Like the social scientists that Palmié and Bronfman have examined, journalists embraced increasingly folklorizing narratives that decried certain superstitious excesses while extolling others as manifestations of national traditions. This transformation was a factor in the rise of the state's managerial approach to the regulation of religious conduct.

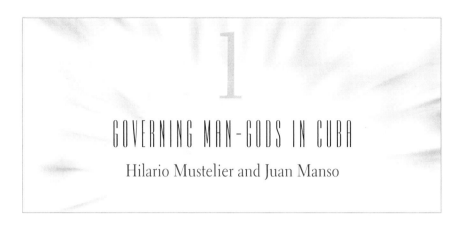

1

GOVERNING MAN-GODS IN CUBA

Hilario Mustelier and Juan Manso

Few locales have been witness to as many theogonies as the Hispanic Caribbean in the late nineteenth and early twentieth centuries.[1] The proliferation of new deities, prophets, and saints and their irruption into the public realm so soon after the calendar welcomed the 1900s caused modernization's boosters throughout the region grave concern. The new arrivals announced that the conditions for progress were not in place everywhere; miscreants blocked the roads to regeneration and threatened to lead the popular classes astray. In Cuba, journals and newspapers ran reports in late 1901 about a man they dubbed mockingly "el Dios nuevo." The "new God" was Hilario Mustelier Garzón, an elderly Afro-Cuban healer whose Spiritist cures attracted hundreds of rural easterners, as well as the unbidden attention of government officials. Mustelier's notoriety proved costly: the press condemned him and he was jailed twice. In 1904, however, even as news of the alleged ritual murder of white children spread throughout the country, touching off a bloody anti-witchcraft campaign, celebratory headlines greeted another Spiritist.[2] Journalists and cure-seekers alike took to calling Juan Manso Estévez, a Spanish veteran of the war in the Philippines, "el Hombre Dios," or "Man God." They credited Manso with uncanny cures and a surfeit of charisma said to inspire devotion in the motley crowds that gathered about him in the Cuban capital.[3]

Manso emerged as a media sensation, albeit after overcoming suspicions and arrests of his own. Many in Havana's well-heeled circles extended warm welcomes, and it was rumored that a few sought his ministrations. Meanwhile, Mustelier was forced out of sight, as journalists bid him sarcastic farewells. Why was Manso endorsed as a healer fit for the new century, while Mustelier paid for his alleged crimes in jail? Was it a matter of race? Of differences in beliefs and practices? Or was there more to their stories?

I propose that the contrasts in the healers' careers had to do with the rise of a governing regime that aimed to do better than punish misbelievers. Under this dispensation, Cuban authorities and the press sought to alter the conditions that gave rise to "fanaticism," thus clearing the route to a modern and rational political order. Manso's and Mustelier's fates attest to a struggle between the political rationality or *governmentality* of the day and the "subjugated knowledges" that man-gods could be said to represent.[4] Mustelier faced prosecution largely because he threatened a state-sponsored regime of knowledge; Manso thrived because his proposal did not register as a challenge. And yet Manso and Mustelier did not practice different Spiritisms. The two man-gods were connected by a spiritual genealogy that reveals the black ancestry of Manso's reputedly European and scientific Spiritism and disputes scholarly accounts that would distinguish too sharply between orthodox doctrine and Creole belief, or pure and syncretic practices. Such distinctions replicate the logic of the man-gods' contemporary critics, who were eager to separate the alien, primitive, and superstitious from the Cuban, modern, and scientific. That Manso came to Spiritism via Mustelier rather than through the writings of Allan Kardec or Conan Doyle argues against teleological assumptions about who imparted which cultural forms to whom. In this instance, Spiritism did not trickle down from the white literate classes, nor did Afro-Cuban religion rise from the bottom of the social hierarchy through capillary attraction.

To make these claims is not to minimize the significance of race in Cuba, where emancipation was a recent achievement (1886) and black citizenship rights remained subject to bitter disputes. Racial differences and the specter of Africa were invoked in the efforts to dismantle Mustelier's ministry. Journalists and politicians, ready to extirpate the "cancerous" growths that ailed the Cuban body politic, often identified Afro-Cubans as agents of contagion. *El Fígaro*, a leading Havana journal, observed with irritation that Mustelier's "cult" revealed just how "deeply rooted superstition and ignorance still [were] among the innocent peasants of Santiago's sierras."[5] Nevertheless, it would be an oversimplification to assert that Mustelier was condemned solely because he was black, or that Manso met with acclaim primarily on account of his color.

Mustelier's long career suggests that the gatherings associated with man-gods became more worrisome to journalists and politicians alike in the uncertain political climate of the early 1900s. A report published in *La Opinión*, an organ of Havana's freethinkers, lends credence to the notion that Mustelier may have been active for fifteen years before his arrest. In 1887, the journal denounced a healer and "messiah" known as "San Hilarión," Mustelier's most widely known title. Though critical, the weekly did not call for repression. Instead, it decried Cubans' putative tendency to seek deliverance through "fantasies" rather than "politics."[6] Such musings may or may not have consoled a readership composed of freethinking autonomists. At the time, however, there was little to be done about wayward Spiritists. Spain's campaign against Spiritism lost some momentum in the late 1880s following the passage of a liberal law of associations (1888) that allowed for the registration of Spiritist groups. Although church and colonial officials continued to denounce Spiritism and curanderismo, vernacular healing practices that many regarded as quackery, neither clergymen nor functionaries were eager to confront men like Mustelier. Repressive actions against Spiritists were rare unless the "propagandists" in question were also involved in separatist agitation.[7]

By the time of the healer's arrest in 1901, the political climate had changed. Although freedom of religion had become the law of the land, neither journalists nor government officials were content with anodyne philosophizing. The end of the War of Independence (1895–98) and the occupation of the island by the United States intensified a decades-old concern with the state of Cuban culture and the appeal of African-derived practices.[8] Gestures and measures aimed at curbing "superstition" became political necessities. In the years between empires, those who wanted to see an independent republic established were under pressure to demonstrate that Cubans were fit to rule themselves, something that American officials questioned. Cubans intent on tempering the revolutionary egalitarianism of the insurgency against Spain, and those who favored annexation to the United States, demanded an end to superstition, too. They cited the persistence of barbarism as a reason to postpone the inauguration of the republic and the extension of suffrage rights to Afro-Cubans. Even Cubans who rejected such calls as betrayals of the patriots' cause agreed that the island was in desperate need of moralizing reforms.[9] Legally established Spiritist societies and some Afro-Cuban *sociedades de color* maintained that education and vice-control measures were needed to ensure the country's progress and the political integration of black and mulatto citizens.

To call attention to these matters of genealogy and governance is to highlight the shortcomings of a scholarly literature that has embraced what Stephan Palmié has called "'idealtypical' forms of belief and practice" in the study of Afro-Cuban religion.[10] Though Mustelier was in fact black, there is no compelling reason to regard his practices as especially "African," just as there is little to suggest that

Manso's were particularly "European." Although it may seem self-evident that Africanness should not be deduced from black skin, or whiteness confused with Europeanness, there is a scholarship of African-derived religions that seems to propose precisely that. Sociologist Roger Bastide offers a particularly clear illustration of this tendency in *The African Religions of Brazil*. While asserting that "it is possible in Brazil to be a Negro without being African and, contrariwise, to be both white and African," Bastide—and many scholars concerned with religion in Cuba—have espoused essentializing understandings of the linkages between blackness and African culture. Clearly perturbed by what he perceived as "adulterated" Afro-Brazilian religion, Bastide declared it impossible for authentic blacks to take part in Umbanda, a Brazilian practice influenced by Spiritism that he saw as a sign of the development of a "semi-European ethnic identity" among mulattoes and acculturated blacks.[11] Accounts of this sort obscure the history of things "African" in modern Cuba. In examining these man-gods one can see that "African" was used to designate more than the race and practices of black slaves and their descendants. "African" was reified in legal, scholarly, and religious domains; it was a qualifier applied to undesirable, allegedly antimodern conduct and a marker indicating just how far freedom of worship would extend.

The notion that man-gods like Mustelier and Manso were leaders of syncretic cults that combined African and European components does not take us far from Bastide's analysis. After all, students of syncretism have long sought to untangle the African and European "elements" that went into the making of hybrid forms, as if these were stable and homogeneous. As David Scott has observed, the study of syncretism in the Caribbean has often taken a "verificationist" form.[12] In order to counter colonial assertions that posited the cultural dispossession of Afro-Caribbean people, many scholars have called on history and anthropology to confirm the existence of surviving African traditions. My own account seeks to reveal the mestizo logic behind the customary story of Spiritism's syncretism and diffusion, and aims to show that when dealing with man-gods, it is nearly impossible to discern original strains. This should not be a surprise; as Jean-Loup Amselle has proposed, the boundaries of a culture and its practices cannot be determined independently "of the interrelationships existing among different cultures, nor of the fixing of such cultures in writing by the emergence of a particular form of state."[13]

The man-gods' careers illuminate the operation of a machinery of government concerned with—as David Scott put it—"disabling non[-]modern forms of life by dismantling their conditions" to generate in their place new conditions capable of producing "governing effects on conduct."[14] The actions of the man-gods' critics were not intended to dispose of problematic individuals. They had a different point of application: to create political and intellectual domains—often called "public opinion"—inscribed in the language of rights and dependent on scientific disciplines that would banish suspect practices and knowledges to the trash heap of progress. Allegedly backward elements of Cuban society were expected to abandon "superstition" by choice in favor of rational understandings and productive behaviors. I do not mean to suggest only that the categories that corralled the man-gods were products of an infatuation with science, nor do I want to imply that Mustelier and Manso's practices were traditional rather than modern. That would be to discount the importance of virulent racism and to distinguish categorically between modernizers and man-gods, as if the latter represented vestiges from the past. Instead, I aim to show that, as the political rationality of government gained ground, Manso, Mustelier, and others could either accept or reject the position that experts and critics assigned them, but they had to communicate in new codes. The man-gods did not resurrect ancient languages; they made Spiritism—a practice that was itself a product of nineteenth-century visions of progress—their own. Their exchanges with the authorities produced a perceptible feedback; though proponents of an often-suspect Spiritism, Manso and Mustelier helped to constitute the reality of other discounted knowledges, notably African "witchcraft," or brujería. Spiritists and so-called witches and wizards and those who would denounce them transformed brujería into a "moral artifact," a tangible object that defined behaviors, policies, and discourses independent of belief.[15] The man-gods' critics, though emphatic in their profession of disbelief, became observers of ritual procedures and catalogers of objects the better to distinguish between the malformed practices of the ignorant and truly criminal activities. Moreover, as I suggest by way of provocation, it appears that some practitioners who fell under suspicion, including Mustelier, saw themselves as extirpators of witchcraft. One might argue that they aimed to heal ailments that the new dispensation conjured.

It must be noted that the Cuban republic did not introduce the political rationality of government to the island; that was already in evidence under Spanish rule, as one can see in Spain's efforts to deal with man-gods in the 1880s. But Manso and Mustelier do reveal changes in the workings of state power. The two healers underscore profound tensions between the republic's legal framework, which purported to guarantee religious freedom, and a growing need to regulate conduct. Although the outcome of this conflict might seem preordained, the victory of government was not definitive. The "new God" is not quite dead.

The Man-God Menace and Cuban Spiritism

The term "man-god" is admittedly imprecise. In Mexico, it has been used in reference to seventeenth-century indigenous messiahs and to describe the popular canonization of nineteenth-century clergymen taken to stand for the king of
Spain. The term has also been applied to the living saints who emerged from
penitential communities in the Brazilian backlands in the 1890s and 1900s. Unlike their Cuban counterparts, several of these figures led peasant millenarian rebellions with no clear connections to Spiritism. In the Cuban context, however,
the term "man-god" had a distinct double valence. Turn-of-the-century critics
seized upon it to underscore the alleged delusions of men like Mustelier. But
there is evidence of other usages, too. For that reason, I write of man-gods with
a measure of self-consciousness, preserving the term as a shorthand and setting
aside for the moment questions of who believed what in order to focus on the
struggles surrounding the label and its application.

Several decades before Mustelier and Manso rose to prominence, cure-seekers
in eastern Cuba used terms such as *hombre dios* when referring to healers who
led congregations that Victor Turner might have dubbed "drums of affliction."[16]
Such groupings consisted of ailing and often dispossessed men and women, including those caught in the tempest of Cuba's anticolonial wars, who after healing their own maladies were inducted into collectives that were summoned to
treat others. As with Turner's cults, the evidence suggests that the ministrations
of man-gods could have politicizing effects, even if these were not always revolutionary in orientation.

Whether they came by their titles through self-ascription or via the accusations
of their detractors, Manso and Mustelier did not hark back to a distant and unenlightened past. The two healers built on recent trends with currency throughout
the wider Caribbean. Man-gods and their female counterparts, often women associated with the Virgin Mary, had been known throughout the Hispanic Caribbean for a quarter century. In the 1880s, for instance, a woman named Rosario
Piedrahita roamed the Cuban province of Villa Clara, where peasants marveled
at her cures. Our Lady of Jiquiabo, as she was known, healed by means of wet
cloths or "hydrotherapeutic compresses," a method that Fernando Ortiz linked
rather fancifully to ancient pagan practices rather than Spiritism.[17]

In 1899, as Puerto Ricans readied themselves for the arrival of the century of
progress, Elenita, who was believed to be the Virgin Mary incarnate, appeared
on a promontory deep in the eastern mountains of that island. A few years later,
José de los Santos Morales, often called "el Hombre-Dios," preached his first

"missions" in northwestern Puerto Rico, launching the Hermanos Cheos move-ment. Similarly, in 1908, a healer called Olivorio Mateo emerged in the Domini-can Republic. In this instance, more than a decade of intermittent persecution culminated with a bloody massacre of the healer's religious encampment that helped to transform Mateo into Dios Olivorio.[18] And figures of this sort were not restricted to Hispanic societies. Following far-reaching revivals in Britain and the United States, Jamaica saw a proliferation of evangelistic prophets in the late nineteenth and early twentieth centuries. Although they were not called man-gods, some, like Alexander Bedward and Leonard P. Howell, two Revival leaders with a profound influence on Rastafari, were known to heal and to intimate their own suprahuman status.[19]

It is surely no coincidence that the period of the man-god's ascendancy through-out the region was framed by extraordinary outbreaks of violence, an institutional void generated by a collapsing colonialism, and multiple threats to the autonomy of rural peoples, especially those residing in Cuba's war-torn eastern region.[20] Scholars have associated conditions of this sort with religious revivals, the birth of new religions, and millennial expectation since the publication of Norman Cohn's classic *The Pursuit of the Millennium* in 1957. While my aim here is to concentrate on legal and knowledge regimes rather than on the factors that might help account for the emergence of man-gods, of which only some were millenar-ians, I should note that I do not find the argument linking man-gods to disasters wholly persuasive. It is difficult to describe the period in question, which lasted several decades, as a protracted crisis without stretching the meaning of the term. It is also possible to find such figures during periods of relative calm.[21]

Though following in the footsteps of numerous predecessors, Manso and Mustelier were not traditionalists. On the contrary, they were innovative, even iconoclastic, figures. Far from claiming the inheritance of folk Catholicism, they presented themselves as practitioners of a modern science-religion. Mustelier and Manso were healers, advocates of collective moral transformations, and sci-entists, too. While trading in esoterica, Spiritists denied the existence of miracles and cast their treatments and otherworldly communications as ill-understood, albeit natural, events regulated by laws that could be deduced through experi-mental observation.

Although most man-gods were spared martyrdom, from the vantage point of the state and its supporters—notably journalists and police officers—the rise of such figures could be cause for alarm. In 1886, Spanish authorities in Cuba, understandably vigilant when it came to disruptions that could aid the separatist movement, commissioned a confidential report on Spiritist activity in Oriente, where it was feared that "fanaticism" might lend itself to political "manipulations." Among other disturbing findings, the report revealed the presence of a man-god in the vicinity of Mayarí. José Pérez, "who takes on the functions of Jesus Christ and is called the new God," was assisted by Manuel Pérez, a self-appointed priest, and their two wives, described as "mediums" in the document.[22] Though they were not involved in the insurgency, Pérez and his followers were suspects by association. After all, Spiritists had been active in the struggle to end Spanish domination and they were among the most acerbic critics of the Catholic Church.[23]

Evidently, the state's suspicions were not always unfounded; some man-gods could spell revolutionary upheavals. An 1886 letter to Oriente's provincial governor justifying the imposition of fines on Spiritist groups mentions a "new sect that appeared in Guantánamo whose chief or sponsor was the mulatto Emilio Lay, entitled God[,] and the black woman Dolores Aranquet[,] entitled the Virgin." The group was said to regard the Afro-Cuban insurgent Gen. Antonio Maceo as "God" or "messiah." Spirit communications had reportedly alerted the group to Maceo's imminent return from exile. The information had led the man-god to post sentries on a hillside overlooking the spot where the general's landfall was anticipated.[24]

Although Mustelier and Manso were not accused of promoting insurrections, it is worth noting that Afro-Cuban leaders in particular could rouse fear of racial conflagrations. In 1886, Oriente's governor received a letter (dated 28 August) warning him that "in the jurisdictions of Bijarú, Encajó, Barajaguá and Mayarí, Spiritist propaganda [had] grown greatly among the people of the countryside, and especially among the colored race, which it [seemed was] being prepared for a race uprising." The agents allegedly responsible for inspiring Afro-Cubans were identified as returning exiles intent on relaunching an anti-Spanish war propelled with "the push of all religions."[25]

Although Spiritist meetings often violated the law of associations in effect until 1888, when Spanish authorities intervened against man-gods and other Spiritists, their actions were usually measured. They dissolved meetings, imposed fines, and arrested ringleaders. Given the upheavals of the day, such restraint is surprising. One would have expected the military to wipe out such threats. And, in fact, there was Circular No. 243 of 3 August 1886 in which the governor general ordered Spiritism "extirpated" throughout the island following the murder of a Spiritist in Holguín.[26] To the consternation of local officials, the murder coincided with a public show of Spiritism-inspired "fanaticism." Only days after the killing, a group of black men and women dressed in sheets walked in procession to Holguín's cemetery, where they chanted, kneeled, and reportedly invoked the spirit of a deceased relative. The participants also said that they were en route to the virgin's sanctuary in El Cobre. Still, mass arrests did not ensue. Only a handful of the most "agitated" pilgrims were arrested.[27]

To be sure, surveillance could be intense. Indeed, the report quoted above was commissioned in the aftermath of the vigil in the cemetery. But even the author of that report counseled patience. Though he conceded that there was some risk that religion would be manipulated to political ends, Jefe provincial Celestino Castellanos pronounced Spiritism in most of Oriente province "free of any tendency that would constitute a danger to public tranquility or the interests of the Government." He cautioned that violent repression would be counterproductive "since the victims would become martyrs or advanced spirits according to them."[28]

Evidently, the concern with Spiritism and man-gods intensified with republican rule. As constitutional guarantees were put in place, man-gods came under increased scrutiny that was justified as an attempt to secure the very rights of citizens. On 23 October 1903, Circular No. 149 was issued following a murder in Bayamo in which a member of a "clandestine" Spiritist association was implicated. The authorities in Havana asked for the names of the suspects and ordered the association shut down if it was found to be unregistered. Havana also reminded the local authorities that the point of a second circular (dated 30 September 1903) was precisely to ensure that all associations were in compliance with the law of associations so that "immoral centers" could be investigated. Following inquiries into several centers, Bayamo's police denounced an illegal Spiritist gathering. Captain Mesa's remarks illuminate the nature of the state's emerging approach to the regulation of religious conduct. Mesa noted that "while it is true that the Constitution of the Republic and other current precepts concerning meetings guarantee citizens the right to congregate freely," he believed that municipal authorities should "tighten their surveillance" of all Spiritist activities "so that this right could be sufficiently guaranteed without serving as a pretext for the consummation of acts that by their nature constitute crimes." Given "the state of ignorance or fanaticism of the congregation," the captain warned, "synotic [sic] experiments and magnetic practices" could result in "the repetition of scenes contrary to culture and civilization."[29]

In spite of all of the circulars, the status of Spiritism remained nearly as uncertain as it had been under Spain. Spanish law had accorded Catholicism the status of state religion and limited the practice of competing faiths. But Spiritism itself had appeared to government officials as an unruly amalgam of practices, only some of which were objectionable. With the U.S. occupation and the subsequent adoption of a liberal constitution, Spiritist societies multiplied, as did the Protestant missions whose work the new freedoms promoted. But in a republic whose dominant discourses increasingly favored secular mores and rhetorical attachment to rationality, Spiritism was tolerated begrudgingly. The science-religion occupied a marginal space between respectable experimental disciplines and quackery. While Spiritists could claim the cachet of an association with anticolonial fervor, and even the imprimatur of intellectuals like Fernando Ortiz, Spiritism was never rid of the suspicion that many practitioners were profit-driven fakes. This, along with issues of public order, contributed to the authorities' reservations toward Mustelier and Manso.

Church, state, and professional authorities continued to perceive man-gods as menacing figures; to them, such healers were superstitious revenants come to rouse the populace and embarrass the country before the civilized world. Man-gods did violence to foundational categories, muddling the lines between knowledge and nonsense, healers and physicians, and superstition and faith. These, of course, were the very distinctions that legislation, infrastructure projects, hygiene programs, Protestant evangelization, and public and missionary education were calling into being at the time that Mustelier and Manso began to capture headlines.

Scholars date the diffusion of Spiritism in Cuba to the 1860s, when the newly systematized body of old and recently minted doctrines arrived from the United States and Europe and began to propagate in spite of legal prohibitions.[30] Initially, the "philosophy," which upheld the perfectibility of the human, spirit communication, multiple spheres of existence, animal magnetism, and nonallopathic healing, circulated largely in the form of books and articles authored by Allan Kardec. Kardec, a Frenchman with medical training who specialized in pedagogy, had long been attracted to the study of mesmerism, clairvoyance, and related phenomena that other men of science were coming to regard as fringe during the first half of the nineteenth century.[31] Nonetheless, Kardec insisted on the natural, physical causes of the occurrences he investigated and eschewed supernatural "idealism" in favor of "positivism." Under his influence, fashionable table-turning and spirit-communications sessions were transformed into systematic inquiries guided by what Kardec regarded as scientific methods. In the course of these investigations, he gathered fifty notebooks containing messages from enlightened souls. These spirits also revealed to Kardec (born Hippolyte Léon Denizard Rivail in 1804) that Allan Kardec had been his name in an earlier incarnation. In 1857, Kardec published *Le livre des esprits*, a volume that codified the lessons of Spiritism in a question-and-answer format, with the "celestial brethren" supplying the answers. Though Kardec was not widely known in British or North American Spiritualist circles, *Le livre des esprits, Qu'est-ceque le spiritisme?* (1859) and *L'évangile selon de spiritisme* (1864) sold widely in translation in Latin America, especially in Cuba, Brazil, and Puerto Rico.[32]

In Cuba as elsewhere, Kardec's marriage of science and spirituality appealed to the privileged literate classes, especially those with liberal, scientific, and anticlerical inclinations. By the 1880s, however, Spiritism was flourishing and gaining a wider following. According to Armando Andrés Bermúdez, a split accompanied this popularization; two sorts of Spiritism began to emerge in the last decades of the nineteenth century. The first sort was anchored in cities, private salons, and registered "centers." Its practitioners favored experiments, communications, and philosophical discussions. The second form of Spiritism emerged in the countryside, attracting "people of a lower cultural level, more inclined to employing material elements such as water, incense, bush leaves, images and crosses, who practiced rites involving chants and collective movements, sometimes of indubitable African [*afroide*] influence."[33] In this case, practical concerns displaced icon-free séances; healing sessions that drew from a variety of systems, including folk remedies, prevailed.[34] Admittedly, the Cuban man-gods—characters that Bermúdez thought shrouded in legend—had no direct precedent in Kardec's teachings; the Frenchman's humanism never went that far. Though he did propose that "transmigration" or reincarnation offered a mechanism for the gradual improvement of the spirit over the course of many lives, Kardec differentiated between "advanced" spirits and God.

Rather than confirming scholarly narratives that emphasize the deviation of the man-gods' brand of Spiritism from Kardec's doctrines, Mustelier and Manso point to the shortcomings of the scholarly account of Spiritism's diffusion and corruption. Salon Spiritism and the more clinically inclined variety had more in common than it appears at first glance.

Bermúdez was neither the first nor the last scholar to maintain the existence of two Spiritisms. Scholars of the standing of Fernando Ortiz have also insisted on such distinctions. In his early work *La filosofía penal del espiritismo* (1915), Ortiz praised (true) Spiritists for their adhesion to science and pronounced them superior to all other religious groups for the primacy they accorded reason over faith. Later, however, Ortiz came to dismiss Juan Manso as a throwback to the seventeenth century who employed the "supernaturalist techniques" of Spain's miracle-makers.[35] More recently, Elizabeth Carrillo and Minerva Rodríguez have argued without much elaboration that Spiritism (and Pentecostalism) spread among the rural poor and the marginal urban classes who were less committed to Catholic orthodoxy and already influenced by syncretic and Afro-Cuban beliefs, a precondition that may have made such populations more receptive to the new traditions.[36]

Two objections may be raised to these accounts. The first, as mentioned above, is that this scholarship preserves the very distinctions that Cuban courts employed in the prosecution of man-gods in the early 1900s. Reliance on this scandalously partial archive makes the proposal of two distinct Spiritisms dubious. While this does not necessarily invalidate the distinction itself, a close examination of the man-gods' Spiritism shows that their faith was not rural and local, nor was Kardec's Spiritism entirely urban and free of syncretism. Mustelier operated in one of the many ruined sugar estates that dotted the eastern landscape in the aftermath of the War of Independence, but his ministry attracted people from a wider region, including residents of the city of Santiago de Cuba. Moreover, the man-god's influence reached urban centers; dozens of Spiritist societies throughout Oriente's cities, ostensibly of the "scientific" variety, bore the name of "San Hilarión." Manso, for his part, crisscrossed the island visiting both rural and urban locales and garnered his greatest triumphs in Havana, where he was embraced by both the poor and sectors of a liberal, middle-class Spiritist movement that he helped revitalize. Science and magic, and reason and superstition, already racialized categories in the dominant discourse, followed the Cuban pattern of race relations, "miscegenating" in spite of the authorities' efforts to ensure the purity of racial, analytical, and juridical categories.

Further, it is necessary to recall that Spiritism was a hybrid well before it arrived in the Cuban countryside. It emerged in embryonic form in New England, shortly after the Civil War, and grew popular among abolitionists and religious nonconformists, and especially those seeking to communicate with the spirits of the dead, a population whose numbers had grown as a result of war and disease. As Spiritism expanded, it became a complex montage of scientific findings, universalized Christian tenets, Swedenborgian philosophy, Asian notions spied darkly through an Orientalist lens, and mesmerism. Though reifying "science" and "progress" and profoundly Eurocentric in its evolutionary schema, Spiritism had a critical bite. Like theosophy, Spiritism could be seen as belonging "within the archives of dissenting western imagination."[37] Practitioners invaded the terrain of medical science and astronomy, corroded the natural-supernatural divide, multiplied the spheres of life, disaggregated the soul into multiple components, and denied scientific "materialism." These were qualities that the man-gods would deploy in proposing their rejected knowledges and therapeutics.

It is impossible to ascertain with precision the number of Spiritists or even Spiritist societies in nineteenth- and early-twentieth-century Cuba. Nonetheless, it is possible to offer some sense of the growth of Spiritism in Oriente, where it predated the man-god's ministry by decades. In August 1886 an observer noted that in barrio Bruñí, located between Mayarí and Songo, "Spiritist meetings among people of color [were] things of old." In October of the same year, Celestino Castellanos found that Spiritist meetings in Songo, Mayarí, Nipe, and Santiago involved men, women, and children gathered in groups of approximately twenty persons. Although most participants were reportedly illiterate, during the meetings prayers were read from a book called the *Diccionario espiritista* in order to "remedy their physical and moral ailments."[38]

Spiritism continued to prosper even after Mustelier's arrest. An inventory by the provincial government reflects that there were 169 legally constituted societies in eastern Cuba alone during the first decades of the twentieth century.[39] Forty-one—including one called Los Hermanos de la Fé de San Hilarión—were located in Santiago de Cuba; twenty-four had their headquarters in Bayamo; twenty-two in Manzanillo; and thirteen in Holguín. Alto Songo, the town closest to Mustelier's home, hosted three Spiritist groups.[40]

An Ailing Man-God in Alto Songo

After four months of intermittent surveillance, on 10 August 1901, Col. Juan Vaillant and a group of Rural Guardsmen arrested sixty-six-year-old healer Hilario Mustelier Garzón.[41] Mustelier was detained at his home in El Quemado, a coffee and cacao farm established on land where the Jagua Baralt sugar mill had once stood, near the town of Alto Songo. He was taken to the hospital in Santiago de Cuba and placed in a cell in the psychiatric ward, a move that crystallized the difference between state-supported medical practices, capable of mobilizing the machinery of discipline, and the ministrations of the man-gods. As the press would have it, Mustelier appeared deranged, but enough doubts lingered as to his condition to warrant a period of observation. Physicians were charged with determining whether the healer was truly an *enagenado*, someone deprived of sense and judgment by reason of mental illness, or a run-of-the-mill confidence man.[42]

The suspicions that weighed against Mustelier in 1901 were evidently significant, but they were not perceived as ponderous enough to require immediate repression. Songo's mayor, J. Arias, charged that Mustelier had "the lowly classes in constant movement, making them believe in frauds and powers that he [said] God [had] conferred upon him." For the mayor the "existence of such an individual [lacked] any great importance of itself." His concern was that groups of as many as 400 "persons of all classes" were gathering regularly around the man's house. Such mobilizations constituted a threat to "public order," particularly at a time when the eastern countryside grew more ungovernable by the day. Bandits, old insurgents, political bosses, and others vied with the central government for authority. In this context, the man-god's actions amounted to a usurpation of the power to convene the citizenry.

Although the mayor and the courts appeared unaware of it, the trial records list more than a few veterans among Mustelier's associates. Had this been known, it surely would have added urgency to the authorities' worries; memories of uprisings by military bosses were fresh in eastern Cuba. Leoncio Tamayo, the secretary of Mustelier's Fraternal San Hilarión, had been a lieutenant with a national regiment of unassigned officers. Daniel Vera, a healing medium who assisted Mustelier, was also a *mambí*; he had been second sergeant in Santiago's Moncada infantry regiment. Other veterans in the healing cult included Manuel Jiménez, a Manzanillo-born man who testified to his "blind faith" in the man-god, and apparently the Dios nuevo himself. In 1902, Mustelier applied for a soldier's pension. Like many others of his social standing, Mustelier was unable to document his participation in the war, and his request was denied.[43]

The motivations behind Mustelier's confinement to a medical facility were scarcely altruistic. His detention in a hospital in lieu of a jail allowed the authorities to preserve order in spite of legal strictures that purported to guarantee freedom of religion. However, Mustelier's mental health examination was more than an expedient rationale for detention. The diagnostic exercise served to redefine policing as a positive, scientific enterprise, a project that rested partly on the experts' ability to make distinctions regarding the etiology of criminal behavior.

In previous months, Arias had attempted to dissuade the healer through intimidation. When those efforts failed, he resolved to arrest Mustelier. In early April 1901, however, Governor Leonardo Rus stayed Arias's hand. "As long as the meetings in the home of the individual popularly called 'El Dios Nuevo' do not disturb public order and morality," the governor sentenced, "they cannot be prevented."[44] Central government, distant from the difficulties of keeping the peace, could aim to abide by the letter of the law. At the local level, however, the quest for an expedient resolution continued. An alternative to the governor's wait-and-see strategy became available when attorney Nicolás Nin y Valiente filed a complaint against Mustelier questioning the healer's competence and thereby recruiting medicine as a direct instrument of state power. Medical intervention removed the man-god from the relatively protected terrain of religion and pathologized the menace he presented in a manner that was consistent with the government of conduct: if "fanaticism" was in fact a malady, it could be treated. Modern medical technology could separate the human from the divine, as it would Siamese twins.

The documents do not indicate the attorney's motivations for filing his suit, nor do they state how long Mustelier was detained in the hospital. It is certain, however, that the man-god was freed before the end of September 1902 because a new set of charges was brought against him then. Although the regulations governing the confinement of the legally insane were in flux during this period, a government aiming to uphold the rule of law was forced to face the facts.[45] The healer may have been eccentric, but even the state's doctors had to concede that he was far from insane.[46]

Mustelier's reclusion at the hospital sufficed of itself to satisfy some critics, who were mindful of the fact that a failure to incarcerate him for good did not necessarily entail a breakdown in the operation of power. After all, the point was not simply to punish a particular man for an all-too-common set of infractions or even to discourage imitators by way of exemplary punishments; the goal was to rearrange the conditions that made Mustelier's challenge possible. In the eyes of his adversaries, the law and the medical profession had desecrated the man-god and neutralized the threat. Just as importantly, in curbing Mustelier and his followers, some journalists felt that the conditions for economic prosperity had been safeguarded, too. The man-god would no longer distract farmers and laborers from their tasks. The farm in El Quemado and its occupants could assume their proper functions after decades of disruptions. It is in this context that one can understand why *El Fígaro* found early cause for celebration in the juxtaposition of two engravings. The first showed Mustelier sitting and the other his empty hospital cell: "Dear readers, there you have him in his [hospital] cell . . . until the law transforms him to his human condition, and he returns to his old ranch, to his vegetable plot, to his coffee plants, forgotten of men and released from the hand of God."[47]

The press was more zealous and less equivocating in its denunciations than the mayor and the governor. Journalists charged that Mustelier encouraged superstition and subjected those who came to him to barbaric treatments, which in this case reportedly included the rather extraordinary recourse of beating patients to exorcise demons.[48] Mustelier was said to head a "miracle-making cult," to have established a temple, to harbor messianic pretensions, and to threaten the peace.

This portrait of Hilario Mustelier Garzón was published upon his release from
a cell in the Hospital de Santiago de Cuba. The hand-drawn halo echoed
journalists' derisive take on the healer. From *El Fígaro*, 8 September 1901.
(Widener Library, Harvard College Library, KJ54)

Mustelier's hospital cell. From *El Fígaro*, 8 September 1901.
(Widener Library, Harvard College Library, KJ54)

The last imputation found some confirmation during the man-god's arrest, when the Rural Guard felt compelled to fire their weapons in the air to avert a riot of the pilgrims congregated around his residence. According to some reports, by the time of the arrest the crowds had reached as many as 1,000 pilgrims. The press was outraged and castigated local authorities for their apparent inaction until Alto Songo's court decided to intervene.[49]

The testimony of Jacinto Duverger, a man who charged Mustelier with assault during a healing session, and statements from several unnamed sources, along with a healthful dosage of speculation, hint at the nature and extent of activities in El Quemado and give some sense of the mores that regulated them.

In hindsight, the scale of the enterprise figures among its most striking features. Mustelier's compound surpassed those established by other man-gods and healers.[50] The complex had the makings of a homegrown sanatorium, complete with multiple dwellings, a temple, prayer chapels, and convalescence quarters, where cure-seekers would stay for as long as twenty days while undergoing treatment. The site struck critics as a travesty; some denounced it as a "grotesque Lourdes" consecrated to the profit of a deified Mustelier, which after all seemed to be the implication behind titles such as Papá Hilarión, San Hilarión, and Dios nuevo. Mustelier's status was far from clear, however. The layering of names and honors suggests that the man-god may have been different things to different people. The man-god offered no synthesis; Mustelier was filled with accretions held in tension. Mustelier, in any case, reported the names by which he was known and appeared to enjoy the praise, but he did not claim divinity.

Duverger's account suggests that Mustelier viewed some of his procedures as treatments for brujería, the very malady that the authorities invoked and sought to counter with their raids on temples, the prosecution of alleged child-murderers, and the arrest of healers like Mustelier himself.[51] Duverger, a seventy-five-year-old Afro-Cuban man, claimed that Mustelier had beaten him after exclaiming, "Tú son brujo" ("You is wizard"). If true, this suggests that brujería as a category had found a measure of acceptance beyond the legal code, the writings of intellectuals, and the pronouncements of the church. Secondly, such usage indicates that man-gods proposed their own solutions to witchcraft without relying on the state's procedures.

A handful of surveillance reports support the notion that Mustelier's followers saw themselves as enemies of witches and wizards. In September and October 1908, a Rural Guardsman from Palma Soriano investigated meetings that Juan Rivery, Domingo Duvalón, head of the Centro Espiritual Público in Dos Caminos, and an unidentified "relative of the new god that was around Songo" conducted in a coffee estate named La Fe. The guardsman concluded that the meeting dealt only with Spiritism and noted that a Cristino Carrión was expelled "because those gathered there regarded him a wizard."[52]

The nature of Mustelier's therapeutics and the inspiration behind what practitioners called "San Hilarión's temple" would have remained elusive if it were not for some fifteen witness accounts gathered in the course of Mustelier's second trial. It is from these documents, which included transcripts of Mustelier's depositions, that one can establish that the healer and his followers were indeed *espiritistas* (Spiritists); that Mustelier's alleged deification was far from clear-cut; and that the temple was connected to a registered Spiritist society. Of the three findings, only the last one can be called a surprise. That Mustelier should have been associated with an organization that began operating with legal authority after the first charges were brought against him challenges the assumption that healing Spiritism was less formalized than its salon counterpart, and indeed complicates the distinction between the two.[53] It also indicates that even when repressive, the political logic of governmentality demanded that rejected knowledges and practices be tolerated if presented under conditions that safeguarded the distinction between the rational, and hence legal, and the primitive, and hence illegal.

Rather than impugning a specific act, in the second trial the prosecution charged Mustelier with *usurpación de funciones*, a crime involving the illegal practice of a profession requiring a degree or a license. The 6 September 1902 indictment maintained that Mustelier had violated Articles 339 and 340 of the penal code and had "attributed himself the title of professor of medicine and had practiced . . . acts appropriate to that profession without legal title." Moreover, he was accused of "usurping the character of a religious minister."[54] Under the new regime, secular as it was, pastoral duties were reserved for experts recognized as such by their respective churches and the state.

The prosecutor's efforts to show that Mustelier issued prescriptions for medicines or other concoctions and that he charged for his services ran into multiple obstacles. Witnesses denied such contentions unanimously. The second count also proved difficult to substantiate. The prosecution was unable to determine which religion Mustelier meant to usurp and was forced to drop the charge in an amended indictment. Ironically, the very "admixtures" that had made Spiritism contemptible in the eyes of the authorities also made it difficult to criminalize. The prosecutor had been inclined to believe that the practices in question were distortions of Catholicism because the "improvised" altar in the temple was "composed of images of the Catholic cult." Mustelier, however, healed by means of magnetic "passes," the recitation of what the lawyers called "made-up prayers," and the administration of "unknown medications," none of which had precedents in Catholic liturgy. Other objects found in the temple remained inscrutable as far as the authorities were concerned. A large table had been located inside. On this surface, there were a wooden cross adorned with flowers and several images depicting Christ's and Mary's Sacred Hearts, the Mystery of the Trinity, and the Crucifixion. But a sign reading "Gloria a San Hilarión" also hung over the "Catholic" objects. In addition, the authorities confiscated a standard bearing an inscription in golden lettering: "La Concepción de Liguaní, F. E. y C. Gloria à nuestro padre San Hilarión."[55]

Given the fate of many other practitioners of suspect religions, it is remarkable that Mustelier was never given the defamatory and potentially deadly moniker of brujo. Indeed, this appears particularly surprising if one considers that only two years later, in the wake of the violent persecution that followed the niña Zoila case, a number of newspapers condemned the whole of Spiritism as nothing more than poorly disguised witchcraft.[56] Mustelier's relative good fortune in avoiding that pernicious label may well have been connected to the inventory of confiscated items. The absence of the ritual accoutrements of what the authorities called witchcraft is notable; there were no drums, "idols," or vessels with decomposing offerings. As Alejandra Bronfman has shown, republican authorities relied on such artifacts to circumvent Article 26 of the constitution, which guaranteed freedom of worship. Prosecutors and police collected decaying matter as evidence of violations of the sanitary code, which became an important instrument for the criminalization of witchcraft. Following confiscation, these artifacts were dispatched on a nomadic journey that took them from courts to a newly established museum at the University of Havana. Once there, the practitioners of anthropological and criminological science put them to use in the construction of evolutionary racial differences, a knowledge that limited the prospects for full Afro-Cuban citizenship.[57]

These complications notwithstanding, Mustelier's prosecutors forged ahead. Much of the questioning in the case was directed precisely at establishing whether Mustelier had presented himself as a divinity or had led others to believe that he held religious office. Ultimately, the point was to remove the hyphen from the man-god dyad in order to condemn Mustelier as a false god.

The most damning testimony was the defendant's own. Indeed, Mustelier appeared to flaunt his transgressions. During his first interview, he asserted "that he practiced as physician in the temple that he has in his residence and that he [was] authorized to do so by the title that he presented before the court." Mustelier even presented the court with a licensing document in support of his claims. He also admitted that he prescribed and supplied medicines to his patients and conceded that he accepted payments, which contradicted earlier statements. During a second appearance before the court, Mustelier added that he employed the fees in providing lighting for the temple. In response to questions, he replied with some bravado that he had received no university training, since "his healing science [came] from above." He then observed that his cures were "so miraculous that he was known as San Hilarión Dios Nuevo."[58]

From a legal standpoint, Mustelier's statements were highly compromising. Yet, rather than suggesting a self-destructive will, Mustelier's remarks hinted that the logic of the man-god was incommensurable with reasons of state. Certainly when considered in light of the information provided by other witnesses, a less incriminating picture emerges. Narciso Palacios, a tavern keeper who resided in El Quemado, revealed that the medications of which the healer spoke were "invisible medicines" rather than material substances. His testimony also showed that Mustelier's manipulations were not beatings but *pases*, the hand motions that Spiritists everywhere employed to activate and direct the universal fluid. According to the witnesses, the temple was a Spiritist center, where "the spiritual religion was professed." A Spiritist society called Fraternal San Hilarión met there regularly, and some of the members, who also had healing talents, assisted Mustelier with his work.[59] It was this organization that provided the funds for the support of the complex.

The bylaws described the fraternal as a "society for psychological studies." Like all so-called scientific Spiritist organizations, its given purpose was "to study all phenomena related to communication between Spirits, between spirits and men, and the laws that regulate these manifestations and our moral, physical, historical and psychological beliefs." Except for its name, nothing in the document suggested the fraternal's connection to the defendant or any other healer.[60]

Given that neither medicines nor payments were involved, and that no proof of religious misrepresentation was forthcoming, the court determined that "the acts of charlatanism" that the defendant had committed "were not particular to any profession, nor of the sort that could be practiced with an official title." Because of its invisibility and because of its disconnection from the official economy, the knowledge of the man-god lay outside the spheres of professional expertise. Once more, the prosecution was unable to secure a conviction. Mustelier was released again in late October 1902. In its sentencing document, the court manifested its frustration, regretting that "not all actions that [were] repugnant to culture and [could lend] stimulus to superstition" were "sanctioned by the Penal Code." These failures expose the distance that separated the state's will to regulate from its incapacity to define all acts of malfeasance in a manner consistent with a hegemonic vision of progress that required both the banishment of the primitive and religious freedom. The same legal code that protected and defined expert competence and in whose name the state acted also enshrined a principle of tolerance that applied to Protestantism, a modern religion for modern citizens, as well as to less respectable faiths.[61]

Nevertheless, the prosecution's efforts against Mustelier must not be counted as total failures. Medicine provided a temporary corrective. And prosecution did force the man-god's followers to regularize their status before the law. Registration as a society offered members some protections, but it also exposed them to official scrutiny. The registration of Fraternal San Hilarión gave the authorities a means for overcoming the stonewalling of the witnesses. The society's bylaws allowed the court to identify participants who may have remained anonymous otherwise.

Identification of society members, however, gave the court no hold on the hundreds of anonymous pilgrims and cure-seekers who visited the temple or those who made their homes within the compound.[62] In its closing statement, the court contented itself with the notion that Mustelier's followers were mostly "peasants from the vicinity," presumably black, "who grew in number thanks to all of those who because of ignorance, superstition or simple curiosity, found it desirable to appear before the defendant." But soon there were other man-gods who impugned the court's assertions and robbed authorities of whatever comfort they had derived from the belief that man-gods were a thing of the past restricted to the backward countryside.

Juan Manso, Man-God and Media Cynosure

After months of itinerant preaching and healing throughout eastern Cuba, Juan Manso arrived in Havana in the summer of 1905. His growing popularity, manifest in the size of the crowds gathering wherever he appeared, had been punctuated by several arrests. In late June, shortly before his arrival in the capital, Manso had served one month's hard labor in Matanzas for healing a woman. According to the Spiritist press in Puerto Rico, which took a keen interest in Manso's activities, Manso was the victim of a provincial governor, whose interests he threatened. The governor was said to own a drugstore, and his brother was reportedly a physician. Earlier, Manso also had been incarcerated in Yaguajay under an unspecified set of charges.[63]

Little in Manso's experience hinted at the scale of his coming success or at his transformation into the media's cynosure. Nonetheless, this rather ascetic healer soon attracted the attention of crowds, the press, and society figures alike. In July 1905, Manso met with a group of Havana's "fat cats." The gathering included people of such note as the editor of *El Mundo*, Próspero Pichardo; Manuel Sobrado, a representative to the Cámara de Delegados; María González, a well-known theosophist; and Dr. Laime, a physician of renown. They, along with reports crediting Manso with miraculous cures, helped put an end to the legal troubles that had plagued the healer.[64] Indeed, by August 1905, thousands of people— reportedly of all classes and colors—were congregating in La Loma de San Juan

Juan Manso administers magnetic passes to Zoila M. Gener. The first victim of
the so-called negros brujos was also named Zoila, but the journal did not
remark on the coincidence. From *El Fígaro*, 30 July 1905.
(Widener Library, Harvard College Library, KJ54)

in the neighborhood of El Cerro to listen to his speeches on Spiritist doctrine and
to receive prayers, advice, and "magnetized" water. Not only did the authorities
allow these congregations to take place with minimal interference, but Manso
was also permitted to build a temple on land donated by two followers.[65]

Even the mainstream press—so adamant in its condemnation of Mustelier—
warmed up to the new man-god. *La Lucha* described Manso as a "humble and
kind Castilian farmer, who [had] carried out some apparently amazing cures in
the interior of the Republic," which in turn had moved a "credulous public" to
call him "Hombre-Dios." Manso, the daily noted, was surrounded by admirers
now, but he had been the victim of "judicial persecution" in Matanzas even

though he did not prescribe any medications or charge for his services. In a curious if unintentional echo of the Spiritist dictum, *La Lucha*'s writer denied that anything supernatural was behind Manso's talents and concluded with an endorsement such as Mustelier never received. "In a free country," the journalist editorialized, "where the President of the Republic has received in [his] Palace the celebrated North-American who calls himself the Prophet Elias, who aims at nothing less than to found a new religion, it would be a true injustice to imprison the harmless Juan Manso. La Lucha has investigated all actions of the so-called Hombre-Dios and has confirmed many of his cures."[66] On this occasion, the republic and its knowledge systems would be affirmed in the assertion of religious freedom rather than in the prosecution of fraud. Such largesse, of course, responded to the perception that this particular man-god was "harmless."

The journalists' goodwill and commitment to the principle of religious freedom were tested days later, when a zealous agent concerned with what he viewed as an affront to "the culture of any civilized country" arrested Manso for practicing medicine illegally.[67] *La Lucha* derided the official as an ignorant *gualdia*—a play on the word *guardia*, or guardsman, that suggested lack of instruction by mimicking "popular" and "black" speech patterns—and later publicized the news of the dismissal of the charges against the Hombre Dios. *El Mundo*, for its part, reacted by publishing an editorial and a series of letters detailing Manso's cures and defending him in the name of Cuba's democratic constitution.[68]

Even Manuel Márquez Sterling, the celebrated journalist who had penned one of *El Fígaro*'s damning articles on Mustelier, softened his rhetoric when confronted with the new man-god, whose ministrations he had observed. While Mustelier had been described as an enemy of reason for violating the integrity of science, Márquez Sterling now congratulated Manso precisely for "opening up" the discipline. The "triumph," he wrote, "of the poor and humble little soldier dressed like Jesus . . . lies in that . . . in order to study the recesses of his Paradise . . . critics need to open up science, to seek its counsel, to listen to it with fixed attention, and explain his successes, for he does have some, [whether] real or produced through suggestion[.]"[69]

Manso's eventual success in avoiding further prosecution in spite of his high-profile activity and his good relations with the press and some official sectors pose a number of intriguing questions if one considers Mustelier's fate only three years earlier. Why was Manso less threatening an interloper into the public sphere? Manso was tolerable because his proposals, though "naïve," could be reconciled with scientific orthodoxy and the political rationality of government. If the healer obfuscated the boundaries of faith and science, he did so without challenging an

evolutionary scheme that made scientific reason the capstone of human achievement. Moreover, Manso defused the menace implicit in every man-god by appearing to reduce the title hombre dios to an unsolicited honorific. Manso and
those who spoke in his name emphasized that his cures supplemented, rather
than supplanted, professional medical treatments. Manso, it was said, healed
those whom doctors could not treat, especially those who suffered from mental
illness or "nervous" disorders.[70] Manso presented himself as a moral crusader
and emphasized that physical cures followed spiritual regeneration. He acknowledged that faith was a crucial component of his therapeutics. For instance, during his interview with Havana's fat cats, one of those in attendance asked Manso
to cure his eyes. The man-god replied that he was not a *curandero* (healer), and
added that if the will of the Father allowed it, and the patient himself willed it,
he would heal himself. The most important thing, Manso said, was "to heal the
spirit."[71]

Mustelier was never able to fend off the suspicion that he headed a cult. Manso
disavowed messianism explicitly. During a Sunday gathering in October of 1905,
two priests approached Manso and asked if he was the messiah they awaited.
Manso replied that God's messenger had come long ago and had not been recognized. He was nothing more than a man.[72]

Race played a role in making the second man-god appear more respectable
and less "backward" than the first. The fact that Manso was white, a Spaniard
born in Avila, conferred no special authority on him, but it shielded him from the
suspicions that fell on blacks and their religious practices during this period. The
portrayal of Mustelier as a charlatan or a self-deluded man was consistent with the
view that blacks were prone to fanaticism and other pathologies of ratiocination.
However, race alone does not explain why Mustelier was condemned or why
Manso was spared. The authorities and the press had been known to denounce
whites who engaged in practices such as divination, card reading, and brujería. If
his proposal had been incompatible with the teleology of progress, Manso could
have been condemned as one of those whites who had fallen victim to African-
inspired superstitions. It was ultimately Manso's willingness to abide by his place
within the institutionalized system of knowledge that made him tolerable.

In his speeches, Manso took care to distance himself from false Spiritists and
from brujos, a feat that Mustelier was never able to accomplish in spite of his
anti-witchcraft treatments. Manso denounced those Spiritists who, like Catholics, allowed pecuniary interests to enter their practices. Moreover, he argued
against the use of charms and other protections as counterproductive. These declarations played well with authorities and journalists. *La Lucha*, for instance,

publicized Manso's tirades against mediums that took advantage of those "who had not been initiated in the scientific theories of Spiritism."[73] In Manso's lips, such accusations served two functions: they condemned anew those whom the courts had found liable for their practices, and they drove home the differences between the scientifically inclined, involuntary man-god and those who were rightfully prosecuted.

Ironically, Manso's therapeutics replicated much of what had been found objectionable in Mustelier's healing repertory. He treated patients by prescribing prayers, water magnetized by "passes," and early-morning baths, all familiar techniques from the Spiritist medicine bag.[74] Indeed, Manso's regime derived directly from Mustelier's techniques. During an interview with a Puerto Rican reporter in Havana, Manso gave an account of his initiation in 1903. According to the narrative, Manso's healing talent first manifested itself during a session at Mustelier's compound in El Quemado. It was there that he acquired the rudiments of Spiritist doctrine. As Manso told it, he cured a feverish person after only one treatment. "Afterwards," he said, "and without my wanting to work as a curandero, many people were healed following my advice; and lately, I have been unable to keep those crowds from coming to me."[75]

The connection between Mustelier and Manso was hardly common knowledge in Cuba, and it is probable that if it had been publicized, Manso's standing among Havana's Spiritists, government officials, and journalists would have been compromised, for in the end they welcomed Manso as a palatable alternative to the African influences and rural ignorance that Mustelier was said to exemplify. The finding is weighty even today. Among other things, it suggests that an Afro-Cuban ancestry lies hidden in the genealogy of Manso's practices, which were declared "rational" and presumed free of African-derived blemishes. "White," "scientific" Spiritism, however, was neither so white nor so scientific. Manso's rationality was constructed in a manner reminiscent of what sociologist Angel G. Quintero Rivera, writing of Puerto Rico, has characterized as a "marooned ethnicity."[76] Not only do African orishas masquerade as Catholic saints, as so many students of syncretism have argued, but seemingly European spirits also "camouflage" their hybridity in a variety of guises.

Incarnations of the Primitive and the Divine

Irony and ambivalence enveloped the man-gods at nearly every turn. The most profoundly ironic of these twists is revealed when one considers the question of belief only to realize that it was state officials and journalists who espoused the most literal-minded understanding of the man-gods. Officials and journalists disdained Mustelier because they regarded him as an atavism. The "new God" was an embodied manifestation of a primitive Cuban self who was feared capable of overwhelming the rational citizen whom the new political rationality sought. Manso was tolerated, of course, but not as a true man-god. Journalists and official supporters stripped him of all ambiguity and sanctity; he was a man-god in name alone. To distinguish Manso from Mustelier, journalists and government officials found it necessary to construct the difference between true Spiritism and a super-stitious, rural variety that drew from a well polluted by Africanness.

Those gathering around Mustelier and Manso were better prepared to deal with tensions, uncertainty, and pluralities of meaning. To some adherents, the Cuban man-gods were healers of commanding moral authority. As such, they deserved honors but not adoration or ritual invocation. To others, however, the man-god designation surpassed the confines of the titular. These practitioners charged Mustelier and Manso with the heady burden of enacting the divine and gathering the faithful under a new covenant. Whether holy men or men approaching gods, they placed demands upon practitioners; they required what a witness in Mustelier's second trial called "fé inquebrantable," their own "un-breakable faith." Such a faith offered a bridge to the past without reifying it. It evoked the memory of Catholic saints capable of intervening here and now, al-luded to and reworked the mysterious mechanism that permitted the incarnation of the godhead in Christ, and refracted the orishas' ride on their children's backs extending the divine's transit through human bodies. Rather than proposing a return to an idealized past, man-gods offered an alternative to the state-sponsored vision of the future. Unlike state officials, Mustelier and Manso did not assert au-thority over expanding domains, nor did they recruit institutional muscle in their cause. They claimed the power to heal, a claim that was broader than it appeared, for it sufficed to short-circuit some of the operations of the dominant regime of knowledge. In asserting their healing power, man-gods challenged the state's mo-nopoly over the body; questioned the very distinction between the physical, the spiritual, and the moral; and denied the professional's monopoly on truth. They gave notice that progress would not be built on a denudation of the sacred, for the so-called primitives had a notion of a progress curbed by divine measures.

In spite of the efforts of state officials, journalists, and scholars, the memory of the Cuban man-gods has proven largely self-governing and independent of the history-making apparatus. Today, this memory appears to have eluded suppres-sion to claim a place in Cuban Spiritism. Manso, the media's cynosure, has been forgotten. Mention of his name is met with indifference and quizzical glances. In Santiago de Cuba, however, Mustelier has survived and has been transformed anew into San Hilarión, African santo, and object of entreaties and prayers.[77] While Mustelier, the man, is no longer remembered, San Hilarión is now regarded as a *corriente* (literally, current or spiritual force).[78] Santiago's Spiritists invoke his name at the opening of sessions so that he may "purify" practitioners and prepare the way for spiritual labor. Appropriately, health is San Hilarión's purview; even today he is known as "el médico divino," a title in use at the time of the arrests.

A tradition that ascribes to the Dios nuevo an African origin in the very distant past has resolved what modernization's boosters found so intractable. Rather than reducing man-gods to manifestations of irrationality or models of toothless piety, Spiritists seem to have forgotten Mustelier's humanity. The man has vacated his body to make way for the god.

2

GOVERNING SAINTS IN PUERTO RICO
Elenita and the Hermanos Cheos

In 1904 and 1905, several Puerto Rican Spiritists and freethinkers were traveling and residing in Cuba, where they contracted a Manso fever that they helped spread in both islands. During their sojourns, they attended the meetings of local societies, promoted the organization of an islandwide Cuban Spiritist federation (modeled after the one established in Puerto Rico in 1903), and sang the healer's praises. These travelers took proselytism seriously; they wrote regularly for *El Iris de Paz*, Puerto Rico's leading Spiritist journal, and sent home dozens of clippings from Cuban publications. Manso, they maintained, represented "a revolution" in the "character" and "way of being" of individuals and their societies. They recommended that Puerto Ricans take Manso's lessons to heart so that "the cause may advance simultaneously in the Antilles, [which are] connected by the same suffering and a single sentiment."[1]

The Puerto Rican Spiritist Federation counted on the man-god's popularity to advance its work. Rosendo Matienzo Cintrón, the faith's foremost propagandist in Puerto Rico, was a formidable intellectual and politician, but he lacked the immediate appeal of the Cuban man-god with a healing touch.[2] Perhaps for this reason, during the first public act of the newly formed Committee for Spiritist Defense and Propaganda, several speakers promised a gathering of "simple peasants" whom Manso would visit on the island. The news was met with enthusiasm, but the Spanish-born healer never came. Spiritists tried to make the best of the situation; they took comfort in the knowledge that although Puerto Rico lacked men of Manso's talent, its need of them was not as urgent as Cuba's. A moral revolution was already afoot in Puerto Rico.[3]

Needed or not, man-gods and woman-virgins of various sorts roamed Puerto

Rico during the early years of the twentieth century; several preceded Manso's rise by several years. Spiritists, however, met them with far less enthusiasm than they had shown the Cuban. Indeed, Puerto Rican Spiritists did not embrace one of their compatriots with a comparable ardor until 1922, when a young woman known as La Samaritana captivated thousands with her water cures. Why did island-born man-gods deserve such scorn even as Manso was upheld as a model?

Unlike their Cuban counterparts, the most commanding figures in Puerto Rico's pantheon of the 1900s were not practitioners of the science-religion. Elenita, a woman who was revealed as Our Lady of Mt. Carmel incarnate, and the Hermanos Cheos, a brotherhood of itinerant preachers known by the names of the saints who "inspired" them, defended Catholicism ferociously. Though the church sometimes mistook them for Spiritists and even Protestants, Elenita and the Cheos were professed enemies of Kardecism and the "sectarian" denominations spreading through the island since the U.S. invasion.[4] The woman-virgin and the preachers known as *inspirados* (literally, inspired ones) also denounced secularizing changes; they opposed civil marriage and divorce and the wresting of cemeteries and hospitals from church control.[5]

This chapter considers Elenita and the Cheos as mediators and as agents of discord between religious practitioners, government officials, and liberal professionals; their movements mark the perimeter of a broad zone of conflict that also knew sporadic consensus. The first section is a synopsis of the ministry of the inspirados and their connections to what could be called a popular missionary tradition. I follow Fernando Picó's assertions regarding self-appointed apologists to argue that the woman-virgin and the living saints could function as intermediaries between the institutional church and Catholic practitioners who for centuries operated autonomously from the clergy and its orthodoxy. As one might expect, not all intermediaries proved equally successful. After a few tempestuous decades during which their charisma fizzled, the Cheos were welcomed into the church. Elenita, whose claims to divinity were difficult to rationalize, remained the object of the hierarchy's suspicions and misgivings. Subsequent sections examine the antagonism between Spiritists and Puerto Rican man-gods, their complex and ambivalent relationship with the Catholic Church, and their attitudes to the state and its plans for the future. Unlike their Cuban counterparts, who tended to face state-led opposition, Puerto Rico's woman-virgin and saints faced their greatest challenges from other religious groups.

In spite of the Puerto Ricans' millenarian take on modern innovations and of their longing for a thoroughly sacralized way of living, state officials and inspirados usually maintained temperate relations. Aware that these preachers could represent voting blocks, politicians took a conciliatory approach when practicable. The inspirados, while disruptive, did not challenge government authority in open ways. Those whom critics called *enviados* (God-sent ones) nourished alternative visions of progress, but their cries for regeneration resounded in many other corners of Puerto Rican society.

Genealogy of the Inspirados

In Puerto Rico, the second half of the nineteenth century witnessed a deepening of the crisis of institutional Catholicism and the emergence of self-appointed practitioners who offset the official cult's languor. Access to the sacraments deteriorated sharply during this period. Priests, generally Spanish-born and dwindling in numbers, remained in town centers distant from a dispersed and overwhelmingly rural population whose needs they could not meet. Canonical marriages decreased dramatically, baptisms were postponed for months and even years, and growing numbers of children were born out of wedlock.[6]

The War of 1898 exacerbated the situation. By 1899 many towns had been left without parish priests, as nearly three dozen Spanish clergymen returned to Spain following the occupation by the United States.[7] Many of those priests who remained were called to double duty, replacing predecessors who had migrated. In addition, the clergy confronted the loss of salaries that had been paid by the state under the Spanish regime. According to the *Boletín Eclesiástico*, in January 1898 there were 137 priests serving eighty-seven parishes throughout Puerto Rico. By 1900, twenty parishes had merged due to a lack of manpower and only ninety-five ministers remained.[8]

The loss of clergy members had a direct impact in the region around San Lorenzo, where Elenita operated, and in Utuado's coffee country, where the Cheos's preaching was especially strong.[9] On 6 October 1898, for instance, Utuado's parish priest was asked to direct the church in Jayuya. In September 1899, San Lorenzo's pastor, Joaquín Saras, already burdened with more than 10,000 dispersed parishioners, took over the church in Juncos.[10]

This pastoral and sacramental crisis, however, did not result in a mass defection from Catholicism. As Picó has suggested, in the end, domestic and popular Catholicism complemented rather than supplanted institutional faith. Picó poses the question of how such a complementarity was achieved, and he suggests that a set of "intermediary" figures holds the key. In the country, he argues, the clergy were substituted by prayer specialists, midwives, healers, unofficial catechists, *padrinos de agua* (godparents who performed baptisms when a child faced the possibility of death before a priest could perform the sacrament), Spiritists, and, significantly, the Cheos.[11]

Following Picó, I propose that the Cheos, as well as Elenita, should be understood as mediators between a compromised institutional cult and a burgeoning, independent-minded set of practitioners. Man-gods and woman-virgins could expose and widen gaps within state systems of discipline, as they did in Cuba. But they also could build bridges between official liturgy and extraofficial devotion, which, contrary to Agosto Cintrón's assessment, were never quite as separate as they appeared.[12] Complementarity, however, did not preclude conflicts. Not all figures seeking to act in an intermediary capacity found the support of the Puerto Rican Church.

The differences between Cuban and Puerto Rican figures should not be exaggerated, however. Man-gods and woman-virgins in both islands functioned in a variety of roles, ranging from the antagonistic to the conciliatory, depending on local meanings and their wider representation. Manso, I have argued, mediated between dominant scientific notions and suspect practices. Puerto Rican inspirados, for their part, generated friction and conflicts in the course of their campaigns. Overall, however, their ministries sought to incorporate the peasantry's evolving faith within the broader framework of the official church.

Unlike in Cuba, where there were man-gods and woman-virgins in the late nineteenth century, in Puerto Rico there is no evidence that any sanctified or deified figures preceded Elenita or the Cheos, who emerged in 1899 and the early 1900s, respectively. Both seem to have reworked the church's "missions" in a way that extended their reach beyond the institution's capacity. During their sporadic tours of the countryside, which intensified in the second half of the nineteenth century as the church attempted to redress the dearth of religious instruction and sacramental participation, gifted priests preached intensively for a few days and then offered the sacraments to those congregated at the designated site.[13] It is surely no coincidence that Elenita and the men and women whom José de los Santos Morales and his associates organized in the Cheo brotherhood were known as *misioneros* and that the events during which they spoke were known as *misiones*.[14] The designations were apt; Elenita and the Cheos were prophetic preachers who traveled to lead devotions in the countryside. A chronicler of the Cheo movement has observed that their preaching was reminiscent of that of the Capuchins in its emphasis on salvation, the approaching day of judgment, and the moral imperatives of Christian life.[15] Above all, officially designated missionaries and their lay counterparts shared a desire to inspire commitment to the sacraments of the church and devotion to the Virgin Mary and the saints. In 1909, for instance, Father Andrés Echevarría of Cayey, a town adjacent to San Lorenzo, alerted the bishop to the "lukewarm" attitude of the faithful, whose commitment to the sacraments left much to be desired. Echevarría recommended that "a long mission of good preachers" be conducted during Lent.[16] In a similar spirit, Elenita and the Cheos were adamant that those who cohabited or had married in civil ceremonies should sanctify their unions. They insisted that children be baptized, sins confessed, and the clergy obeyed. This last principle was encapsulated in the Cheo refrain: "God in heaven and the priest on earth."[17]

The enviados and the church also coincided in the defense of Catholic doctrine. The Cheos and Elenita affirmed the divinity of the Virgin and the saints precisely at the time when such doctrines were coming under criticism. Protestants charged that Catholics deified Mary and challenged the dogma of her immaculate conception; Spiritists dismissed saints and demons as the inheritance of the church's medieval obscurantism and its present-day opportunism. And the secularly minded questioned the entire celestial court on the grounds that such beliefs promoted superstitions among the ignorant. The institutional church had responded to these challenges, already present in nineteenth-century Spanish liberalism, with a variety of strategies. These included missions, the promotion of novel devotions such as the Sacred Heart, the creation of lay associations such as the all-women's Hijas de María (Daughters of Mary), and the extension of greater tolerance to practices that had been condemned during the eighteenth century. In the context of the late 1800s, home altars, lay-led prayers, sung rosaries, and other practices that the church had denounced earlier were revalorized as manifestations of a Catholic "tradition" that could curb challenges to the faith.[18] In this regard at least, the inspirados' missions coincided with the objectives of the church; it was their independent-mindedness and their apparent claims to sanctity that the hierarchy found objectionable.

Elenita and the Cheos were known to perform occasional cures. This talent, however, was not their principal claim to fame. Their cures were one more manifestation of their association with a divine person, whose attributes included the ability to heal, among other modes of intercession. Elenita left her followers a spring that she promised would be a healing "balm" to those who used its waters with faith.[19] This particular therapeutic regime, it should be noted, carried Marian echoes and buttressed Elenita's claim of identity with the Virgin. As her followers surely knew, saintly apparitions in Europe and the Americas often revealed miraculous springs that would become the focus of pilgrimages.[20] For their part, several Cheo preachers also healed during their missions. Before leaving Peñuelas for Ponce in 1907, José Rodríguez Medina, the preacher who joined Morales to constitute the Cheo brotherhood, instructed his listeners to erect an altar to the Virgin and to decorate it with flowers. These flowers, he announced, could cure otherwise intractable ailments. Rodríguez Medina's words found a dramatic confirmation several months later when a disabled teenager recovered from paralysis after bathing in flower-infused water.[21] Finally, Carlos Torres, a seventeen-year-old candidate who later restored the Cheos from their decay, underwent a period of testing prior to his admission into the brotherhood. For nine years (1921–30), he traversed the island preaching and visiting the sick as an unpaid "rural nurse."[22]

Between Catholicism and the Church

The church's reaction to the woman-virgin and the peripatetic corps of preachers was not uniform. Local clergy and the church hierarchy often disagreed in their judgments. Moreover, perceptions varied regarding Elenita and the Cheos. These ambivalences and divergences are noteworthy, especially when one considers the convergence of interests outlined above. Though they were rarely persecuted, misioneros could not count on the warmth of the ecclesiastical fold.

The divisions among the clergy cannot be explained easily in terms of rank. Overall, clerical opinions appear highly individualized. Parish priests disagreed with each others' assessments of the inspirados, and bishops equivocated, cautioning against unauthorized preaching and urging priests to take advantage of the situation. Both rank-and-file priests and the hierarchy, however, grew more tolerant of the Cheos over time.

Some parish priests, who were in better positions to evaluate their unsolicited aides than the bishops, recognized the inspirados' successes in motivating large numbers to fill the churches and seek out the sacraments. In 1901, soon after the inspirados made their appearance, Father Santiago Estrago, parish priest of Quebradillas, wrote the bishop that, thanks to the preachers, Spiritism had been vanquished, many had returned to the church, and those who had married civilly were now seeking the sacrament. People were also praying assiduously; in only nine days, Father Estrago had blessed 3,000 rosaries and a good number of crucifixes.[23]

Years later, in 1916, Manuel José de Palacio, Utuado's Capuchin parish priest, was still reassuring the bishop that the Cheos were obedient Catholics. The Cheos's influence, de Palacio added, was responsible for "the diminution of cohabitation and for the failure to thrive of Protestantism and Spiritism in those barrios where they have their supporters."[24] Father Pedro Puras, San Lorenzo's parish priest, issued a similarly positive assessment of Elenita's labors. Two years after her passing in 1909, Puras wrote the bishop a letter intended to defend his support of a Cheo preacher and Elenita's record:

> There is no doubt that before the Missionary they call *Nuestra Madre* arrived, they were all barbarians in barrios Espino, Jagual and Quebrada Honda [San Lorenzo]; they were all cohabitating; they were not baptized; gambling, drunkenness and crime were entrenched there. Every day there were deaths and stabbings, and many were even buried on the mountain.
> Not even a post of the Spanish Guardia Civil managed to fix those people, [even] living among them. That woman gave them light, she converted them, showed them the way, and after her death that man [Cheo brother Francisco Núñez] gives them the same advice, and because of this, I have them all in church on Sundays to confess and take communion. Don't I have cause to be thankful and to encourage him in this labor?[25]

San Lorenzo's parish records support Father Puras's account of Elenita's impact. The books reflect that fifty-three couples were married on a single day in May 1901. Moreover, oral history maintains that those weddings took place around midnight, when Elenita arrived from the country with hundreds of her followers, roused Father Joaquín Saras from his sleep, and asked him to perform the ceremonies.[26] In contrast, the records reveal that just between forty and fifty weddings per year were celebrated between 1895 and 1898, the years prior to the misionera's arrival. In 1899, the year that the hurricane of San Ciriaco devastated the island and left more than 3,000 dead, only twelve marriages were performed.[27] And the crisis extended to the following year when only twenty-four weddings took place. But in 1901, at which time the misionera was well established, the church had begun to recover from the invasion, and the worst of the hurricane's fallout had been addressed, Father Saras married 132 couples, a number that remained unsurpassed until 1917.[28]

All evidence suggests that Elenita had a noticeable impact on sacramental practice and that more marriages were celebrated once her ministry had begun. But these improvements appear to have been the result of roundups of the unmarried rather than of a continuous stream of couples seeking the sacrament. The recovery of 1901 was exceptional, and it was not sustained during Elenita's decade-long mission. Indeed, that peak was followed by several years when fewer than fifty weddings were celebrated.

In spite of the effectiveness of the inspirados advocacy of the sacraments, many members of the clergy, including parish priests, regarded them with suspicion and even derision. Jaime Reyes cites witnesses who reported that Father Puras himself had dismissed Elenita at first, referring to her as a *buruquena* (crab) because when she arrived in San Lorenzo she took up residence by a boulder.[29] Shortly after holding his first missions, José de los Santos Morales confronted the clergy's animosity, too. During a visit to Utuado in July 1900, Father José Lebrón refused to hear Morales's confession. After mass, when the congregation urged "the Angel" to preach in front of the church, Lebrón forbade it. Morales, who was evidently well aware of what the recent divorce of church and state meant, disregarded the priest and declared that the square was a public place. The priest's request to have Morales arrested fell on deaf ears.[30] Other confrontations took place in Villalba, where the priest ordered an unusually large congregation to vacate the church, suspecting that the increased attendance was a Cheo's doing.[31]

Though they insisted on the importance of obedience, Elenita and the Cheos challenged the clergy's monopoly on authority. They preached at a time when that was the prerogative of ordained ministers, and their words carried more authority than many priests managed to exert. Some priests resented being reduced to sacramental functions; that is, to the performance of rites at the instigation of the inspirados. At the very least, the Cheos and Elenita challenged dogma and churchly authority; they pried open the door to public revelations that the church had declared shut centuries earlier. According to Esteban Santaella Rivera, "Cheo Catholics" credited inspirados with preaching both "what was written and what was not."[32] Their revelations were new, direct, and made public in ways that superseded ordinary sources of religious knowledge.

Some members of the clergy perceived glimmers of Protestantism and Spiritism in Elenita and the Cheos's preaching. Even these critics, however, conceded that the enviados were efficacious in ways that advanced the interests of the church. In 1915, a priest who heard Brother Policarpo Rodríguez preach summed up his impressions of the Cheo mission as follows: "Everything O.K., except that it sort of reminded me of a Protestant revival."[33] In contrast, Francisco Vicario, a Paulist priest charged with a parish church in Ponce, reported in a 1909 article that a "multitude of these inspirados and inspiradas (in my judgment Spiritists, crazy people and fanatics)" had made an appearance near Ponce some two years earlier. Though he called them "preaching devils," Vicario acknowledged that "twenty zealous missionaries traversing the country continuously would not have done one hundredth of what these wretches did, who neither listen to Mass, nor confess because they say they have full grace[.]"[34]

Even if inaccurate, the priests' suspicions were not entirely unfounded. Elenita's and the Cheos's misiones shared some formal features with Protestant evangelizing and had more than a passing resemblance to Spiritist practices. As Nélida Agosto Cintrón and Liliam del Carmen Rodríguez Pérez have observed, both Protestants and inspirados relied on preaching and the establishment of chapels in the countryside, where there were few Catholic temples.[35] The Cheos, in fact made a priority of this, building dozens of chapels throughout the island, several of them in Montaña Santa, where Elenita lived and preached. Sociologist Juan José Baldrich has noted that Cheo chapels were established in regions dominated by coffee and tobacco agriculture. The brotherhood appealed especially to these rural workers, among whom the Socialist Party and labor organizing also prospered.[36] Ironically, it was precisely in response to Protestant evangelizing that many misioneros took up their callings. Although there were several active preachers before Protestant missionaries arrived on the island in significant numbers, Cheo efforts intensified considerably in response to Protestantism.[37]

Contrary to the first priest's assertion, everything was not "O.K." with the anointed evangelists; the inspirados referred to themselves in ways that suggested to others that they were on intimate terms with saints and divine persons. This perturbed some clergymen. Sympathetic priests like de Palacio insisted that "the inspiration with which some of them say they have been favored, must be interpreted in the sense of protection, special assistance, [and] not in the sense that theology gives to this word."[38] Others, however, were less charitable in their interpretation of Cheo claims and were troubled by people's tendency to call José de los Santos Morales, the brotherhood's leader, "Hombre Dios." Even the priest who found Brother Polo's mission "O.K." balked when that preacher demanded his listeners' obedience and claimed that none could tell if he was truly inspired or not. As the priest put it, "It seems dangerous. They all listened as if he were inspired by St. Mark, as far as I could tell." Though referring to events that took place in Ponce seven years earlier, Vicario's misgivings were remarkably like those of his brethren of the cloth. Among those untutored preachers, Vicario wrote sarcastically, "the entire celestial court" was represented, having "abandoned the delights of glory to 'introduce' themselves in these 'innocent' creatures."[39]

If the Cheos skirted sanctification, Elenita left fewer doubts. Not only did she fail to correct those pilgrims who addressed her as the Virgin, but she also made claims to divinity through a series of titles of increasing stature. According to Father Rafael Torres Oliver, the woman-virgin was first known as Elenita. The surname "de Jesús" was soon attached, and this change was followed by the use of the title "sister."[40] Eventually, those appellations gave way to "Madre Redentora," a controversial honorific ordinarily reserved for the Virgin Mary herself. Further, a series of testimonies collected in the 1980s by Father Jaime Reyes suggests that Elenita revealed her identity to select followers, notably a circle of young girls who accompanied her, who then spread the word. Elenita was believed capable of ascending to heaven at will.[41] Then, as today, Vuestra Madre, as she is often called, is credited with miracles that lend credence to her claims.[42]

The hierarchy was never certain of what to make of Elenita's and the Cheos's assertions, and it wavered on the issue to the extent that it could. In 1910, Bishop William A. Jones published a circular cautioning parish priests against those "who[,] calling themselves with the names of saints and even with others of divine persons, make converts in the countryside with their preaching on religious motifs." The bishop, however, recommended "discretion and prudence" without passing unequivocal judgment on the so-called enviados. He recommended that if priests could avoid being associated with the suspect characters, they "could take advantage of the good that such preachers do . . . in exhorting them [listeners] to the observance of the precepts of the Catholic Religion[.]"[43]

In regard to the Cheos, the church ended its wait-and-see policy and eventually resolved to grant them recognition. A formal investigation, in whose course a number of priests—including the sympathetic Capuchins—were consulted, convinced the bishop that tolerance was warranted.[44] Provided that the Cheos discontinued the practice of praying publicly for their saint's inspiration, their activities were to be encouraged. This process concluded in 1927, when the church admitted the brotherhood, appointed its first spiritual director, and approved a formal set of bylaws.

In contrast, Elenita and the devotions surrounding her were treated with trepidation. She "changed" or passed away in 1909, but the hierarchy remained profoundly suspicious of both the woman-virgin and the Cheo brother who could be found in her company in barrio Espino. The matter came to a head in 1911, when the bishop censured Father Puras. (The priest had already been involved in controversies with the hierarchy over financial matters and with local and military authorities in Caguas.)[45] Puras had written a letter to a newspaper defending Cheo Francisco Núñez from charges leveled against him in a freethinkers' journal. Puras also had his photo taken with the Cheo at the entrance of a cave site associated with Elenita.[46] The bishop castigated Puras for being "the first priest to publicly join those called ENVIADOS in this island . . . which may be prejudicial to the Church." The letter also charged San Lorenzo's pastor with neglecting his duties in order to "foment superstition among the ignorant."[47] Although the letter did not depose Puras, the bishop refused to attend a celebration in San Lorenzo where his presence was expected. Puras left Puerto Rico soon after.

Spiritists and Antagonists

Though they failed to see that the church had no unified stance toward the in-spirados, Spiritists were sagacious in their judgments. They suspected that the hierarchy stood ready to profit from these preachers if that could be managed. In 1902, Agustina Guffain recited a satirical poem before a group of Spiritists gathered in an elegant theater in Mayagüez. Her verses accused "Rome" of de-ceiving the gullible masses through the dual appeal of "foolish traditions" and a few "chosen ones" whose inspiration she proclaimed an "absurd story."[48] Spiritists also viewed Elenita as an instrument of the clerical ambition. An item published in 1902 reported that "a woman dressed like the sisters of Charity" had been in Cayey urging people to marry in church. The journalist reporting on the event concluded his short piece with this leading question: "Who doubts that there is *someone* else behind this?"[49]

Unlike the Catholic hierarchy, Spiritists had no reason to equivocate when it came to the inspirados. From the vantage point of the proponents of the ra-tionalist faith, Elenita and the Cheos were "winged peasants" whose activities underscored just how ludicrous "Romanism" was. From early on, the woman-virgin and the man-god and the saints flanking them stood on the front lines of the conflict between a burgeoning Spiritism and a threatened church. Even before the Cheos emerged as such, Spiritists condemned itinerant lay preachers and scoffed at priests who applauded their efforts. In 1901, *El Iris de Paz*, a Spir-itist journal from the western city of Mayagüez, mocked Quebradillas's parish priest for claiming "that the blessed little angels . . . have converted everybody there, beginning with Spiritists, who have abjured their beliefs." It was more than wounded pride, however, that urged the editorialist to add: "It would seem that in this campaign, we have Saint Raphael, Saint Gabriel, and a few saints who have fled the celestial court to hold an anti-freethinking *tournée* and uplift an anemic religious spirit. And I ask: in what sort of state is Roman Apostolic belief when the army of parish priests and Paulists has not been sufficient, and God has found it necessary to send to earth some of his out of work courtesans to convert us?"[50]

Spiritist hostilities were amply reciprocated, of course. Elenita and the Cheos regarded Spiritists as their own enemies because the latter had declared them-selves enemies of the Catholic Church. Scuffles between the rationalist and the inspired camps were frequent in propaganda outlets and in public debates, with some encounters reportedly deteriorating into riots. According to Santaella Rivera, a contest between Spiritists and Catholics took place in Ponce's barrio Cantera in 1908. Ponce was then the largest city in the island, a center of Spiritist and Protestant activity, and a frequent site of Cheo missions. The contest took the form of a question-and-answer match. Morales represented Catholicism, and a José Luis Gamón, who was stumped at the very first question, represented the opposition. When Morales declared the victory of Catholicism, a gathering of 20,000 reportedly cheered. The Spiritists, or perhaps the police, responded by firing their guns in the air. The shots sparked a fracas. Several participants were arrested, including Cheo leaders Morales and Rodríguez.[51]

Oral tradition maintains that confrontations, albeit of a lesser scale, also took place during misiones. According to these narratives, both Elenita and the Cheos faced off with several crypto-Spiritists, that is, Spiritists who attended without disclosing their true faith and with the intention of discrediting the speakers. In these instances, Elenita and the Cheos were able to foretell the intentions of the interlopers and to defeat them, a talent that followers deemed as proof of the enviados' gifts. The enviados also were credited with the conversion of several Spiritist miscreants. Morales, for instance, was said to have saved Domingo Quiñones, a well-known follower of the Cheos who used to transcribe their speeches from memory and have leaflets printed for distribution.[52]

In a typical confrontation, Brother Polo, along with José Rodríguez, was said to have wagered with a Spiritist that he would be unable to recall even ten words of their preaching. In the course of the mission, which charged Spiritists with lighting candles to God and the devil, the Spiritist fell unconscious. Polo then approached him saying that because of the time he had wasted in that religion, the Spiritist now had "the demon sleeping in his conscience."[53]

Elenita faced off with Spiritists and masons with results that affirmed her claims to perfect knowledge. Though historically masonry has been associated with Protestantism, in turn-of-the-century Puerto Rico, masons and Spiritists were allied; they shared some of the same journals, a commitment to free thought, and the enmity of the Catholic Church.[54] In Charco Azul (San Lorenzo), Elenita is said to have warned her followers that several men had left the towns of Arroyo and Guayama with the intention of killing her. She sent several of her followers to find them and had the would-be killers' leader, a Joaquín Rosa, brought to her. Upon Rosa's arriving before her, his horse is said to have kneeled down. Elenita then unmasked Rosa as a mason and ordered him to walk barefoot for a year as a penance for his trespass.[55] The incident, it should be noted, had an unmistakable

Marian timbre. One of Puerto Rico's most beloved virgins, Our Lady of Hormigueros, performed a similar miracle in the seventeenth century. A man faced with a charging bull had invoked the Virgin's name, and she had delivered him from danger by causing the animal to kneel.[56]

Elenita's encounters with her enemies left her followers persuaded of her immortality. According to a witness, a Spiritist once fired several shots at the woman-virgin. In response, Elenita lifted the scapular off her shoulders and gathered the bullets in the folds of her skirt.[57]

While some clergymen granted that the inspirados had slowed the spread of Spiritist doctrines, some suspected them of being tainted by Spiritism themselves. Journalists contributed to the priests' impressions when they referred to Cheos and Spiritists as if they were one and the same group.[58] An anonymous writer for *El Ideal Católico* charged that the "new plague began germinating in soil fertilized by Spiritism" and that the very same "diabolical doctrine" inspired "these new propaganda agents."[59] Fear of Spiritist deception remained one of the clergy's main concerns. The same author questioned the inspirados' seeming allegiance to the church, alleging it was a ruse that provided camouflage for their true beliefs. From this vantage point, the inspirados were crypto-Spiritists who threatened the integrity of Catholicism. The article recounted the story of a parish priest who had been deceived by a sly Spiritist woman. Though this "poisoned soul" was a diligent churchgoer, while receiving the sacrament of confession she let the priest know that she owed her virtues to the direction of Saint Raphael and Saint Anthony. When the priest asked her to forsake these communications and to accept his guidance instead, the woman reportedly left the church in a rage. Later, she abandoned "religious practice and ended up contracting civil marriage with another *santón* [literally, 'big saint']." The bishop's misgivings, while less colorfully phrased, were of a piece. In his 1910 circular, Bishop William A. Jones remarked that there was "something" about the preachers that "smelled of Spiritism."[60] In retrospect, the identification of that "something" did not require a particularly keen nose.

The Cheos talked of their inspiration—of their connection to the saints "for whom they spoke"—in ways that insinuated identification with the divine and something resembling Spiritist mediumship. Spiritists maintained that some individuals had a God-given gift for communication with the celestial brethren, spirits that could assist human beings in their long trek to perfection and that humans, in turn, could teach so that they, too, would evolve. Mediums relied on automatic writing, visualization, and codes involving audible raps to communicate with otherworldly realms.[61]

Some students of the Cheo movement have ascribed its "Spiritist flavor" to the preachers' lack of instruction.[62] Such interpretations, however, gloss over the possibility that the Cheos shared a widespread vernacular understanding of human-divine communications. The few accounts of Cheo preaching that have survived indicate that they understood inspiration through metaphors suggestive of communications via a link and the existence of a celestial abode that was extraterrestrial in character. After reviewing this evidence, the critic from *El Ideal Católico* concluded rather simplistically but with some justification that "the angels and enviados [were] Spiritists, and of the worst kind." The reasoning of the orthodox Catholic went as follows: the inspirados legitimated their mission by saying that they were obeying orders from spirits, already a sign of Spiritist action, according to Kardec's teachings. Moreover, they said that the saints communicated with them through a "thread" and that they could not resist the force that impelled them to preach those revelations.[63] From a conservative Catholic outlook, all of these could be signs of demonic intervention.

Some of this critic's impressions were borne out on 17 July 1906, when a Cheo sister preached a mission in a private home in barrio Real, Ponce. She spoke for St. Francis of Sienna, and she did so in the first person, referring to the female body that the saint took as belonging to his *escogida*, or "chosen one."[64] A displacement of the senses and a relinquishing of the physical to the divine person, as the preacher made clear in the opening invocation, made this multiple habitation of the same body possible: "May the Holy Sacrament of the Altar be praised and sanctified with the blessings of the Father, the Son and the Holy Spirit. . . . From the Celestial Motherland, I come extending my hand. Receive the blessing that we send you, [the blessing] of the Father, the Son and the Holy Spirit, I detach myself from the Celestial Motherland, the five corporeal senses of this body disappear and the five spiritual senses penetrate her[.]"[65]

St. Francis's explanation implied that his was a temporary tenancy of the body rather than a permanent claim of ownership. There is evidence that some in the Cheos's audience understood the matter differently, however. In their eyes, the presence of the divine left a permanent imprint. Many believed that Morales, who spoke for St. John, was a spiritual being who required no nourishment. Believing him to be the apostle himself, few offered him any food or drink during his early travels around the island. Similar things were said of Elenita, who was reputed to eat little more than the occasional sour lime.[66]

Elenita, nonetheless, was difficult to typify as a Spiritist medium under the influence of a disembodied being. Her misiones were not a matter of inspiration; her claims to divinity were less equivocal. She did not speak for the Virgin. Rather, she spoke for herself. All the same, Elenita was at times mistaken for a Spiritist or worse. Some believed her to be a witch on account of her clairvoyance and her miraculous power over the material world.[67]

Elenita's reception, however, suggests that distinctions between Spiritists and Catholics may not have been drawn as quickly, nor as sharply, as the vitriolic newspaper exchanges between the two camps would suggest. As Picó has argued in regard to the role of the country espiritista, in practice Spiritism and Catholicism constituted a dispersed field of religious practices capable of mediating between the extremes of institutional Catholicism and the Spiritism of the journals. Indeed, there are indications that in the early days of her mission, Elenita was able to transit between the two groups. According to one witness account, in 1899, before she settled in San Lorenzo, Elenita preached in the rural barrios of Caguas. There she conducted a number of missions in the home of Spiritist Manuel Muñoz, who also invited her to stay as his guest. Though Elenita remained there for a time, witnesses point out that she did not find the house to her liking, presumably because of her host's practices.[68]

Regardless of the apparent and actual similarities between the two, Spiritists scoffed at the suggestion that the inspirados might be counted among the proponents of the science-religion. Rather than calling them Spiritists (espiritistas), purists referred to Elenita, the Cheos, and the variegated lot of untutored practitioners with the epithet *espiriteros*. They dismissed mediums who strayed by attending Mass and mocked all "mediums with patrons." Faced with the practices of the majority of the population, Spiritists could only ask sardonically: "In truth, isn't this delicious for those of us who pride ourselves in being the *standard* in matters of progress and the like?"[69]

The difficulty of ascertaining precisely whether the practices of the man-gods and the woman-virgin originated in the popular cult of the saints, as some scholars suggest,[70] or in Spiritism, as critics charged, highlights once more that ascriptions of "tradition" are treacherous. Those attempting to defend or condemn the preachers for their loyalty to a particular religion confronted (and confront today) the very obstacles that faced Mustelier's prosecutors: who could distinguish between Catholics and Spiritists when the inspirados' power sprang from the very tensions and ambivalence in categories?

The State, Tolerance, and Electoral Politics

Rumors relating the inspirados to crime, disorder, and promiscuity circulated occasionally in the religious press. *El Ideal Católico* suggested that members of the *partidas sediciosas* (seditious bands) that had terrorized the countryside with their score-settling after Spanish colonialism ended may have joined the enviados, whose ranks also welcomed ex-convicts and bandits.[71] For their part, Spiritists upbraided the likes of Brother Pancho for indulging in nearly every known vice and castigated a "little Che brother" for bigamy.[72] The state, however, did not lend much credence to these charges; nor did officials appear especially alarmed by the inspirados' alleged connections to criminal activities. Unlike the Cuban state, when confronted with the inspirados, Puerto Rico's authorities generally remained at the sidelines. The police did arrest Cheos on occasion, as occurred after the riot that followed the contest of religions. But just as often, state agents were absent from the scene or intervened in a supportive role. The inspirados' followers seem to have regarded judges and police officers without acrimony and went so far as to enlist their assistance in protecting preachers from their adversaries.[73]

This tentative peace emerged after a period when the authorities tested the strength and resolve of the inspirados and their followers. Early on, the authorities attempted to slow the mobilization of the countryside that the preachers were propelling. They did this under pressure from coffee growers, who found that the preachers disrupted work rhythms on their haciendas. Sometime between 1907 and 1909, José Rodríguez Medina and Morales led a mission in the home of Poche Joglar in Ponce's mountainous district. There they were confronted by two police officers on horseback who arrived with orders to arrest the two leaders. Growers from the region, the police said, had filed a complaint against the Cheos, whom they charged with the loss of their coffee crops. Workers were attending misiones, often protracted affairs involving hours and even days of travel, instead of harvesting the beans. The officers, however, were unable to detain the suspects on that first outing. They could not identify the wanted men, and, even worse, they could not control their mounts. According to Rodríguez Medina, when police refused the Cheos's requests to allow them to appear before the judge on their own the following day, a great storm broke out. This scared the policemen's horses, which buckled and trembled, "bending their front legs as if they were trying to pray."[74]

As promised, the next day, Morales and his companion made the long march to Ponce. Along the way, thousands, including many coffee workers, joined them. A leaflet with the news of the arrests was passed from hand to hand. By the time the brothers appeared before Judge Felipe Casalduc, as many as 15,000 were gathered in the city. When the judge repeated the coffee growers' charge, Morales replied by saying that peoples' attendance was strictly voluntary. The judge agreed.

If there were any doubts as to the strength of the movement, they were dispelled immediately following the Cheos's release. The brothers had been sent home through a back door, without the gathering's knowledge. The crowd threatened to set fire to the city if the Cheos were not released before five in the afternoon. Fearful that the police would be unable to avert a riot, the judge took a carriage to collect the men before the deadline. Morales refused to go back, but he permitted Rodríguez Medina to do so. Rodríguez Medina defused the situation with the announcement that a mission would be held elsewhere that very evening. According to Rodríguez Medina's account, which Santaella Rivera cites, the Cheos's success on this day was unqualified. Not only did they escape incarceration, but they also secured Casalduc's support and scored a victory against Spiritism. Rosendo Matienzo Cintrón, it was said, had followed the crowd from Ponce, heard the preaching, and said politely to the Cheos: "Allow me to welcome you. We are at your service. From now on, things will change." Nonetheless, after this experience Morales resolved to avoid conflict and ceased to hold missions during the peak of the harvest.[75]

Elenita was never arrested, nor do local authorities seem to have considered her a threat. On the contrary, at least in San Lorenzo the local judge considered propaganda in favor of Catholicism desirable and supported Elenita, as well as church-sanctioned missionaries. On 9 October 1909, only days after the woman-virgin's death certificate was issued, Joaquín Crespo, a resident of Elenita's own barrio Espino, wrote the bishop. Crespo requested authorization to "continue in the same propaganda endeavors" as "the lady who called herself Elenita and later Madre Redentora." He also asked the bishop to send a missionary to carry on her campaign, which he claimed had transformed "precincts that were in a thicket into a garden of rich and fragrant flowers." In his letter, Crespo gave every indication that the local judge had acted as an intermediary between Elenita's followers and the official church. It was the judge who notified the bishop of the lady's apparent demise, and it was through the judge that the bishop was to reply to Crespo's request on behalf of San Lorenzo's laity.[76]

The state's attitude toward the enviados is difficult to reconcile with the rhetoric of many state officials regarding healers, prophets, and other agents of so-called superstition. Whereas physicians and rationalists in government posts condemned the religious and medical practices of the peasantry, much was tolerated in practice. A number of factors may be adduced by way of explanation. In spite of the change in colonial administrations and the boost this gave to the challengers of the church's monopolies, many judges, mayors, and police officers continued to adhere to Catholicism. Moreover, while potentially menacing, Elenita and the Cheos were seldom involved in outbreaks of violence. For the most part the inspirados kept to themselves, preaching in private homes throughout the countryside, a tendency that lends some qualified support to Quintero Rivera's characterization of Puerto Rican popular religion as a sort of marronage.[77]

In spite of the occasional charges of collusion with the partidas sediciosas, the inspirados may have benefited from comparison to the political factions that turned town squares into battle zones during election periods or to the so-called bandits that roamed the country pillaging and burning. Indeed, there is little evidence to support Zayas Micheli's assertion that the Cheos and Elenita should be regarded as moralizing equivalents to the partidas that so troubled the colonial and judicial authorities in the months following the U.S. invasion.[78] On the contrary, if their defenders are to be believed, the presence of the inspirados contributed to reductions in the incidence of the very crimes and vices that the state sought to curtail. Pronouncements against gambling, drunkenness, sexual depredations, and even cruelty to animals were leitmotifs of the Cheos's and Elenita's preaching. In a letter to the bishop expressing both his doubts and his excitement, the parish priest of Quebradillas appeared so moved by the transformation in the peasantry's conduct that he was prepared to contemplate the possibility that the inspirados were truly on to something: "Rough and rustic creatures as they are, they have acquired a preeminence over that great corrupt mass and have driven to submission hearts hardened by crime in a manner that only a supernatural force would have managed. . . . I can assure you that Aguada's parish priests . . . , as well as Hatillo's and the one who writes this, find ourselves confused, and we all believe that there is *something* superior to our intelligence that we cannot explain, for these creatures . . . have accomplished things that cannot be imagined[.]"[79]

Whether the much-lauded reduction in violence and crime actually occurred is difficult to substantiate. The records of police activity in San Lorenzo do not allow for direct comparisons between the periods preceding and following Elenita's ministry. Police logs from May to November 1904, however, suggest that the violence that was said to characterize San Lorenzo's and the island's rural life prior to the woman-virgin's arrival in 1899 had abated somewhat. Conditions, however, remained far from idyllic. During these six months in the middle of Elenita's stay in barrio Espino, police reported twenty counts of disorderly conduct (including fights); thirteen violations of the sanitation code; ten instances of animal cruelty; seven charges for illegal weapons; five thefts; five acts of aggression; five violations on the road (?); and two incidents involving disturbances of the peace. In short, the total number of arrests was sixty-seven among a population estimated at approximately 15,000.[80] The arrests carried out in San Lorenzo deviated somewhat from the islandwide pattern for this period. No gambling-related arrests took place, and the town did appear to have a lower rate of arrests for violent crimes shortly before such rates decreased islandwide. This lends some credence to Crespo's and Puras's claims but is far from conclusive. According to Kelvin Santiago-Valles, the leading causes for arrests in Puerto Rico in 1903 were, in descending order, disorderly conduct, gambling, assault, theft, and violations to the sanitation code. In 1905, however, disorderly conduct remained at the top but violations to the sanitary code had come to occupy the second spot, followed by gambling, assault, and theft.[81]

Other factors may have contributed to the perception of a reduction in crime in the first decade of the century. As mentioned above, the years between 1898 and 1900 were exceptionally violent throughout the island. (Santiago-Valles counts 130 murders in 1899 and only 41 in 1902). These were the days of the partidas and their vindictive acts. In addition, newspaper reports of homicides and aggravated assaults nearly trebled. These years were also racked by public outbursts of political violence, like the election-period riots in Caguas and Cayey in 1900.[82] The passing of these difficult days may have fostered a perception that crime was decreasing.

The demands of realpolitik contributed a good deal to staying the hand of the authorities when it came to the enviados and their followers, particularly in the later stages of the Cheo ministry. Howsoever state officials may have derided the ignorance of their compatriots in the hills, electoral politics had its own set of rules. Politicians, especially those in the *prohacendado* Unionist Party that dominated island politics until the 1920s, found it hard to resist a ready-made block of potential voters. Santaella Rivera reports that during election periods Unionist leaders were frequent visitors to the place pilgrims called *el trono* (the throne), the main Cheo chapel in Puerto Plata, Jayuya. Later on, the authoritarian José de los Santos Morales flirted with politics himself, running for office under the Unionist ticket. This identification with the party is not surprising; during this period the Unionists stood for a defense of the enterprises that provided livelihoods for much of the Cheos constituency. The party also championed the rights of the church against encroachment from other sectors.

Given the limitations of the evidence at hand, Rodríguez Pérez is justified in denying that the Cheos were uniformly pro-Unionist.[83] However, indications that pro-Unionist or at least anti-Republican sympathies predominated among the following of the woman-virgin and the sainted brotherhood should not be ignored. In his letter to Father Puras, San Juan's bishop charged that the parish priest had shown a desire to exacerbate rather than conciliate the animus of his adversaries, whom he did not identify. Puras replied with a revealing set of remarks. First, he identified his enemies as "impious atheists and some republicans (since the countryside is all republican, and that is not my fault)." Second, Puras accused a Sergio Mangual and a Cruz Mangual of spreading rumors against him because he had refused to "destroy" Brother Pancho, as Republicans had requested. According to Puras, these two men, "who have never set foot in Church, and who as recently as yesterday [bailed out] an anarchist," were clearly unworthy of the bishop's trust.

Though Puras may have been right about the extent of the Republicans' animosities toward Brother Pancho, he exaggerated when he intimated that the party's hostility extended to the church as a whole. Only a month before the exchange with the bishop, Puras himself had invited Cruz Mangual and his wife, along with local notables, to attend the blessing of the newly remodeled parish church. Chances are that Mangual had not refused to contribute to the project, as Puras now claimed in his letter to the bishop. Puras's own earlier account claimed that even Spiritists and Protestants contributed to the renovation fund. Even the most rancorous of adversaries in Puerto Rico's religious conflicts of the turn of the century declared the occasional truce.[84]

The Present, the Future, and the Need for Regeneration

Though enviados and the state managed to tolerate one another, often with an eye to strategic advantages, their perceptions of the changes gathering momentum since the mid-nineteenth century were decidedly at odds. Boosters who regarded the desirability of modernization as self-evident dominated the state and its bureaucracy. While Elenita and the Cheos were never opponents of technology and structural improvements as such, they did oppose the secularization of public order and knowledge that accompanied development. They viewed the markers of state-sponsored progress as omens of things to come. To Elenita and the Cheos the completion of such projects underscored the urgency of repentance and regeneration. In their prophecies, development—the construction of roads and the arrival of automobiles, airplanes, and communications technologies—figured prominently as a sign of the end of times.

When St. Francis of Sienna called for listeners to make amends and abandon sin, he assured them that "we are in the promised times," hence the urgency of the need for change now. Indeed, according to the saint, Puerto Rico was living on borrowed time. Hurricane San Ciriaco, the greatest disaster to befall the island to that date, had initiated a fifteen-minute countdown to the end. Mercifully, God had granted the island a respite, thanks to the intercession of "that Mother of Mercy." The saint urged the faithful to repent, that is, to renounce the quest for material gain, as well as the attachments to fashion, dancing, gambling, and drinking that fostered dissoluteness and crime. The point, however, was not to produce the improved citizenry that the state sought. St. Francis favored allegiance to a higher moral and religious code and condemned "the damned laws of men that cause so many souls to be lost." In order to release the soul from the body's hedonistic bondage, he recommended confession, good prayers, wearing the "holy scapulars of [Our Lady of] Carmel," carrying three crosses, and continued attendance to the missions.

Elenita, for her part, looked upon the future with a jaundiced eye. Though she pronounced the twentieth century a "century of light," her prophecies lent those words an ironic tone.[85] She anticipated times of disorder and wholesale corruption a few generations hence. Respect would be lost; children and parents would forsake one another; families would be torn asunder; there would be a universal war; and the world would take its last faltering steps as communism, an order predicated on godlessness, ascended to power. Puerto Rico itself would fall before the forces of chaos, its progress no more than a mirage. The country would be covered with roads; food and money would abound; men would "walk on the air" and ride on "headless horses and carriages without teams of oxen." But when people started speaking without seeing their interlocutors, presumably through telephones, the end would be at hand. Puerto Rico's farmlands would bear no fruits; people would refuse to work the soil; crowded hospitals would hand out poison; and true religion would fall prey to apathy and false prophets. Elenita would return near the end, but once again priests would fail to believe. In the end, the living and the dead would be judged in barrio Espino, San Lorenzo.

Neither the Cheos, as Rodríguez Pérez contends astutely, nor Elenita should be called full-fledged millenarians if by that term one means to designate those who felt compelled to hasten the coming of God's kingdom. Rather than instructing their followers on how to bring about the awaited end, the enviados urged their audiences to mend their ways so as to avert catastrophe or to ready themselves for the inevitable. What Rodríguez Pérez calls the Cheos's "prophetism," however, was ripe with millennial expectation, as can be readily seen from the descriptions of their prophecies above. Rodríguez Pérez refuses to classify the Cheos as a "messianic movement," arguing that they did not promote violence, as Brazilian messiahs supposedly did, nor did they declare any preacher to be a savior or deity. Whereas the first part of her argument is convincing in regard to the Cheos, the latter claim is problematic. The Cheos's involvement in violence was sporadic and begrudging. Morales never made any effort to realize his youthful dream of constituting a Catholic army capable of vanquishing by arms the enemies of the faith.[86] However, the preacher's claim to sanctity was far from clear-cut. While Rodríguez Pérez and Santaella Rivera may be correct in saying that no one regarded José de los Santos as God himself, few regarded him as an ordinary man. At the very least, some suggested he was a living saint. Others went further, as I have argued above. For her part, Elenita never called herself a messiah. But she certainly claimed a redemptive role, as indicated by her prophesied return at the end of times and by the title she assumed: "Redeeming Mother."

Although they may have been the principal propagandists of millennial fears and hopes in the island, Elenita and the Cheos were not alone in their calls for regeneration. During the first decades of the twentieth century, such cries rose from all quarters in a disconcerting din. Expectations for the future varied from the chiliastic pessimism of the enviados to the confident optimism of Spiritists and modernizers. But there was a remarkable consensus regarding the present: one way or another, it all had to change.

Spiritists sounded their calls shortly after American officers sounded off the march of U.S. troops throughout the island. In some respects, their agenda intersected that of state builders and Catholic moralists. Spiritists, like the enviados, the church hierarchy, and many turn-of-the-century physicians frowned upon gambling and regarded alcohol with suspicion, recommending temperance. Like state-builders and Protestant missionaries, they were advocates of education. But in many respects, the project was all their own. Following the founding of an islandwide Spiritist federation, they agitated for the abolition of the death penalty, for prison reform, for the introduction of lay "moral education" in the schools, and for the "moral and material improvement of the proletariat." The principle guiding their advocacy was a faith in the possibility of rehabilitation: victims and perpetrators alike suffered from ignorance, which could be corrected with instruction.

Even though they found the present sobering, Spiritists were hopeful. They derived hope from the conviction that progress was a law of nature. Kardec and his followers, many of whom were keen on Social Darwinism, transposed regnant notions of evolution to celestial strata.[87] Reincarnation operated in the spiritual plane just as natural selection did among earth's organisms. Each subsequent existence permitted the spirit to "advance" toward perfection. In 1901, Rosendo Matienzo Cintrón, who had recently abandoned a court bench in Ponce to join Puerto Rico's governing executive council, began a campaign to propagate these views. In public lectures, newspaper serials, and books he announced that "all of history is nothing but a demonstration of human progress, and this progress means nothing other than that man's faculties grow ceaselessly."[88] His optimism found corroboration with the spirits themselves, who urged men and women to take heart. In "From Beyond the Grave," a regular feature in *El Iris de Paz*, a "progress-loving spirit" assured those dedicated to "the regenerating enterprise" that "the hordes of obscurantism" would be vanquished now that a new century "of transcendental transformations of the psychic as well as the moral orders" had "dawned" for humanity.[89]

The church concurred that there was a pressing need for regeneration. In fact, the hierarchy's assessment of early-twentieth-century Puerto Rico was often grimmer than the Spiritists', a judgment that was no doubt colored by the erosion of the position of the church as a whole. However, the clergy objected to the Spiritist and Protestant argument that the church and its teachings were responsible for the island's moral turpitude. They also contested the unidirectional notion of progress that Spiritists espoused. In the course of a protracted polemic, the church argued that the answer to the island's problems lay in a return to the fundamentals of the Catholic faith. In a series of twenty articles titled "Social Regeneration—The Salvation of Puerto Rico," Jáuregui, apparently a priest, summarized the ecclesiastical take: "We defined regeneration and explained what this word means to us. We pointed at the words of our Holy Father Pope Pious X as demonstration that the Catechism was the best means for the regeneration of society. We followed this with a study of the causes of social degeneration, focusing on the main ones: ignorance and concupiscence."[90]

Others denounced the Spiritists' idea of progress as a "rationalist" misperception. In a retort to Matienzo Cintrón, *El Ideal Católico* argued that no "revolution," a term that stood for regeneration in Spiritist parlance, had ever led to true advancement. The journal charged that the use of science "for a social and religious unhinging" was no progress at all, for it only spelled the "triumph of the principles of avarice and sensuality." True progress, the Catholic journalist argued, lay in "knowing, serving and loving our Lord God." Only by living in accordance with divine design would man reach his ultimate perfection.[91]

It should be mentioned parenthetically that Protestant missionaries also found Puerto Rico a den of material deprivation, ignorance, and moral destitution. Like the Spiritists, they held the dual legacies of Catholicism and Spanish colonialism responsible. And they offered several correctives, including the Gospel and American know-how. With the assistance of U.S. authorities, they launched a civilizing mission that aimed to address spiritual and mundane needs in tandem. Their efforts concentrated in three areas: education, care for the indigent, and evangelizing.

Professionals, particularly those involved in the program-building of the early 1900s, echoed religious clamor for regeneration, though this time in the language of hygiene and contagion. In Puerto Rico, as elsewhere in Latin America, physicians were particularly outspoken. Dr. Manuel Quevedo Báez, for example, declared in the newly founded *Boletín de la Asociación Médica de Puerto Rico* (1903) that government had a dual responsibility to ensure material advancement as well as moral progress through "moral prophylaxis."[92] Medical professionals, for their part, should treat individuals and also society for those infirmities with an ethical etiology. The eugenics-tinged list included many ailments that the Lombroso school of criminology had identified. Alcoholism, prostitution, mental retardation, criminality, superstition, and quackery, all of which were believed to cause the degradation of genetic "types," preoccupied doctors through the first half of the twentieth century.[93]

Though regenerative regimes varied, religious and lay proponents often coincided in the redemptive functions they assigned Puerto Rican women. Spiritists counted on them to instruct their families, and especially their children, in the discoveries of the science-religion. The Catholic hierarchy, well aware of men's apathy, expected women to maintain tradition and faith in the home. Physicians, for their part, sought to cut off disease vectors that originated in pregnancy and motherhood and asked women to bring their homemaking and child-rearing practices into conformity with scientific norms. Catholics, Spiritists, and inspirados, I argue below, followed different routes to a common destination; they all imagined women as the strongholds of the faith and assigned them a leading but ultimately subordinate role in their crusades.

Contesting Women

The turn of the twentieth century witnessed bitter contests for the allegiances of Puerto Rico's rural population and especially for the support of women. Though

Protestants, Catholics, and Spiritists charted very different courses to regeneration, all parties concurred in their strategic assessments: Women were the key to their hopes and ambitions for the future. This climate of opinion created new opportunities for women, who took on roles as public intermediaries with remarkable success. Women's participation, however, did not entail the triumph of a protofeminist agenda. Most imagined regeneration in more or less patriarchal terms. That was certainly the case with the peripatetic misioneras, with Elenita, and even with many Spiritist leaders.

El Ideal Católico, one of the church's defensive organs, feared that men were hopelessly lost to the church. Now that Spiritists and Protestants had launched proselytizing offensives, apostasy was sure to follow. When men were not actively hostile to Catholicism, the newspaper sentenced, they were mired in "glacial indifference." Those who would reaffirm the "one true Religion" found their solace in women. Disregarding women's eminence in the Spiritist movement, they affirmed that Puerto Rican women were "Catholic in their totality." Moreover, they viewed women as the key to the restitution of moral order; they would bring their families to the ecclesiastic fold and animate the regeneration of the island through their feminine and maternal virtues. Devotion, restraint, and sacrifice would save the island. Women would return Puerto Rico to the values of old and the sacraments. As the Catholic organ put it, "After God, we base the hopes we have for the future in them; the moral and religious regeneration of this people will be reached through her."[94]

Spiritist propaganda also made women the motors of moral revolution.[95] For that reason, Spiritist speakers and organs sought to bring women to the science-religion. Besides their appeals to scientific reason and progress, propagandists proclaimed that Spiritism was the route to women's liberation from ignorance and subjection. Liberation, however, was often as much about women's rights as it was about combating Catholicism. Emancipation from the bondage of the church was a precondition to the exercise of women's individual freedoms. José Reyes Calderón, editor of *El Racionalista Cristiano* and one of several travelers who had brought news of Manso to Puerto Rico, illustrated this point in one of his articles. While celebrating the opportunities for regeneration that the convergence of Spiritism and a "liberal" administration—that is, American neocolonialism—offered women and the island, he urged women to take on the clergy. Though women were not recognized as political actors with citizenship rights, Reyes assigned women enormous political responsibilities. Women, Reyes argued, were "called upon to play a role of great importance in the life of this country, lending it, with the vigorous exercise of its spirit, the contingent of her intellectual forces, which shall propel the coming generation along the holy road to progress." "But to conquer this advance," he cautioned, it would be "necessary for her to appear free of all clerical tutelage before her home and her own free conscience." Reyes pled: "Oh! Puerto Rican woman, wake up and emancipate yourself from the Catholic yoke, for that shall be your redemption through which you shall conquer your legitimate rights on the stage of civilization and progress."[96]

Puerto Rican Spiritists, however, assumed ambiguous stances when it came to women's rights. In Puerto Rico, as in the United States, reformist impulses coexisted with a desire to limit women's roles in the public sphere.[97] Spiritism offered Puerto Rican women the first opportunities for religious leadership outside of nunneries. Women occupied positions of note in the Spiritist press and in other organizations within the movement. Agustina Guffain, for instance, founded and edited *El Iris de Paz* in 1901. When the Spiritist Federation was created two years later, the assembly named Guffain's journal its official organ and elected her honorary president.[98] Though no tally is available, Puerto Rican women were also reputed to constitute the majority of mediums in Spiritist societies and were believed to dominate the ranks of espiritistas who practiced autonomously and eclectically throughout the countryside, much to the chagrin of purists.

But mediumship itself was a complicated vehicle for women's deliverance. Though it could challenge the silence expected of women in public, the operation usually required an altered state, which ultimately authorized speech. In a sense, many women mediums did not speak with their own voices. Spirits rather than their living conduits could be credited for the skills women displayed. It is true that Spiritists advocated civil marriage, divorce, and voting rights and countenanced women's participation in the professions. But Spiritist cries often echoed some of the patriarch's favorite lines, as occurred when they insisted on the link between femininity and devotion, and again when they enlisted women—now equipped with the new possibilities that Spiritism opened up—in the service of their children and husbands for the sake of the regeneration of the island.

While encouraging women to rise to the level of men, or at least close to it, some Spiritists continued to regard womanhood as a "natural" encumbrance. A spirit's reincarnation in a female body could imply a relatively low ranking on the scale that measured progress toward perfection. Only Spiritism offered women a way to rise above their lot. During a moment of tempered fatalism, a female Spiritist writer put it thus: "Woman, for your expiation, today you have a casing that forces you (unless you uplift yourself) to be a slave to men, to suffer innumerable humiliations, to be a mere wet nurse rather than a mother to your children[.]"[99]

Radical as Spiritism's advocacy of women's rights appeared to the church, practitioners of the science-religion could draw the outer boundaries of women's freedom close to where tradition had supposedly set them. When Francisca Suárez argued that Spiritist women surpassed all others in their three fundamental roles—daughter, wife, and mother—she was hardly delivering a revolutionary manifesto. Reverberations of the cult of true womanhood, the din of the women's rights lecture hall, and the sounds of women's natural predisposition to piety rose simultaneously in the Spiritist cry. As a daughter, Suárez explained, a Spiritist woman watched over family harmony. As a spouse, she married for love, though she continued to respect her husband's will as if it were her own. And as a mother, she was concerned with raising rational Christians and with the fate of unfortunate youths. Outside of the home, she was an effective propagandist. And knowing that idleness only breeds vice, she was also laborious and seldom given to vanity. "Pious par excellence," such a woman would "turn her home into a sanctuary in which she will officiate as a priestess to duty, adoring God in spirit and truth; she will have no secrets for her life's companion, unlike Catholic women who place Rome's priest between her husband and herself[.]"[100]

As Suárez demonstrated, the contest between Spiritists and Catholics often focused on questions of marriage. The Spiritist clamor for changes to the institution was more than a matter of legal reform. In large part, marriage was hotly contested because the church regarded it as a sacrament, a zone of exclusive ecclesiastical privilege. Priests feared that even those who had no intention of "abjuring" Catholicism as such would insist on the right to marry outside the church, as Matías Cancel and Juana Nieves did in late 1898, to the irritation of the Lares parish priest. The church feared that the lower cost of civil ceremonies and the perception that state-sanctioned weddings were somehow more legitimate would continue to reduce the number of church weddings.[101]

Though Spiritists also regarded consensual unions as undesirable, they objected to the hierarchy's efforts to put an end to the increasingly widespread practice of cohabitation through ecclesiastical sanction. After all, the church's struggle to bolster the sacraments was directly at odds with a Spiritist agenda bent on breaking ecclesiastical monopolies and reinforcing the boundaries between church and state. It is for this reason that both sides used the prevalence of civil versus ecclesiastical marriages as a gauge of their progress toward regeneration and of their standing in Puerto Rico's religious contests.[102] And it was also for this reason that the inspirados urged their followers so ardently to sanctify their unions in church.

The church's trust in women may have been inflated, but it was not misplaced.

As Santaella Rivera and Agosto Cintrón have observed, it was precisely rural women who first rose to defend Catholicism from the challenges of Spiritism, Protestantism, and the government's secularism. The role of the intermediaries, those who bridged the gaps between the church and Catholic practice, was gendered female at the outset, and only gradually did men come into play. A young woman remembered only as Hermana Eudosia was the first to take on the part. She began speaking in Quebradillas in 1899 on the feast day dedicated to the Virgin's celestial ascent (15 August), scarcely seven days after Hurricane San Ciriaco struck the island. Though little is known of Eudosia's preaching, it is clear that she had a direct influence over the Cheos's missions. Eusebio Quiles, who later inspired Morales to initiate his ministry, was himself galvanized by the nineteen-year-old sister's preaching.[103]

In many respects, the inspirados lived by values and gender norms that they shared with the institutional church and, as shown above, with some reform-minded Spiritists as well. Women preached with the authority that those who observed proper conduct to the point of saintliness could demand. And yet, in taking on public roles, these women also deviated from the norm. This deviation, however, cannot be reduced to what Rodríguez Pérez has called Elenita's rupture with "machismo." As Agosto Cintrón has shown, Elenita resolved the contradiction of being both a misionera and a good Catholic woman through an invocation of Marian authority and the promotion of a hypernomian code of conduct that remained generally consistent with patriarchal norms. Elenita's charisma held dominant, androcentric values in temporary abeyance. But upon her passing, authority reverted to such men as Brother Pancho and the priests who came to Montaña Santa periodically to say Mass. An overview of the careers of some inspiradas shows that women associated with the Cheo movement had less autonomy than Elenita, who, in calling herself the Virgin, deprived all mortals of authority over her life.[104]

The turn-of-the-century religious awakenings held opportunities for women, but these were more tightly regulated than it first appears. Eudosia died after only a three-year ministry, when Morales was just fifteen. In subsequent years, many other women would figure prominently within and outside of the brotherhood. But here, too, the role of women was gradually circumscribed until the Cheos refused to admit them as evangelists. Safety concerns and the responsibilities of motherhood and matrimony, as Morales and other leaders defined them, were thought to preclude an itinerant, public life. Women were not readmitted into the brotherhood until 1974, when the congregation was well past its prime.[105]

Among Cheos, womanhood posed obstacles that childhood did not. Eugenia

Torres Soto, better known as Hermana Geña, was among the most noted Cheo preachers. She began her career (also on 15 August) as a girl of twelve, after one of Morales's missions helped "spread the preachers' fever" throughout her barrio in Peñuelas. She gained recognition from Morales and returned home to preach for a number of years, often traveling in the company of her mother. Later, however, Morales sent Geña to Ponce, saying that no one could be a good prophet at home. After Brother Pancho's death, she relocated anew, this time to San Lorenzo and then to Caguas. But when Sister Geña married, the three principal Cheo leaders—Morales, Rodríguez, and Pedro Laboy—put an end to her missions. As a girl in her mother's care, Geña could move about with relative freedom. But as a married woman, no such behavior was allowed.

Unhappy in her marriage, Sister Geña moved again to Ponce, where she worked at a sanatorium until her husband's death. Only widowhood made it possible for the preacher to return to her ministry. But having been liberated from the vows of marriage, she found it necessary to renounce the duties of motherhood, too. Geña relinquished her two children to the care of Ponce's orphanages and only when wholly "free again" did she return to public life. In order to do this she was favored with exemptions from Monsignor Byrne, who approved her children's admission in orphanages, and from Morales, who allowed the sister to hold missions again in 1938.[106]

While initially tolerant of female preaching, the inspirados' understanding of gender roles generally reinforced sexual mores that weighed heavily on women. Both males and females were admonished to renounce the gratification of the body, but it was women's mobility and contacts with men that were most firmly regulated. Beyond observing absolute celibacy herself, Elenita ascribed immense value to chastity. She surrounded herself with a group of young girls, always virgins, whom she instructed in housekeeping and religious duties. These girls were the only persons to share any sort of ordinary contact with the misionera, for she insisted that no others should touch her. Elenita made a point of sending chaperones along with the girls to prevent inappropriate trysts and sexual violence, and on the occasions when the girls moved about unescorted, they were told not to fear because a "guard dog" accompanied them wherever they went. Girls who fell in love were excluded from her company. Some girls, however, remained virgins for life, as Elenita had prophesied.[107]

During her life at Montaña Santa, Elenita's words were peremptory; both men and women obeyed them as commands. Elenita's style was no less authoritarian than Morales's. Cheo preachers insisted on the virtue of absolute obedience, and Morales was quick to expel those who did not respond with haste and conviction.

Elenita was similarly autocratic. She did not consult others, nor did she abide by their opinions. Moreover, she could tell when obedience had been begrudging or when her orders had been disregarded.

Elenita's authority, however, flowed from several sources. As a woman, it should be noted, she remained unmarried and unattached to any organization. This meant that unlike Sister Geña, she never had obligations to husband, child, or *principal*. Beyond that, however, Elenita's power had the imprint of divine agency. She spoke not as a woman but as the Virgin herself. As shown above, this identification was revealed in a variety of pronouncements and made concrete in Elenita's appearance and conduct. Her observance of purity was so strict as to make her more than merely virginlike.

While affording her access to prerogatives ordinarily reserved for men, Elenita's identification with the Virgin had high costs. It certainly was not a formula for the emancipation of women. Even if one does not go as far as Agosto Cintrón, who argues that "the exaltation of the Virgin Mary as a feminine ideal was predicated upon a denigrating view of Mary and the whole of humanity, but especially of women," it is clear that Elenita's vision was predicated upon patriarchal conventions.[108] Though she took on a role closed to most women of her day, access to such power required a strict enforcement of tenets that valued women primarily as virgins, mothers, and wives.

Saints Remembered and Forgotten

In Cuba and Puerto Rico, man-gods, woman-virgins, and living saints demarcated zones of contest between religion and the state and dominant and subaltern visions. The conflicts varied, however, according to local context, as did the loyalties of inspired men and women themselves. Indeed, the complexity of the conflicts was such that facile binarisms such as church versus state, traditional versus modern, or Catholic versus Spiritist can scarcely be sustained. Whereas in Cuba, Manso and Mustelier were associated with Spiritism, in Puerto Rico, Elenita and the Cheos declared themselves paladins of Catholicism and enemies of the science-religion. The first entered into a struggle with the republic's authorities, while the second were primarily concerned with religious competitors. Nonetheless, both Cubans and Puerto Ricans proposed alternative visions of the future and questioned state-sponsored notions of progress. Elenita and the Cheos went as far as to connect development and the day of judgment. Yet the inspirados were not traditionalists in the common usage of the term.

The Puerto Rican figures are instructive in that they highlight the qualified and contradictory nature of the engagements generated by the irruption of man-gods and saints into the public sphere. Not only do Elenita and the Cheos remind us that the suspicions of the powerful (in government, the church, or elsewhere) did not always translate into repression, as the Cuban figures already made plain, but they demonstrate that man-gods and inspirados could also serve mediating functions. Elenita and the Cheos did more than provoke ruptures; they negotiated a sort of peace between institutional Catholicism and the quotidian practices of the majority at a moment when the church faced serious challenges from Spiritism, Protestantism, and secularism. As shown above, women were the first to take up the role of the intermediary, partly in response to multiple religious and secular appeals to mothers and wives to become agents for the regeneration of the island.

The mediator's role was itself hard-fought. And as one would expect, there were both short- and long-term losers in this game. In spite of their intentions, Elenita and the Cheos roused the hostility of some within the church. The Cheos, whose claims to sanctification were recast in accord with ecclesiastical orthodoxy, eventually gained the hierarchy's endorsement. Ironically, the churchly embrace appears to have suffocated the brotherhood. Only a few years after official recognition, the group's energies had largely dissipated. Today, the brotherhood subsists with a reduced membership. The hierarchy's gradual softening toward the Cheos did not extend to Elenita or her memory. The woman-virgin, who left little doubt as to her claims to divinity, continues to generate controversies to this day. While some members of the clergy and even the former bishop of Caguas have been open to the possibility that Elenita might be recognized some day as a legitimate apparition, the church has indicated its unwillingness to do that.[109] The sanctuary honoring Our Lady of Mt. Carmel, established in Montaña Santa shortly after Elenita's "change," remains open to the public. But the church has discouraged pilgrimages and devotions honoring "Vuestra Madre" in an effort to stave off a revival of the holy site that took place during the 1980s. The sanctuary is not what it once was, but it survives: Catholics, Spiritists, New Agers, and the simply curious pray in Montaña Santa, where people also collect water from a healing spring. Elenita continues to appear in visions to the faithful, and the outcome of her prophetic pronouncements is eagerly, albeit quietly, awaited.

3
GOVERNING WITCHCRAFT
Journalists and Brujos in Republican Cuba

The year 1919 opened a grim new chapter in the annals of what scholar Ernesto Chávez Alvarez has called the "militant Negrophobia" of the Cuban republic. This year witnessed a public fright of witchcraft, or brujería, that seems to have bordered upon genuine panic. White families circled the wagons, many fearing or claiming to fear that their children would be abducted and sacrificed by the negros brujos, a group of blacks imagined in counterpoint to the familiar black figures who had long been entrusted with child-care responsibilities in many households. Because of the scare and its surveillance tactics many Afro-Cubans, especially males, were confronted with life-threatening suspicions. According to contemporary reports, black men carrying a bundle or a bag (in which ritual implements or sacrificial remains could be hidden), passing through an unfamiliar neighborhood, or participating in a celebration that involved drumming, or anyone who happened to resemble the vague description of a suspect could find himself accused of witchcraft, kidnapping, and even murder. The consequences of these accusations could be somber indeed, as witnessed by the lynchings in Regla and Matanzas and other similar attempts at vigilante justice. Among the first decades of this century, the memory of 1919 is surpassed in its brutality only by recollections of 1912, the year in which Afro-Cubans said to support the Partido Independiente de Color were cut down in a massacre that claimed thousands of lives.[1]

Fear of the sort of witchcraft that preyed upon children was not precisely new; it had been around since at least the nineteenth century, when Spanish authorities accused runaway slaves who raided estates in eastern Cuba and liberated their slaves of abducting white children only to kill them in barbaric rituals. Such concerns were reactivated in 1918–19 by a widely reported series of alleged abductions and murders.[2] Although most of these were later shown to have nothing to do with brujos, the supposed crimes inspired such dread that a grave threat was conjured. One consequence of the scare was that atrocities as barbarous as those that white infants supposedly suffered were visited upon black adults. On 28 January 1919, for instance, a Jamaican man named Williams (or Menem, according to *El Mundo*) was taken from police custody and dragged behind a horse through Regla's streets until he was dead. According to the newspapers, the mob was convinced that Williams was a brujo and that he had intended to lure and kidnap a white girl to whom he had offered candy. Williams's identity as a savage was confirmed after the fact by an impossibly fragile narrative; it was said that this man had purchased his hat in Colón, which, according to rumors and news reports, was a center of witchcraft activity.

Several papers celebrated the lynching. *El Día*, for instance, remarked that paradoxical as it seemed, this killing was "a step toward civilization," a sentiment that found echoes elsewhere. *La Prensa* also praised the action at first, but a few days later the newspaper published an account by a white worker who denied that Williams had ever been a brujo. The source suggested instead that Williams had been killed because of a labor dispute in which Jamaicans had been hired as scabs.[3] Whatever the immediate motivation, Williams's death was the bloody and foreseeable denouement to a pattern of discursive and physical violence that had been long in developing and that would last for some years still. Time and again, rumors and the news of the day combined with other interests and the demands of a civilizing and modernizing mission into an exceedingly volatile mixture.

Even more than Williams's gruesome killing, the spark that touched off the terrors and repression of 1919 was the *crimen de la niña Cecilia*, a crime that, like all others of its ilk, was known to great effect by the name of the infantile victim. According to the many reports circulating in the press, in June 1919, José Claro Reyes and a cabal of four male and two female accomplices seized and killed a three-year-old "white" girl from Matanzas. The negros brujos, it was believed, sacrificed the girl in a macabre religious ceremony in an effort to heal some patients. In the course of the ritual, they were said to have extracted the girl's viscera and removed her heart. Most disturbing of all, they were also believed to have eaten some of these parts, perhaps salting some of the remains in order to preserve them.

Cecilia's disappearance caused unrest in Matanzas, which resulted in the imposition of martial law and unleashed a campaign to ferret out practitioners of Afro-Cuban religions, much of which could be construed as brujería because this category of criminal activity was porous and ill-defined at best.[4] Even before a body had been located, the military authorities charged with the investigation were looking for brujos, who in the officers' minds made for the likeliest culprits. Eight alleged witches and wizards were arrested, and one reportedly committed suicide while in custody on 28 June 1919. When his body was brought before Reyes, the suspected mastermind of the crime, he broke under the implicit threat and reportedly revealed the place where he had buried the girl's body.[5] And, indeed, a mutilated body was found where Reyes indicated, although there was no certainty that the child was truly Cecilia. News of the finding spread throughout the city, and by evening a riotous crowd had gathered in front of Fort San Severino, where Reyes and his alleged accomplices were held. The mob demanded that the authorities turn over the inmates, but the soldiers refused and fired on the crowd, killing two men. The guards, however, soon balanced the score, for they also killed the adult male suspects in their custody, charging that they had attempted to escape amid the confusion. Later, in April 1919, the court released the two women and a male survivor, and the press was forced to concede that at least some of these people could have had no hand in the crime.

Fatal though it proved, this act of mob justice by proxy did not assuage fears in Matanzas. The threat of brujería, it would seem, could not be expiated even with the immolation of half a dozen men. In the weeks that followed the killings, the press reported on at least ten attempted kidnappings and murders throughout Matanzas and elsewhere in the island, especially in the province of Havana. Some of the reports named specific children, such as Rosa, the young daughter of a police lieutenant involved in the investigation of Cecilia's murder, whose alleged victimizer was nearly lynched himself en route to the police station and again later in a confrontation between the police and a mob.[6] Other reports, however, only referred to unnamed victims and to failed "attempts." Yet others were no more than oracular exercises and transparent rumormongering. On 7 July, for instance, the *Heraldo de Cuba* issued a warning against the possible excesses of the witch hunt in Matanzas. The article that broached such reservations ran under a headline that left some doubt as to the sincerity of the newspaper's concern; the block letters read: "Ogun has asked for more human flesh and Shango needs more children's blood to purify and elevate its spirit." This was followed a few days later by a piece in which reporter Pedro M. García warned that Saint Barbara, a saint associated with the orisha Changó in Santería, had ordered two future crimes to be committed in Jovellanos.[7]

There can be no doubt that the press—by its relentless coverage, its inflammatory commentary, its alarmist pronouncements, and its demands for punitive intervention—did a great deal to fuel the witchcraft scares. Chávez Alvarez, Aline Helg, Stephan Palmié, and Alejandra Bronfman all concur in this regard, and their opinion is corroborated by contemporary testimonies of reporters who congratulated themselves for their role in ridding Cuba of superstition and crime and by the denunciations of prominent Afro-Cubans who faulted the press for its sensationalism. Evidently, journalists did more than recount these stories; they were directly involved in the affairs they covered. They accompanied or guided investigators and police to the sites of crimes; they interviewed suspects along with judicial officials, and they even served as witnesses for the prosecution in several cases. Press accounts, moreover, frequently provided the raw materials for erudite analyses, as was most notably the case with *Los negros brujos* (1906). As others have observed, Fernando Ortiz wrote the book that launched him into intellectual celebrity while outside of Cuba and largely on the basis of press clippings and correspondence with informants. The volume, Chávez Alvarez has shown, became in turn a sort of manual for the prosecution of brujos and the interpretation of their motives.

In spite of all this, to maintain that the fears surrounding brujería and Afro-Cubans were the product of a racist conspiracy headed by newspapermen and set in motion by the machinations of the press overstates the case and obfuscates some important dynamics. As Palmié and Bronfman both argue, the creation of the category called brujería, with all of its dismal consequences, came about as a result of a collective social and intellectual enterprise in which anthropological, legal, police, and press discourses constituted one another in the terms proposed by positivist criminology. The press, then, was not alone in contributing to the atmosphere that made repression of Afro-Cubans appear both sensible and necessary. As seen above, a minority sector of the white-dominated press voiced occasional criticisms of the campaign against blacks and their religious practices. More importantly, some Afro-Cuban leaders used their own papers and other publications that would listen to register their dissenting views. Rather than detailing the inner workings of a conspiracy, this chapter seeks to untangle the involvement of the press in the collective operations that generated the witchcraft scares.

I suggest that, rather than dreaming up stories, the press and others interested in deploying narratives about the ritual killing of white children functioned within the parameters of a genre, or to speak with Palmié, a "discursive regime." Reportage and even rumor were ruled by conventions that appealed to the "common sense" and the scholarly wisdom of the day. Moreover, the rumors and misinformation that the press propagated with such eagerness may not have been always the cynical fabrications of those who controlled the media. Indeed, the relationship between the press and the reportedly indignant citizenry was less one-sided than it first appears. The press did shape "public opinion," but the public also had some impact on reportage. In a similar vein, the persecution of Afro-Cubans on account of their practices, while certainly responding to the interests of the elite, was at times also mediated by individual interests, including those of some practitioners of Afro-Cuban religions. Although these practitioners were unable to control or direct the repression, they were sometimes able to manipulate the machinery of discipline to their own private ends.

The *Asesinato* Ritual as a Genre

In spite of the signal role played by Cecilia's murder, the scare of 1919 cannot be attributed to a single event or to a single type of practice. The repression and its discourses bundled ñáñigos and their gangster-infested "secret societies" with stories of ignorant healers who endangered public health, charlatans who took advantage of "public credulity," and narratives of abduction and child sacrifice. All of these and unexpected others, such as Catholic processions, were cast as evidence of a generalized, twentieth-century recrudescence of superstition, obscurantism, and backwardness. I focus here only on the last type of crime, mainly because this was the one that preoccupied journalists, even if it did not result in a great number of arrests.[8] Ñañiguismo, though vigorously prosecuted under the new regime, was waning by the second and third decades of the century; its criminalization, moreover, owed its origins to a late colonial initiative that the republican authorities carried on. In contrast, the most abhorrent acts of brujería, what the authorities called "ritual murders," appear to be of a distinctly modern vintage. These were properly republican horrors that the law was ill-equipped to handle.[9]

As adverted above, the conflicts between the republic and the brujos were not the only instances of friction between the new order and religion when the republic first tried to balance the interests of "freedom" with those of "civilization." Indeed, conflicts of the sort could be said to characterize the advent of republican modernization. Although Afro-Cuban child-murderers were indubitably singled out for the harshest treatment, it should be remembered that the state attempted to regulate a number of religious practices at this time, in spite of the formal guarantees of freedom of religion. As they launched the first waves of the antibrujo repression, the authorities turned their attention to Catholicism, particularly to those expressions that served as public occasions for popular celebration and elite pageantry. Late in November 1904, for instance, representatives to the House debated the merits of a bill banning religious processions through the streets. Enrique Villuendas, a frank supporter of the measure, expressed surprise that after six years of the new regime persons trying to revive conquered traditions should remain active. He argued further that religious tolerance only obtained in countries living in ignorance.[10] Havana's Catholics responded to these efforts with a challenge; rather than abiding by the ban on their 8 December procession honoring the Virgin (La Purísima Concepción), thousands marched through the streets and more than 10,000 gathered in front of Havana's cathedral for the celebration that followed.[11]

Strictly speaking, the so-called ritual murders should not be called events or occurrences but rather recurrences. As Chávez Alvarez has observed, Cecilia's crime of 1919 belongs in a gruesome cycle. By his count, there were at least eight such crimes alleged in the years between 1904 and 1923.[12] My own count, which is far from systematic, brings the number to well over three dozen in the period between 1903 and 1943.[13] This figure includes prosecuted cases as well as rumored and attempted kidnappings and murders reported in the press and the popular police chronicles of those days. This count excludes, of course, the dozens of kidnappings for ransom and other forms of banditry common during the first decades of the century that reporters endeavored to distinguish from the acts of brujos, even when the two could prove difficult to differentiate.[14]

The paradigmatic or defining incident was the much-publicized *crimen de la niña Zoila*, which took place in Güira de Melena, Havana province, in 1904. The official reconstruction of the event went something like this: an elderly African-born man and "known brujo" called Domingo Bocourt diagnosed the premature deaths of Juana Tabares's newborns as the result of a *daño* (literally, harm) caused by whites during the days of slavery.[15] He resolved to heal the woman with the blood of a white infant, and to this end he recruited another man to find a suitable victim and commit the crime. This man, Víctor Molina, along with an African-born accomplice, kidnapped twenty-month-old Zoila and murdered her in order to use her blood, heart, and entrails in a series of witchcraft rituals. They then recruited another two men to assist them in hiding the body. Although the evidence was largely circumstantial, the suspects—all of whom were connected to an Afro-Cuban association known as the Congos Reales—were convicted and received lengthy prison sentences. Bocourt and Molina were singled out for even harsher punishment and received death sentences. Aline Helg, whose account I have just summarized, notes in her analysis precisely the point I wish to highlight here. She observes that "in reality, it seems that the strength of the 'public rumor,' its correspondence to deeply held stereotypes and the conviction of the journalists determined the fate of the accused from the outset."[16]

After the successful prosecution of Zoila's alleged killers, press and judicial accounts of kidnappings and ritual murders acquired a formulaic quality. Indeed it could be said that Zoila transformed public rumors and common wisdom into a genre whose contours can be easily outlined. Generally, the narratives of these crimes begin with a description of a decent, hardworking family whose chief joy is their young children. The assault of a black stranger or casual acquaintance, usually male and at first also African-born, soon breaks into the idyllic scene, causing a general alarm. A search designed to beat out the culprits is conducted throughout the area, and one or more centers of brujería are uncovered or, in many cases, rediscovered, for their existence is generally a matter of common knowledge. A likely perpetrator, often linked to a group of accomplices, emerges, and soon the motivations for the attack surface. The brujos, moved either by their superstitious logic or by their criminal instincts, usually intend to heal a relative, a friend, or a paying client. Typically, the ailments include sterility or chronic afflictions such as tuberculosis and rheumatism. The blood (and often the heart and viscera) of a white child is required for the treatment.

In the course of telling such stories, reporters also condemned superstition and witchcraft, demanded particular government actions, exhorted the public in one direction or another, and even proposed prophylactic and punitive policies to contend with the brujería problem they had helped diagnose and constitute. These denunciatory incursions were not mere moralizing asides. Commentary on the need to extirpate backwardness and these criminal affronts to culture and civilization was an expected part of the discursive regime upon which Cubans attempted to construct the edifice of republican modernity.

Although no one individual or agency was capable of controlling the entire spectrum of popular and learned discourses associated with the ritual-murder genre, the willful deployment and manipulation of Zoila-like narratives was possible at times. In fact, Zoila's story would haunt more than a few Afro-Cubans for decades. Among those victims, one might count Desiderio Padrón, a twenty-five-year-old black man who was arrested on New Year's Day 1910.[17] He was accused of attempting to abduct a white girl named Esperanza from her home in El Gabriel on Christmas eve. Several witnesses placed Padrón near the house where the girl lived, but there were few indications as to his motives and no way to confirm the suspicion that brujería was implicated in the attack. Zoila's case, however, offered a scenario that could be extended to incriminate the suspect, who claimed that he had been looking for work around there and that the girl

Zoila's burial in El Gabriel's cemetery. From *El Fígaro*, 4 December 1904.
(Widener Library, Harvard College Library, KJ54)

had been scared of him when he walked by, "as white people are often scared of blacks." According to a Rural Guardsman named Guerra, Padrón's crime confirmed rumors that had reached him months earlier when it was said that brujos were plotting to commit a robbery or perhaps a new kidnapping. Guerra speculated further that it was "very possible that someone would now try to commit a new abduction to do with her something analogous to what was done with Zoila, since the brujos have the custom of performing cures among themselves using the blood of a white girl." The only snag in the proposed plot was that no sick person had turned up; Padrón himself appeared healthy. After some pointed questioning, however, a complete montage was erected in conformity with niña Zoila's precedent. During his second appearance before the court, Guerra noted that even though Padrón had lived for some time with a "very light-skinned mestiza," they had not had any children. Zoila, he recalled, had been killed precisely to cure a reproductive ailment. El Gabriel's reputation as a hotbed of witchcraft dating back to the days of the 1904 crime and the presence in town of a group known as "Los Congos" that celebrated *bembés* (feasts involving drumming and dancing) lent additional credence to Guerra's notion that "in this town there are many brujos capable of taking this girl as they did some time ago with Zoila."[18] Circumstance and speculations marked Padrón as a likelier brujo than most.

By the 1920s, the child-murder genre was sufficiently entrenched as to permit falsification. In 1922, for instance, the death of a girl named Cuca was reported in Camagüey. *El País* covered the crime and editorialized that it was cowardly that ten or twenty brujos had not paid for the crime with their lives. It was later determined, however, that the child's death had been accidental and that the mother had mutilated the body in an effort to simulate a ritual murder because she was afraid to confront her husband with the news.[19] Among other reasons, the incident is significant because it hints at the public's manipulation of the press in a move that reverses the more usual understanding. Here it is not the public who is led astray by the stratagems of the press but rather the other way around. That the press and the public were both willing to circulate such narratives is itself noteworthy.

The child-murder genre functioned by means of exclusion as much as through mimesis. In the course of narrating the *crímenes*, efforts were made to downplay those aspects of particular cases whose retelling might require a revision of the prototypical forms. The image that mobilized government and vigilantes alike was that of a black perpetrator victimizing a white child, as had allegedly occurred in Zoila's case. Not accidentally, there seems to have been some resistance to revising the race-specific casting of the ideal type of crime when counterevidence surfaced. This reluctance was manifested with Cecilia, who was called white in spite of evidence suggesting that she was in fact a light-skinned mulatto.[20] While it is possible that misidentification played a part, it seems just as likely that the ascription simply ensured conformity to the usual tale. This reading is supported by similar instances, perhaps nowhere more painfully evident than in the 1923 case of a seven-year-old Afro-Cuban girl named Justina. The court records leave little doubt that this child was indeed the victim of brutal torments at the hands of her own family. It seems that her father, Guillermo Alvarez, her stepmother,

Caridad Hernández, and others starved her, beat her, bled her, and burnt her with cigars during ceremonies intended to rid the family of evil influences and heal sick participants.[21] The newspapers, El Mundo among them, apparently failed to notice the ways in which the story deviated from the standard account and publicized the case as one more instance of brujería-related crime. Others, like the noted criminologist Israel Castellanos, however, noticed that something was amiss. Justina, after all, had not been murdered; she was black rather than white; and most importantly to Castellanos, she was singled out for this procedure as an individual rather than selected at random on account of her race, as was supposedly the custom in ritual murders. Unable to reconcile Justina's story with the criminological construction of witchcraft, Castellanos proposed a bizarre resolution. Though criminals and perhaps even ñáñigos, Justina's victimizers could not be brujos:

> The lovers from Marianao . . . constitute a criminal couple. Her brain
> is deficient in its evolution; his [brain] lacks independent reactions.
> Caridad is a female of wicked passions; he is a man without scruples for
> crime. Both belong to the social subsoil, to the basest strata of the crimi-
> nal world. Caridad knows the ñáñigos' jargon. All of them use it without
> shame in front of the authorities. None of them know the sacred jargon,
> the secret language of the fetishists of good faith. The submission, docility,
> humility and the lack of pride of Bocu, Pina, Papá Silvestre and the "Rey
> Congo" are lacking in Justina's frustrated assassins[.][22]

It should be emphasized, nonetheless, that Castellanos's move was a revisionist one; he aimed to correct the record and to reinstate a useful genre. As Castellanos acknowledged, his was an exceptional view. Chroniclers and the public saw Alvarez as an émulo, or a copy, of Zoila's killer. Rafael Roche Monteagudo, once Havana's chief of police and later a writer on crime and superstition, had no doubt that Alvarez deserved the sobriquet "el brujo Guillermo." And the police officers charged with the investigation certainly understood Justina's case as another instance of witchcraft. They showed no concern with the deviant character of the story, finding what they required for prosecution in an increasingly capacious variety of crime called witchcraft. Indeed, on 25 August 1923, judicial police officer Antonio Gayoso wrote the judge in the case that the accused "are fervent believers in the practices of witchcraft, which is called Lucumí religion."[23] He added that Caridad was a priestess and that after a divination ritual, she had convinced the others to subject the girl to such trials as were ordered by the saint. The object was to rid the girl of the evil influence of her dead mother and later to initiate her in the faith. Failing this procedure, the girl would reportedly die from the injuries sustained in a process that would render her into a facsimile of the popular Saint Lázaro, a crippled saint.

Although there was much that was formulaic about the construction of these accounts, the ritual-murder genre as a whole was far from static. Zoila's story provided a framework. This meant that the form could accommodate subtleties, innovations, and new concerns and that it certainly could be deployed at different times to varying ends. In the first decades of the century, for instance, the accounts were insistent in suggesting that the connections among practitioners were far-reaching enough that brujos could be described as constituting a network or a "sect." Angel Espinosa, the author of a 1905 booklet on Zoila's case, described Bocourt and his alleged accomplices as a "conciliabulus" and referred to the brujos as *"esa tenebrosa colectividad,"* or "that sinister assembly."[24] By the 1940s, however, the brujo sphere of influence seemed to be limited to more immediate and domestic spaces, and the efforts to cast brujería as a broad-based conspiracy faded.

It is also germane to point out that not all of the enduring elements of the ritual-murder genre nor the anti-witchcraft campaigns themselves can be traced back to Zoila. In October 1904, a month before the child's disappearance, for instance, *El Mundo* reported on police raids and the prosecution of healers, grave robbers, and other brujos in various spots throughout the island. Other important themes also appear to have been incorporated into the repertoire from sources other than Zoila's case. The most notable of these themes is perhaps a recurrent preoccupation with the monstrous sexual desires of blacks, especially brujos and immigrants from the Caribbean. References to the brujos' depravity cropped up in rumor and allegations particularly after the murder and supposed rape of a girl in Vedado in July 1904, several months before Zoila's disappearance. According to the prosecutor, a soil peddler known to the public by the nickname Tin Tan broke into a house and murdered a ten-year-old white girl named Celia when she resisted his sexual attack. The first physician to examine the victim provided the only evidence for this reconstruction of events when he remarked that there was trauma indicative of rape and sodomy. In the eyes of the press and the public, that comment established the motivation even though a subsequent autopsy revealed that no sexual assault had occurred. The court, for its part, was forced to acknowledge that Tin Tan's motives for breaking into Celia's house remained unknown, but it still found him guilty of murder and sentenced him to death.[25]

The press and the intelligentsia portrayed Tin Tan as the sexual predator par excellence for years. Some accounts also managed to draw ex post facto connections to the practice of brujería, something that the court had not attempted to do in the prosecution of Tin Tan. Indeed, the only physical evidence that could have substantiated such a link—however cryptically—was a wooden box containing blood-soaked coals found near Celia's body. These mysterious objects were mentioned in the initial inventory of the crime scene, but it seems that they were never discussed again in the course of the trial. After Zoila disappeared, however, reporters like *El Mundo*'s Eduardo Varela Zequeira drew analogies between the two cases he was covering and brought Celia's death within the margins of the genre of ritual murders. Reports on the two crimes appeared in tandem, at times in adjacent columns. The strategy was hardly subtle, but for those who missed the point, Varela Zequeira was willing to spell it out: "These superstitious and lascivious blacks are capable of committing all kinds of excesses; we should put an end to their criminal activity."[26]

Flimsy as the evidence for sexual depredation was, allegations of that sort became rather commonplace after Celia's case. While not always present, such charges were a notable part of the child abduction and murder genre. Although the prototypical perpetrator was usually a black male, this was not always the case. In February 1906, for example, two agents of the special police arrested Julia Torres, a healer from Guanabacoa, after receiving a tip via an anonymous letter. Multiple items related to "witchcraft" also were seized from her home. The charge, which the detectives found credible, was that this woman who allegedly healed by means of witchcraft and sorcery [*hechicería*] was in search of a white girl to "deflower her and use the blood in *trabajos* [in this context, witchcraft ceremonies]."[27]

Many of the narratives emerging after 1919 emphasized the non-Cuban origins of many brujos, pointing more persistently than before at Haitians and Jamaicans who were then arriving on the island in large numbers.[28] Some viewed West Indians as having a particular proclivity toward pedophilia, which motivated their criminal actions even more than brujería. After Williams's murder in Regla at the hands of a mob, a reporter visited the area to interview witnesses and victims of several alleged abduction attempts. In the course of the visit, he ran into those who assured him that the lynched man "was part of a crew that worked in the oil deposits and . . . that these individuals are not brujos but rather degenerate beings that want to satisfy their perversity on innocent girls."[29] All of these suspicions, of course, resonated rather well with a corpus of scholarly literature that had already established black hypersexuality as an ethnographic fact. In his scholarly characterization of brujería, criminologist Israel Castellanos, for instance, wrote that lewdness was not an aberration but an inherited trait of Afro-Cuban brujos.

He argued further that because of this "evolutionary deficiency, their amorous sentiments carr[ied] with them an instinctive and brutal desire for possession."[30]

Finally, partisan politics and electoral jockeying played an important part in shaping and propagating witchcraft scares, which often seemed to flare up during election years. Justina's torment of 1918 and the events of 1919 did not inject politics into the anti-witchcraft polemic, but they certainly brought such matters into the limelight shortly before elections that ended with the Liberal defeat. In the wake of Cecilia's disappearance, some papers gave brujería an explicitly partisan meaning. Brujos and Liberales were said to have secret connections. Several politicians were charged—with good reason, as it turned out—with courting the brujo vote, and even with being practitioners themselves. In Matanzas, too, there were allegations of a brujo-Liberal confabulation. During the first weeks of July 1919, for instance, the *Heraldo de Cuba* accused Senator Vera Verdura of intervening to ensure the release of Cecilia's suspected killers. In Pinar del Río there were complaints that the witch hunt served as cover for the arrest and harassment of Liberal politicians and activists.[31] After the crime in Marianao, *El Día* invited and "summoned" reactions and proposals from black leaders, many of whom made it a point to note that white politicians were partly responsible for encouraging superstition, since they courted brujos and their centers whenever elections approached. There was something to the persistent final charge. As Alejandro de la Fuente has argued, Afro-Cubans, who represented about a third of the electorate in republican Cuba, were an essential constituency. As electoral pressures mounted, rhetorical denunciation made way for realpolitiks.[32]

The Press, "the only enduring power"

A few years after the inauguration of the republic, the Cuban press still searched for its place in the new order. In April 1904, representatives from all of Havana's newspapers gathered at the Ateneo to form Cuba's first successful press association. Eduardo Varela Zequeira, the reporter who covered niña Zoila's and niña Ceila's murders for *El Mundo*, and Manuel Márquez Sterling, a well-known patriot and man of letters with an interest in brujería, were both elected to the new board.[33] In an article celebrating the constitution of the organization, Márquez Sterling put forth a mission statement of sorts. He argued that in Cuba, journalists had proven themselves to be great fighters and that the press had shown itself to be "perhaps the only enduring power" amid the tumults of the revolution. He predicted that America's and Spain's press associations would someday constitute "a true force of resistance against political excesses, social evolutions propelled by ignorance, vice and the disloyalty of the ambitious." In a self-aggrandizing moment, he also proposed that the Cuban press was intellectually superior to politicians and morally above the society that it served.[34] In short, Márquez Sterling appointed journalists guardians of order, culture, and morality.

In spite of the grandiose assertions, in its incipient stage the association was primarily a trade organization with a defensive agenda. At its founding, its principal aim was to forge professional class identifications capable of bridging the chasm of partisan loyalties that separated newspapermen in spite of their shared interests.[35] The association's first public interventions, beyond the call for unity and professional regulation, were defenses of journalists whose public statements had resulted in state sanctions and incarcerations in violation of the freedoms enshrined in the republic's new constitution. In its 15 July 1905 editorial, for instance, *La Lucha* reported that its Campechuela correspondent had been arrested, charged, and incarcerated because of political statements he uttered at a public event that offended the local chief of police. The paper charged that this "Bedouin" had superseded the limits of his authority and assumed powers that would be outside of his reach in any "civilized country." The editor urged the press to "begin functioning as an all-powerful power" and pushed the president of the Press Association to convene his executive committee and to demand the journalist's immediate release. Failing that, the editor urged, the association should lead "the charge against a government that tolerates such things." *La Lucha* reminded readers that *expedienteo*, or the practice of keeping surveillance files of subversives, was (or should be) a thing of the old regime.[36]

If the arrests of journalists gave the association a chance to test the limits of the republic's legal frameworks and to galvanize its membership, Zoila's murder, which occurred only months after the group was founded, gave journalists a chance to try out their civilizing role. In his own "¡Pobrecita Zoila!," a gloss on the grief brought by the child's burial in December 1904, Márquez Sterling wrote of the brujos and their ignorance as an embarrassment to the country. He also noted ominously that after the funeral "the people cried out for the punishment of the culprits" and added, "according to the press, the excitement bordered on delirium." Before closing, however, the author found occasion to explicate his vision of the relationship between the press and the public and to laud his colleagues' part in the affair: "Zoila's name covers these weeks' news in mournful colors. The public that reads the papers rides astride on the reporters' backs and has been unable to think of anything but her."[37]

Perhaps the first to realize the enormity of the opportunity before journalists was Varela Zequeira, a well-seasoned newspaperman who had covered Gen. Antonio Maceo's campaign in western Cuba, and who later rose to the rank of lieutenant colonel in the insurgent army. Varela Zequeira used the pages of *El Mundo* to publicize the case, to castigate the authorities for their inaction, and to fuel a public outrage that could be presented as a mandate for repression.[38] His contemporaries recognized the impact of the series that Varela authored. In 1905, for instance, the author of *El destino de una criatura o la víctima de la superstición* credited Varela Zequeira, alongside "mass public vindication," with the assignment of Special Judge Manuel Landa to investigate Zoila's case. So moved was this author that in the six-page *décima* (a poetic form known for its ten-verse structure) he composed as a memorial to Zoila, he dedicated a few verses in praise of the dual disciplinary powers of the press and the judiciary: "The press was the court's / most powerful assistant / relaying it all / to Landa without fail."[39]

The press took on the full range of its auxiliary responsibilities early in the anti-witchcraft campaigns. Besides being the motor behind the prosecution of Bocourt and his associates in Zoila's case, Varela Zequeira himself served as a prosecution witness on a number of occasions. On 26 July 1904, he appeared before a court to testify on the substance of an interview with Tin Tan and some witnesses that *La Discusión* had published only the day before.[40] Other reporters did similarly when required. In 1910, for instance, Enrique Domínguez Hidalgo, who was also a correspondent for *La Discusión*, declared before the court that the information that appeared under his byline was indeed correct. The relevant article, which reported that a meeting of brujos had taken place near to where the attempted kidnapping of Esperanza had occurred, was read in court and added to the trial record. Although Domínguez Hidalgo could not offer independent proof, nor reveal the names of those who had confided in him, the information was certainly of use to the prosecution. In this case, the evidence was thin (though perhaps no more so than usual): the lone adult witness had not seen Desiderio Padrón carry off the child and the suspect's connection to witchcraft was tenuous.[41]

Varela Zequeira and others, it seems, also made it a habit to accompany the police during their raids on suspected centers of witchcraft. A picture taken during the investigation of niña Luisa's murder in Alacranes shows him and his colleague José C. Pérez, along with the rural police captain, the judge in the case, and several police scribes.[42] And lest it be thought that the camera captured an unusual convergence, it should be noted that there were many other reporters who developed similarly close working relationships with the police and the judiciary. Roche Monteagudo reported, for instance, that while he was a police officer he was assisted by Conrado Planas of *La Discusión* in preventing the murder of a child who was supposedly about to be sacrificed by brujos in Guanabacoa. Although the anonymous tip had not included an address, Roche Monteagudo credits his companion for tricking a cab driver into taking them to the proper destination. Conrado Planas, incidentally, was later appointed municipal judge in a Havana district, thereby closing the circle.[43] Roche Monteagudo also observed that it was Pedro García, author and sometime correspondent for the *Heraldo de Cuba*, who established beyond a doubt the fate of niña Cecilia. García, as it turns out, was the very man to whom a retarded boy, whom the police had already interrogated, confessed that Reyes and his other relatives had killed the girl and eaten her viscera.[44] Given the nature of his involvement, it should come as no surprise that a portrait was taken of García standing next to two military officers while María Faustina López was interrogated in connection to the murder of yet another child, this time a boy named Marcelo.[45]

If the impact of the press's participation in anti-witchcraft activity were judged solely by the arrest and conviction rate, journalists and politicians would appear to have failed in their mission. If other criteria are employed, however, their efforts must be deemed grim successes. Their influence on police officers, politicians, scholars, and even the lynch mobs was large by any measure. Moreover, the genre that these reporters helped to create endured beyond the period of active persecution. All indications are that the narratives of murdered children circulated orally for decades, and many Cubans today recall them as occupying a special place in their catalog of childhood fears. Beyond that, however, it is also possible to trace the trajectory of the stories in print long after the repressive peak that Cecilia's case marked. This suggests, among other things, that the genre had an autonomous existence and that it was capable of reproducing itself over time.

The last specific reports of abduction attempts by brujos appear to have been publicized in *Bohemia* in 1943. In that year, José Quílez Vicente penned a series of reports under the title "Por Las rutas tenebrosas de la Santería." The first episode highlighted three separate attempted kidnappings in Pinar del Río. To my knowledge, these were the first such incidents claimed since 1936. Without going into the specifics of the cases, one should note that Quílez Vicente's narratives contained many familiar elements, blacks, brujos, white children, healing rituals, and condemnations of backwardness among them. These accounts, however, also showed some variations in emphasis and some changes in the dynamic that linked the press to the judiciary and the police. Here the kidnappers, who were still black, were said to rely on third parties to commit their crimes. Perhaps more significantly, however, newer narratives emphasizing the destructive effects of

The press, the judge, and the police convene in Alacranes, where Luisa Valdés
Herrera was reportedly killed. In the photo: (1) Arturo Rivas, court stenographer;
(2) Rural Guard Captain Iglesias; (3) Eduardo Varela Zequeira of *El Mundo*;
(4) Juan Soler, court stenographer; (5) Judge Godofredo Díaz; and
(6) José C. Pérez of *La Discusión*. From *El Fígaro*, 21 June 1908.
(Widener Library, Harvard College Library, KJ54)

witchcraft within both black and white families victimized by brujo swindlers
now accompanied the older stories whose protagonists were usually black strangers
with little connection to the infants.[46] Quílez Vicente also took pains to include
in the series a number of accounts of European witchcraft, by which he aimed
to show that the practice of brujería was not an exclusively black or Cuban phenomenon.[47] Finally, Quílez Vicente's comments about the reticence of judicial
officials to reveal any information deserve special attention. This was quite a deviation from the practice of a few decades earlier.

Indeed, many changes were afoot. By Quílez Vicente's time, old-style brujería
was becoming the stuff of "legend," as he put it. With modernizing optimism,
he explained that "time has gone by and the progress of our era, contact with
other races of superior cultural level, the mixing of bloods, and the desire for
improvement through education and studies, has been banishing those terrible
ceremonies."[48] Perhaps for these reasons Quílez Vicente was less willing than his
predecessors to be categorical in his assertion that brujería lurked behind the new
kidnapping attempts. However irresolute, the redeployment of these narratives
could still imply dangers for Afro-Cubans. By Quílez Vicente's own account, in

1943 a deaf and mute black teenager—nineteen-year-old Eufrasio Pimienta—was nearly lynched in a San Luis field. He was believed to have attempted to abduct three-year-old, blond Panchito from his home.

The Public and Its Indignation

Journalists like Varela Zequeira reached their greatest rhetorical excesses when purporting to speak for a public whose indignation they reported and inspired. The identities of these otherwise nameless actors were shifting and problematic, however. A passing review of the sections above shows that in some respects the press relied on the trope of the public as a rhetorical device. Through this device, for instance, Varela Zequeira and E. H. Moreno, a reporter for *La Lucha*, pressured judicial and government officials to appoint Landa special judge in Zoila's case, all in the name of the "supreme judge" of "public opinion." Reporters elsewhere emulated this strategy to demand tough measures in particular instances and to congratulate authorities when they acquiesced. The public, nonetheless, was more than a fiction. Actors lacking official posts or professional roles to play did intervene throughout the anti-witchcraft campaigns in a variety of capacities. The papers' readership, the victims of the brujo's alleged frauds, the anonymous informants, the demonstrators and protesters, the crowds who trailed authorities and journalists throughout the countryside, those attending court trials, and even the unruly lynch mobs were at times included within this exceedingly elastic category.

Although undoubtedly manipulated at times, public actors preserved a good measure of autonomous agency throughout. Varela Zequeira's defensive assertions that he had no intention of "tipping the balance of public opinion" in any particular direction certainly do not suffice to exonerate the press from charges of partiality. Similarly, his claim that his reports linking Zoila's disappearance to witchcraft were largely the result of confidences and tips he obtained from "brujos" is suspect at best.[49] Ultimately, however, the evidence does support the thrust of Varela Zequeira's statements; it became difficult to know whether the press was pushing its readers or whether the opposite was the case. If one returns to the circumstances leading to Landa's appointment, for instance, one must acknowledge that collective action had a leading part in the drama that unfolded in El Gabriel and Güira de Melena. Local discontent with the performance of the original judge assigned to the case, who had already released the suspects once, resulted in pleas for a new magistrate and in ominously threatening acts. According to *La Lucha*, a delegation of some fifty men rode into town on 29 November 1904 to demand from the prosecutor overseeing the case such an appointment. The press intercepted the men and attempted to quell their tempers, only to have them return moments later for a final dialogue with Varela Zequeira and Moreno. Landa's entrance on the scene had the makings of a grand occasion. Men on horseback were at hand again, but this time only to greet the train carrying the new judge. A gathered crowd cheered and a delegation of children honored Landa, who then delivered an impromptu speech from a balcony. A similar scene was repeated ten days later, when a body thought to be Zoila's was found.[50] The man who had gained fame with Tin Tan's conviction appeared headed for another victory.

It should be emphasized that Landa's investigative success owed a great deal to the very public who cheered him and their representatives in the press. Immediately upon arriving in town, the judge had bulletins posted requesting that any party with knowledge of the case come forward. Unlike his predecessors, who according to Moreno wasted the many efforts of "all the inhabitants" of the town, their investigations, and their "thousand conjectures," Varela Zequeira observed that under Landa "the case is strengthening by the moment, and it is noteworthy that the rumors being circulated are later confirmed to be rather exact, as if the popular classes had adopted this as a system of contributing information to the process[.]"[51]

Journalists, in fact, did report on rumors, gossip, and overheard stories with regularity. Rumor, it appears, also played a role in shaping the responses of the authorities. Pedro M. García's alarmist piece noted, for instance, that rumblings about plans for another murder in Jovellanos, along with public demands for protection, reached the army. On the basis of these bits of intelligence, patrols were dispatched throughout the region and several Afro-Cubans were arrested. García, it seems, was also well aware that rumors created suspense and made for good hooks. He closed the article with a titillating pitch: "I have a sensational rumor related to niño Onelio's crime that I will communicate on my next piece."[52]

Though they constantly evoked them, the press was vague when it came to naming and identifying who constituted their public. They singled out some important witnesses, to be sure, but for the most part, "the riders," "public opinion," "*el pueblo*," and other such terms that they employed routinely had a disembodied quality. When indignant, that is, when acting in the name of civilizing righteousness, the press referred to an undifferentiated mass, which spoke as nearly as one as a chorus. Descriptions of individuals and of race and class composition are rare and mentioned only in asides, if at all. Indeed, the press presented itself largely as the echo of these reportedly consonant voices.

The reports reveal, however, that the outraged public in fact did not include all Cubans, as the narratives first suggested. In an extended statement in which Varela Zequeira denied the notion that Zoila's murder might be proof of racial hatred within Cuban society, the journalist argued that the perpetrators were aberrations, "perverse scoundrels" who took advantage of the sorry legacy of slavery, which made Afro-Cubans easy prey. At the peak of his verbose flight, Varela Zequeira intimated, however, that it was rare to find Cubans of color within the indignant public. As he so indelicately put it, "Güira de Melena's and El Gabriel's residents of the colored race should know, that *El Mundo* has not seen their withdrawal from those public demonstrations which have taken place in celebration of the successes achieved in the discovery of Zoila's murderers, as evidence of their having joined forces with the wicked, fleeing from the persecutors of the crime, too, but has rather taken it as a sign of the shame that they—free, moral and cultured men—felt at this savage occurrence."[53]

The evidence suggests that the exclusion of black Cubans from the public was patrolled and jealously guarded. (And it is not hard to see that Varela Zequeira and others wished that many newly empowered citizens of color would also withdraw from the political fray.) In those instances when Afro-Cubans voiced dissenting views and broke ranks with the public that the reporters and the judiciary had constituted, they were penalized summarily. Nowhere is this more succinctly illustrated than in the case of mestizo Nicolás Santuce Núñez, a resident of Havana who was arrested in 1919 for criticizing the actions of a court that had condemned an alleged bruja to thirty days' incarceration. Santuce Núñez had reportedly remarked that the sentence was "an abuse," adding that it was well enough that "machos" be condemned but that women should be spared. The reporter, for his part, sentenced smugly: "So that he would not keep on criticizing, they sent him to jail."[54]

Black Voices and a White Public

Although it was evident that the scares and the repression were built upon a putative relationship between blackness and brujería, there were repeated attempts to deny that the policing of Afro-Cubans and their religious practices was motivated by racism. Intellectuals, politicians and reporters, who were mostly white, promulgated the notion that the persecution of brujería was color blind. Ruy Lugo-Viña's op-ed piece illustrates the sorts of arguments put forth at the height of the 1919 anti-witchcraft mobilization in an effort to uphold the notions of racial equality before the law. Lugo-Viña argued that the rage of the "white multitude" was not due to racial hatred, "because that hatred does not exist among the various ethnic factors of our social conglomerate." "If the killers were white," he added, "the rage of those who condemn the abominations of fetishism would crash against them too[;] the people do not go after them because they are black but because they are brujos."[55]

Sophisticated intellectuals also joined in defending legal action against brujos. Without denying that injustices and excesses had been committed in practice, Fernando Ortiz put his considerable reputation behind the call for the extirpation of criminal superstition. In a well-known address before the Cuban legislative body, where the introduction of new measures against witchcraft was being debated, Ortiz declared war on "both black and white witchcraft" while he cautioned against vindictive motivations.[56]

The defense of color-blind impartiality under such circumstances required some contortions, of course. But as Aline Helg has shown in her thoroughgoing review of the writings and pronouncements of Cuba's black leaders, at first the denunciations of the racist underpinnings of this pernicious reportage genre were limited in scope. Many expressed a faith in both modernization and the promise of a color-blind republic. Following Zoila's murder, prominent Afro-Cuban leaders responded with calls for the regeneration of the black race and for the abandonment of backward practices. They argued that Zoila's case was an isolated incident and noted that the practice of brujería was by no means limited to blacks, among whom this was primarily a subclass phenomenon. They do not always appear, however, to have questioned the charges against Bocourt or the narrative that accompanied them. Rafael Serra, editor of *El Nuevo Criollo* and a black politician associated with Estrada Palma, described "Africanism" as an "enormous octopus of innumerable and immeasurable tentacles that stretches out completely and increasingly over all our social body." His paper, however, also condemned the efforts of the white press to stigmatize all Afro-Cubans through the brujo's figure and denounced the selective application of justice when it came to blacks.[57]

Previsión, the organ for the Partido Independiente de Color, was more forceful in statements against the brujo bogeyman. But it, too, urged Afro-Cubans to renounce "atavistic" practices while simultaneously condemning mainstream coverage of the alleged crimes as an attempt to disqualify Afro-Cubans from participation in the nation's political sphere.[58]

Though still condemning "ignorance" and "superstition," by 1918 some Afro-Cubans were more openly contesting mainstream press accounts, challenging government measures, and denouncing the racist strategies of the anti-witchcraft talk. During the months of August and September, a number of black journalists, politicians, and intellectuals responded to *El Día's* challenge to lead the black masses whom they represented away from brujería. Ramiro Neyra Lanza, the publisher of *La Antorcha*, was among those who answered the call. His response denied that witchcraft was a black problem that Afro-Cubans had to correct, arguing instead that this was a Cuban problem that all Cubans had to address. Neyra Lanza charged further that whites, and rich whites at that, could be counted among practitioners and that they were the principal promoters of these beliefs. These men, he said, courted brujos in exchange for votes. Finally, Neyra Lansa turned the socioracial explanations favored by the elite on their head. He connected witchcraft and superstition to social inequalities and lack of access to power, contending that such beliefs existed "only where there are 'better' and 'worse' [people] without any reason, where the 'worse' ones go to the 'saint' to solve their problems," which could not be addressed in any other way.[59]

By 1919, the Afro-Cuban critique of a repression that was then applauding the barbarity of the lynch mobs was, if anything, more urgent and better organized. The newly inaugurated Club Atenas—whose membership included Afro-Cuban professionals and intellectuals from Havana—and *La Antorcha* were among those organizations that took steps to counter the racist impetus behind the coverage and the violence it unleashed. The first group published a manifesto accusing the press of fomenting mob violence, while the second echoed the charge in a special supplement and called for Afro-Cubans "to stand up and resist the savage assault."[60] Important Afro-Cuban figures also took their concerns directly to the authorities. Indeed, for a time the witch hunt of 1919 galvanized Afro-Cubans.

At the grassroots level, there are indications that some Afro-Cubans were also engaged in open resistance, in spite of the obvious risks involved. On 30 June 1919, for instance, a raid in Havana's Jesús María neighborhood nearly turned into a riotous showdown. As the police loaded three ambulances with suspects and cult items, a group of black men gathered to protest, and they reportedly attempted to attack the officers. A sergeant and three others were called from the station to disperse the men by force. A few minutes later, however, the protesters tried to ambush the police officers. The police drove away hurriedly, without engaging the men, but the press observed that the incident could well have resulted in deaths. *La Lucha* argued that the officers could have fired in self-defense but that they restrained themselves, fearing that they would be thought to have taken such action too lightly. The reporter warned, nonetheless, that a second incident should not go unpunished.

Not all Afro-Cubans, however, were in a position to challenge the measures and discourses activated in the course of the anti-witchcraft scares. In 1919, too, one finds the likes of Cresencio Valladares, who seems to have felt compelled to accept the stories on the terms given and to offer an apologia for the repressive actions taken by the authorities. Indeed, Valladares's zealousness rings like that of the convert. Writing soon after the horrors that followed Cecilia's death in Matanzas, Valladares remarked:

> Such barbarities pain a great deal because the moral responsibility always falls on our race, to the extreme that the one who writes has seen white children run from him because they suppose that I might be one of those brujos who carry out such inconceivable acts. Do parents do wrong in preparing their children in this regard? I do not believe they do. The preservation instinct demands it. . . .
>
> Who is guilty for these scandalous acts? The excessive tolerance for brujos, self-taught physicians [empíricos], healers, Spiritists, charlatans, bembé participants and many others in the same industry. . . .
>
> Government in the first place, and then the great men of the black race, and ultimately all of society are the cause for these acts that progress would have destroyed a long time ago, if the tolerance I am pointing out had not intervened.[61]

Somewhere between the defiance of some Afro-Cubans and the pragmatism of the letter writer, there were also individual interventions aimed to channel the public repression of brujería to private ends. Among the latter sort, one might point at Arturo Gómez, a man of "mestizo race" who denounced to the secret police a healer who had been treating him. Gómez, it seemed at first, was simply dissatisfied with the treatment Lucio Veitia—whom he now called a brujo—had given him. He claimed that after subjecting himself to the prescribed regimen, he had only gotten worse. The documents, however, make it clear that Gómez was an initiate (ahijado) in Veitia's temple, that he had an affair with a married woman from the same temple, and that Veitia disapproved. Gómez feared that his former benefactor had caused him harm (echado daño) through witchcraft. In his efforts to defend himself from the brujo's powers, Gómez retaliated by summoning the powers of the state. And the strategy proved efficacious; within hours, the police had arrived at Veitia's house, where a celebration was taking place, arresting all participants.[62]

Upon occasion the much-vilified brujos also managed to voice their views, in spite of a press that saw its function as one of "translation" of reportedly "incomprehensible" utterances. The statements from these African and Afro-Cuban men and women are revealing, even if they say little about their beliefs. First, they show that the persecution of witchcraft and the characterization of Afro-Cuban beliefs that accompanied it struck some practitioners as so far-fetched as to provoke disbelief, and, second, that in the face of opprobrious circumstances, many brujos responded to the campaign as a challenge to their dignity and their very humanity.

Bocourt's recorded encounters with the press and the judiciary illuminate the first point. In one of his many enlightening moments, Varela Zequeira admitted that his quotations of the old healer's statements during an interview conducted shortly before the executions—in which he reportedly confessed—were not exact: "As the reader might suppose, Domingo Bocourt did not use the same words we are using now during his declarations; but these are the precise equivalents of those he pronounced in his imperfect way of expressing himself."[63] Varela Zequeira and other reporters, however, had had no trouble understanding Bocourt's puzzlement at the moment of his first release from jail. At that point, the old man is said to have reassured others that nothing would happen to him because he had done nothing wrong. He even went as far as joking that he had bewitched the judge to obtain his release.[64]

A similar disbelief is evident among the defendants in other cases as well. Even in 1919, when it was clear that the authorities where unwilling to make too many distinctions between Afro-Cuban religious practices and brujería, many refused to accept the proposed equivalence. People accused of witchcraft often admitted to practicing the "religión lucumí" but denied charges of fraud, brujería, or the illegal practice of medicine. In a typical instance, Belén González, a woman prosecuted for being a bruja and a curandera, told the court that she could not understand why she was being prosecuted. She had done nothing wrong. As to the incriminating objects found in her home, she said that these were Lucumí items and that she believed in them "because it was the religion of her land." She added that "she harmed no one nor was any brujería practiced in her home."[65] Others, of course, felt that the danger of possessing such objects was too great and the probability of defending themselves successfully too slim to be worth the risk. Shortly after Zoila's murder, for instance, the streets were said to be littered with ritual objects from many home altars.

Other statements reveal self-affirming assertions of individual worth among the victims of the anti-witchcraft crusade. It is only in this light that one can understand why Adela la Conga, who was charged with harboring Bocourt and Zoila's other killers in her home, refused to walk with a Rural Guardsman when she was summoned by the court. Adela demanded instead to be taken by train, adding that she was "una señora de su casa," that is to say, a respectable lady worthy of considerations that the press and the authorities found laughable.[66]

Though betraying malign intentions and schemes within schemes, the witchcraft scares that shook the Cuban republic during the first decades of the twentieth century cannot be called conspiracies in any strict sense of the term. These recurring tremors obtained from the confluence of political interests, anxieties over citizenship, legal and scholarly practices, a modernizing fever, and a certain way of narrating so-called superstition. The crime stories that the press sought and crafted were indeed stories. But they were not just stories.

4

SELF-GOVERNING SPIRITS

La Samaritana and Puerto Rico's Espiriteros

Sometime in the mid-nineteenth century Spiritism arrived in Puerto Rico in suitcases and wrapped parcels. Students returning from European universities, travelers, and purveyors of forbidden tracts brought back to the island books, periodicals, and investigative practices that circulated first via informal circuits. Before the first centers were organized—reportedly in Mayagüez during the late 1870s or early 1880s—Spiritism found a home in a district of the island's incipient *ciudad letrada*, which at the time offered some refuge from a church and a state suspicious of rationalist doctrines that preached the gospel of progress.[1] This city of letters emerged as a discursive space, as possibility, before it was ever realized materially. Its architects, whose labors Silvia Alvarez-Curbelo chronicles in *Un país del porvenir*, were for the most part learned and propertied men consumed with what she has called a "zeal for modernity."[2] The desire to make Puerto Rico modern was manifest in the quest for integration into the world economy, in abolitionist agitation, and in the *letrados'* effort to craft a new role for themselves as experts capable of reordering society. Spiritists, many of whom shared the letrados' modernizing zeal, as did Manuel Corchado y Juarbe, Puerto Rico's representative to the Spanish Cortes who favored abolition and Spiritist instruction in schools, aimed at a wholesale social regeneration through individual advancement. Spiritism was suffused with an ethos of self-improvement that saw in the future utopian possibilities. Progress was inevitable; it was a matter of natural law.[3]

Spiritists kept company with masons, freethinkers, and liberals in the island. They also saw themselves as part of a cosmopolitan vanguard poised to bring forth a new age. Before they could attend international congresses, Spiritists bought and published journals and read treatises, most notably those of Allan Kardec, a Frenchman who systematized communications from celestial brethren to offer scientific proof of life after death in an interplanetary realm. Through these publications, Puerto Ricans kept up-to-date about organizational developments and experimental advances in European and American capitals. They rallied around the promise of science and a powerful anticlerical rhetoric. The church was to them an institutional enemy and a symbol of backwardness; it stood for the dogmatic abuse of reason and the denial of the rights of modern citizenship, most notably the individual's freedoms of thought and expression.[4]

Most Spiritists understood their practices as a philosophy or discipline rather than a religion as such. Instead of beliefs, Spiritists maintained that they shared a methodology for studying the spiritual world. All the same, Kardec's *Book of the Spirits* (1856) and his subsequent volumes put forth a series of principles that Spiritists regarded both as experimental findings and as the culmination of the Christian message. The most notable among these held that (1) the soul was immortal; (2) there were multiple, inhabited worlds, just as there were multiple lives; (3) souls perfected themselves over a long series of incarnations; and, finally, (4) communication between those incarnated on Earth and spirits in other worlds could be carried out through mediums. Indeed, Kardec held that spirits and the living could aid each other to attain progress. Because incarnated human beings carried with them both the lessons and the karmic debts they acquired in past lives, and because they remained susceptible to influence from high and lowly spirits, progress depended on charity, moral education, and, to a lesser extent, healing. The spirits, if unenlightened, could arrest people's progress but would afford human beings an opportunity to act charitably in their aid and to advance in that manner. If evolved, spirits would assist human beings by sharing their wisdom and by availing them of their healing magnetic fluids.

Spirit-mongers

Puerto Rican Spiritists celebrated the arrival of the twentieth century (and the inauguration of a new political regime) with expectations of unfettered technological gains, political democracy, and the secularization of religious fiefdoms. During the first decade of the century, Spiritists had reasons to feel optimistic. Their institutions—centers, hospitals, orphanages, libraries, and a federation founded in 1903—grew at a swift pace. Rosendo Matienzo Cintrón, a leading politician and a tireless propagandist of Kardec's doctrines, scored repeated victories at the ballot box. Spiritists were confident that the struggles to reform gender relations, end the death penalty, ban alcohol, and offer lay education and medical services to all would finally usher in the modern age they had awaited for decades. And they found hope in international developments, too. Though seemingly unaware of Haya de la Torre's work in Peru, Spiritists in Puerto Rico welcomed Camille Flammarion's widely reported experimental "discoveries," Francisco Madero's reforms in Mexico, and Spirit communications from all corners reassuring them that the future was at hand.[5]

Nonetheless, Spiritism remained vulnerable. Even among reform-minded modernizers, Kardec's teachings never attained full respectability. The ascent of positivism made Spiritist doctrines appear as a fanciful mysticism, since they posited the existence of a realm that could not be apprehended through the senses. And Spiritist efforts to produce positive proof of their tenets were not entirely persuasive. Equally troubling was Spiritism's tendency to inspire what critics and lukewarm sympathizers both regarded as "religious mistakes" among the untutored. As early as 1878, Francisco del Valle Atiles warned in *El Buscapié* that while Spiritism was a good doctrine, it was already becoming popular among poor and uneducated people who were distorting it to its detriment.[6]

Lest usurpers bring discredit to Kardec's philosophy, learned adherents assayed to distinguish between true Spiritists (espiritistas) and those they would denounce as spirit-mongers (espiriteros). This distinction was built in the fashion of the ciudad letrada. In many respects, the difference was a fragile one, and it was conjured discursively without being fully realized materially. As Spiritist journals emphasized, true Spiritists were educated, rational, and scientific. Spirit-mongers were afflicted with backwardness (*atraso*). The most visible symptoms of this state included ignorance, evident in illiteracy and in the use of uncouth language in speech and spirit communications; in superstition, manifest in the use of candles, icons, altars, and holy water; and less directly, in blackness, which many Spiritists associated with primitiveness and spiritual immaturity.

Unlike their counterparts elsewhere, most notably Brazil, Puerto Rican Spiritists proved more effective as conjurers of utopias than as builders of enduring institutions.[7] By the 1920s, the organizational momentum of Spiritism was waning and the science-religion sat on the unstable ground between orthodox experimental disciplines and the ill-repute of popular "superstition." While advocates could still claim the support of some experts, charges that Spiritism was not a proper science and that many practitioners were profit-driven fakes were never silenced. The 150 Spiritist organizations reportedly operating in the island in 1923 gave signs of being past their prime.[8] Nothing that dentist Francisco Ponte

Jiménez, president of the Federation of Spiritists of Puerto Rico, could write in *El Libro de Puerto Rico* regarding the advance of Spiritism could change the facts. Rosendo Matienzo Cintrón had died. *El Iris de Paz* and *El Buen Sentido*, two leading Spiritist journals, had both folded. Other publications were launched in the 1920s and 1930s, but they did not bring Spiritism out of its slump. By 1934 the federation had so deteriorated that the entire board of directors was replaced following charges that the incumbents had been "passive" for too long. Once more, those who remained in the federation suggested that the revitalization of Spiritism demanded that "black occultism" and curanderismo be condemned.[9]

Ironically, La Samaritana, a healer of the sort that Spiritists had long dismissed as a spirit-monger, emerged as one of the few visible signs of Spiritist vitality in the early 1920s. Although the religious character of La Samaritana's ministry was never precisely clear (and some, including the healer's family, maintain that hers was a lay Catholic mission of the sort that became popular in the island after 1898), many Spiritist leaders claimed the healer as their own.[10] To these Spiritists, La Samaritana's enormous popularity signaled that the movement was not defeated in spite of its institutional decline; progress was still possible. When the federation celebrated its assembly in 1922, the organizers made sure that the healer from San Lorenzo found her way to San Juan's Municipal Theater, where she was honored in spite of public criticism from journalists and physicians and protests from a group of dissident Spiritists who saw in the healer a return to the irrational ways of old. Though a divisive presence, La Samaritana helped to reinvigorate the Spiritist movement. Soon after the crowds began congregating around La Samaritana, federation leaders predicted that the number of Spiritists would surpass that of every other denomination in the eastern region of the island.[11]

There is nothing exceptionally unusual about the dynamics of rejection and appropriation surrounding La Samaritana. Scholars of religion have long been aware that cleavages of this sort commonly separate popular from official religiosity.[12] Spiritists elsewhere have also been known to condemn and elevate exotic figures simultaneously. A Mexican healer known as Santa Teresa (Teresa de Urrea, 1873–1906) was forced to flee Mexico for the United States during the late porfiriato. She was reputed to have inspired several rebellions, notably an 1891 Tarahumara uprising in Tomochic. After moving to Arizona and Texas, Santa Teresa continued to attract thousands of pilgrims, many of whom opposed Porfirio Díaz. By the early 1900s, however, Santa Teresa had left the border region. For a few years she continued to effect widely reported cures on stages throughout the United States but later desisted, saying that her promoters had exploited the public.[13]

During the first decades of the twentieth century, numerous healers, many of whom were also prophets and local leaders, emerged amid public controversy throughout the Caribbean and Brazil. In the southwestern Dominican Republic, Olivorio Mateo, better known as Dios Olivorio, suffered over a decade of persecution (1910–22) at the hands of Dominican and U.S. authorities and was ultimately killed along with two dozen of his followers. Journalists expressed relief that the disgraceful *olivoristas* and the obstacle to progress they represented finally had been cleared. Though he was affiliated with local *caudillos*, the suspicion that he harbored political ambitions of his own always surrounded Olivorio. Closer in spirit and practice to La Samaritana was perhaps Cuba's Antoñica Izquierdo, a hydrotherapist from Pinar de Río who attracted multitudes of peasants and who also ran afoul of the authorities when it was learned in 1936 that she had urged women not to take part in electoral politics.[14] Although the particulars vary, scholars have regarded most of these healers as instances of resistance to modernization and state-building. These figures also have been thought to personify the distances separating official, urban religious practices and rural sensibilities. While I do not disagree with those interpretations, the account below seeks to interrogate precisely how the barriers between learned Spiritism and popular spirit-mongering were erected. Spiritists' ambivalent attitudes to race played a prominent role in this effort. Moreover, I aim to show that La Samaritana's practices implied a reworking of modernizing pursuits rather than a wholesale rejection of the project that the architects of the ciudad letrada sketched. La Samaritana's treatments were aimed at healing supplicants and Puerto Rican society at large. However, instead of seeking to eradicate all maladies, as modern reformers and physicians hoped, La Samaritana attempted to harness affliction to morally transformative ends. Paraphrasing freely from Victor Turner's classic ethnography, I argue that La Samaritana understood healing as an operation within a complex economy of affliction.[15]

My aim, then, is not simply to call attention to the racist underpinnings of Spiritism. Arcadio Díaz-Quiñones has brought those into plain view and has shown that the Spiritist doctrine of transmigration that inspired Fernando Ortiz's transculturation concept was founded on a hierarchical understanding of progress and race.[16] Kardec maintained that souls perfected themselves gradually over the course of multiple lives or incarnations. But he relegated souls incarnated in black bodies, especially those of Africans, to the lower rungs of the ladder of progress. This would pose a problem for La Samaritana's Spiritist supporters, who had to explain whether it was possible for a truly superior spirit to manifest itself through a dark-skinned *jíbara*.

Besides putting onstage the racial drama built around La Samaritana, I examine the relationship between Spiritists and so-called spirit-mongers as an instance that speaks to the shortcomings of the transculturation, or syncretism, model, as it is usually deployed to explain the development of Spiritism in its folk-versus-scientific or "Kardecist" variants. In her influential works on Puerto Rican Spiritism, Joan Koss has argued that the Spiritist "cult" emerged in the middle of the nineteenth century among anticlerical and anti-Spanish, liberal professionals who sought reforms but who eschewed revolutionary upheavals. According to Koss, neither Kardec nor his first disciples in the island placed much emphasis on healing as such. That would come later with the intervention of "lower-class Puerto Ricans who adopted that [healing] aspect almost immediately, syncretizing Kardecist beliefs and practices with the traditional techniques of healing and Catholic modalities."[17] Although I concede readily that the principles of what I am calling the economy of affliction could function as a bridge between various constituencies and religious practices in the island, the events in San Lorenzo complicate the story: they remind us, first, that Spiritist doctrine did not trickle down the social pyramid unopposed and, second, that practices originating at the bottom were also taken up at the top once their origins had been obscured. Those who thought of themselves as true Spiritists denounced spirit-mongers as corrupting the doctrine. But the distinction between Spiritists and spirit-mongers should not be taken for granted.

Julia Vázquez, La Samaritana

In the spring and summer of 1922, thousands of pilgrims and novelty-seekers traveled on foot, horseback, and truck beds to a distant spot high in the mountains of the town of San Lorenzo. The travelers were mostly latter-day *jíbaros*, rural people who had joined the island's expanding agroproletariat. Most came seeking the promise of cures, bringing along their ailing relatives and carrying on hammocks those who could not walk on account of their age or afflictions. On the way, they assisted the *desahuciados*, those suffering from conditions that physicians had declared beyond hope. Their destination was a horse ranch and farm in barrio Hato where crowds of as many as 10,000 people waited patiently for a group meeting with Julia Vázquez (1893–1986).[18]

The talented *médica* had been growing in her neighbors' esteem for several years without attracting media attention.[19] Known locally as *La Niñita* (literally, little girl), by the time the multitudes began to arrive at her doorstep, Vázquez was a single woman in her late twenties. Though it is difficult to determine precisely how her talents were interpreted at the earliest stages, the title "médica," which translated literally means physician, might offer some indication. Those congregating in barrio Hato reportedly favored the title over the generic "curander(a)," or healer; *santiguador(a)*, a specialist who cured by means of prayers, oils, and abdominal rubs; or *curiosos*, which designated self-taught medical practitioners. The word "médica" linked Vázquez to earlier figures, giving her a lineage that made her recognizable to her following and deplorable in critics' eyes. To the latter, the new healer was only the latest manifestation of Puerto Ricans' unrepentant "superstition," a term they brandished as a weapon. Vázquez reminded them, for instance, of the "Médica de Puerta de Tierra," a woman who had achieved notoriety in 1914 when she performed surgeries by means of magnetic hand passes. Seeing in Vázquez no more than a variation on a recurring folly, Dr. Jr. M. Argaiz, a physician from Vega Baja, wondered just how badly this new médica would tarnish Puerto Rico's reputation as a civilized country. The fact that the women's appeal was not limited to the ignorant struck the doctor as a particularly stinging indictment: "What will they say of us as a civilized people? Are there a people among whom the majority, not only of the ignorant but also of those who pride themselves on some culture, can be deceived with greater ease? Can there be a people who having just suffered deceit fall victim to the very same treachery?"[20]

Dr. Argaiz aside, there were differences between the two médicas. Vázquez did not perform spiritual surgery. Still, she achieved a prominence that far surpassed her predecessor's. By 1922, Julia Vázquez's name had begun to echo far beyond San Lorenzo, as the press took notice of the gatherings at the property where she lived with her family of tenant farmers (*agregados*).[21] Stories of her feats made their way across the island. It was said that "La Samaritana," as she was now dubbed in news items, communicated with spirits. It was said, too, that she performed miracles and healed the sick using only water.

Word of mouth and the unrelenting attention of journalists ensured that La Samaritana would become one of the most widely publicized figures of her day. Features in newspapers and magazines documented in detail the goings-on in barrio Hato. Supporters and detractors debated the healer's merits in letters, editorials, and columns. Vázquez was even the subject of an early blockbuster in Puerto Rican cinema, the unimaginatively titled *La Samaritana de San Lorenzo*.

The crowd in San Lorenzo. From *Puerto Rico Ilustrado*, 2 September 1922.
(General Research Division, The New York Public Library,
Astor, Lenox and Tilden Foundations)

The popularity of Coll and Co.'s film was such that when it premiered in San Juan's Rialto Theater in late July 1922, ticket sales had to be suspended. The throng of moviegoers swelled to such proportions that it blocked traffic along a main avenue.[22] Even on film La Samaritana was apt to disturb order.

La Samaritana's reception was as varied as the roster of travelers and pilgrims making their way to barrio Hato suggests. Crowds grew especially thick on Thursdays and Fridays, the days that Vázquez's spirit guides had designated for her public work. Journalists and self-styled investigators; society ladies, politicians, and physicians; blacks, whites, and people of many hues; Catholics, Protestants, Spiritists, and those who, in the words of an observer, seemed to have "forgotten" their formal religious affiliations came in droves to see the young woman.[23]

La Samaritana's first and most sympathetic audience consisted of the rural poor, who rallied around her as they had done earlier with such prophetic figures as the Cheos, members of a brotherhood of lay itinerant preachers, and Elenita, the Virgin Mary incarnate who lived in San Lorenzo between 1899 and 1909 and with whom Vázquez was identified at times.[24] Jíbaros had good reasons to see La Samaritana as one of their own. Like much of the rural population, Julia Vázquez was illiterate. She began to work at a young age as a seamstress and later took a job in town at a tobacco factory. In these respects, at least, she was emblematic of the lot of many women of her class and generation who sought wage-paying labor as the rural order of old agonized.

Although I do not argue that La Samaritana owed her popularity primarily to a crisis in the rural world, as the most influential functionalist accounts of millennialism and prophetism would suggest, one must acknowledge that the early 1920s were hard times indeed.[25] During this period, agricultural laborers in Puerto Rico's mountains were faced with the collapse of the coffee economy and the loss of the precarious autonomy that this crop had allowed them. As investments poured into the region from the United States, tobacco also ceased to offer an alternative to industrial capital and its labor regime. In San Lorenzo, where large farms, cigar factories, and U.S. tobacco trusts were dominant, nineteenth-century arrangements eroded swiftly. To La Samaritana and those around her, the new economic and political orders brought some improvements, especially in infrastructure and public health, and also new forms of marginalization, proletarianization, and militancy. Between 1919 and 1921, more than 100 strikes involving 30,000 workers broke out throughout the island. Thousands of displaced men sought refuge in the growing cities and in the U.S. armed forces.[26] Recruiting stations throughout rural Puerto Rico made men in uniform a common sign of the times, a trend that may help explain the prominence of soldiers in La Samaritana's early visions.

But it would be facile to suggest that La Samaritana attracted multitudes simply because she shared the plight of the majority. One need only recall that there were numerous healers with close ties to those they served who never achieved celebrity.[27] Several factors made the difference with the médica from San Lorenzo. Media attention combined with improved transportation and roadways to give her a broad sphere of influence. But the media's and the public's interests owed a good deal to the intervention of the group of Spiritists that included several federation leaders who orchestrated a skillful propaganda campaign in La Samaritana's favor. Under the guidance of Juan Jiménez García, an ex-president of the federation, they held press conferences, staged rallies, and distributed leaflets. Enterprising companies like the National Photo Novelty Sales Agency soon joined in, selling buttons and postcards featuring the healer's likeness.[28] This campaign and the counterclaims it called forth made of barrio Hato a discursive battleground where the state of civilization in Puerto Rico and the island's prospects for social regeneration were debated. Finally, La Samaritana's own understanding of illness and the therapies that derived from it help explain her remarkable popularity. She appealed to multiple constituencies, ranging from Spiritists, to so-called folk Catholics, to freethinkers of various descriptions.

For all the commotion, La Samaritana's was a minimalist kind of hydrotherapy. She treated her patients with prescriptions of *agua fluidizada*, a practice well known to Spiritists everywhere and familiar to Puerto Ricans at least since the last decade of the nineteenth century. As early as 1892, Dr. Manuel Guzmán Rodríguez, a physician from Añasco, denounced Spiritism as an attempt to restore medieval customs. The doctor claimed the use of magnetized water mimicked practices involving holy water.[29]

Unlike Catholics, who regarded the springs in apparition sites as having been blessed by a divine presence, many Spiritists viewed water as a vehicle for the transmission of natural, magnetic currents. They disavowed miracles and denied the involvement of divine persons. All the same, the medicine dispensed in barrio Hato was redolent with meanings for Catholics, too. The water that La Samaritana dispensed was procured from springs (a feature found routinely in country shrines in Puerto Rico and elsewhere) near her home and was later "magnetized" while the médica was in communication with her guide, a spirit identified as none other than San Lorenzo's old parish priest. Visitors then took the water home and did what both Spiritists and Catholics had been accustomed to doing with healing water: they drank it, applied it on compresses, or rubbed it over ailing parts according to their own needs or to the regimen the healer prescribed. Those who could not make the trip had neighbors and relatives bring back containers filled with water.

Whereas allopathic physicians and their supporters ultimately aimed to eliminate suffering, La Samaritana saw afflictions as opportunities to transcend frailty and sin and to access unearthly realms. Rather than seeking the eradication of affliction, La Samaritana's practice was an effort to redeploy it. Those healed in barrio Hato surpassed the limits of the order that appeared natural in order to attain physical health. But the treatment implied more than that; it was also an intervention in favor of moral regeneration and spiritual advancement for society.

Though La Samaritana appealed to Catholics accustomed to offering up their suffering to the divine in the context of pilgrimages and the fulfillment of promises to the saints, her proposal did not strike supporters as traditionalist. Many Spiritists embraced La Samaritana precisely because they saw in her practice the ethos of self-improvement that enveloped their movement.[30] In their eyes, La Samaritana stood for progress.

While it seems clear that the principles of the economy of affliction cut across multiple faiths and practices, La Samaritana represented more than eclecticism. Rather than reconciling Catholic and Spiritist notions of health, affliction, and regeneration, La Samaritana revealed that when it came to healing, there was a plurality of understandings at work. These intersecting notions could engage in dialogue as easily as they could lapse into conflict. Barrio Hato's attractiveness resided in its polysemantic practices rather than its ability to amalgamate. The point has been made before, but it remains significant especially because scholars have written of the dynamics surrounding health, sanitation, and healing after 1898 as characterized by the confrontation of two approaches: U.S. health policy and Puerto Rican traditions. The latter are often presented as a relatively undifferentiated mix of curanderismo, Spiritism, and folk Catholicism rather than as a plural and conflict-ridden field in its own right.[31]

La Samaritana as an Obstacle to Progress

The first to call Vázquez "La Samaritana" seems to have been a critic who likened the springs of barrio Hato to Jacob's well and compared the médica to the Samaritan woman from whom Christ received a drink of water.[32] The commentator did not mean to elevate the médica to biblical stature. On the contrary, he referred to her as a "modern-day Samaritan" in an effort to insinuate that Vázquez was promiscuous and hence unworthy of the public's trust. The Samaritan of the Bible story was a woman of suspect virtue. The new name stuck and soon displaced Vázquez's other titles. But the smear strategy failed. Vázquez's followers appropriated "La Samaritana," transforming the sobriquet into an honorific.[33]

Since there was nothing to indicate La Samaritana's lack of chastity, one might wonder why her critic sought to discredit her in this particular way. The answer to that question has to do with the ways in which class, gender, color, and public health policies intersected to sustain the order prevailing in Puerto Rico around the time of World War I. La Samaritana was a poor woman of color who walked into the limelight only a few years after the conclusion of a fierce and controversial antiprostitution campaign. In the final months of 1918, more than 1,000 women, many poor and nonwhite, were arrested in police sweeps.[34] As concern with sexually dangerous women reached its peak, working-class radicals in the Federación Libre de Trabajadores, a leading labor organization that included a significant number of female tobacco workers like Vázquez, took up the defense of prostitutes against what they perceived as an unconstitutional, antiworker crackdown. To suggest that Vázquez was promiscuous was to do more than to discredit her personally; it was to associate her with a group of women that public officials regarded as a health hazard and a moral scourge. It was also to go beyond denying Vázquez's ability to heal to say that she was responsible for the spread of the very maladies that authorities aimed to eradicate.

To many critics, La Samaritana's color lent further credence to the charges of dissoluteness. The unhealthful libidinousness of black women and mulattoes was a truism of nineteenth-century arts and thought. Since the 1880s, letrados like Salvador Brau and Francisco del Valle Atiles had blamed the island's backward and unsanitary condition on blacks, whom they likened to parasites, on anemic "white" peasant women, and on miscegenation. As Benigno Trigo shows, this formulation downplayed the sanitary threat that the letrados themselves posed to colonial officials and secured for the former a position of indirect authority as guardians of public health.[35] Needless to say, such constructions also precluded the possibility of finding health through a jíbara of color.

Ironically, La Samaritana's race was itself the subject of disputes. It seems that the observers colored her according to their opinions of her ministry. La Samaritana's detractors described her as black and homely.[36] Meanwhile, her defenders insisted that photographs made La Samaritana appear darker than she truly was. Even census enumerators were split when it came to assessing color. The 1920s census counts Vázquez as white, but the enumerator of the 1930 census classified her as "de color."[37] Vázquez herself seems to have remained silent on this matter; she did not claim an identity predicated upon her color and did not mobilize followings along racial lines.

Timing complicated matters for La Samaritana in other ways, too. These were years of political turmoil. Puerto Rican women, including noted Spiritists like Rosario Bellber, had begun to agitate for suffrage; black Puerto Ricans were making political demands through the Republican and Socialist Parties; and labor was displaying an unprecedented strength. And all this was occurring well within sight of barrio Hato. In 1920, shortly before the general elections and only two years before the mass gatherings in barrio Hato, workers in San Lorenzo's tobacco and sugar industries struck for better salaries and improved working conditions. Much to the exasperation of owners, the Socialist Party assisted the strikers. The electoral ballots cast in San Lorenzo show that the workers reciprocated the favor. Although the Unionists won the election, Socialists took the second largest block of votes. In 1924, the Socialists consolidated their gains with a second-place showing islandwide.[38]

La Samaritana's emergence precisely when labor and socialism were making such strides aroused suspicions of politicking in the guise of religion. In July 1922, at the height of La Samaritana's popularity, Spiritists and Socialists launched in Caguas a simultaneous series of propaganda and recruitment meetings.[39] The coincidence was not lost upon critics, who accused La Samaritana of serving partisan interests. Some contended that Socialists and Spiritists were responsible for retarding Puerto Rico's progress and condemned them both. According to one such critic, "Socialist and Spiritist tricksters [walked] across valleys and mountains exploiting that rural part of our country where illiteracy still reigns" to exploit "the lack of awareness of the mindless masses and create a cult[.]"[40]

But opposition to La Samaritana involved more than timing. Journalists, physicians, health officials, and many Spiritists would have found Vázquez objectionable even in the absence of Socialist advances and antiprostitution campaigns. La Samaritana's activities were disruptive enough on their own terms. Vázquez literally caused the social margins to overflow their proper channels. Residents of Barceloneta complained that an alarming number of panhandlers had come to town asking for money to go to San Lorenzo. In May 1922, "a true rain of beggars" also struck Caguas, a town located at a convenient stopping point on the route to the springs. The unwelcome travelers plagued pedestrians, interfered with commerce, and disturbed offices and places of industry. The homeless presence in the streets of Caguas must have appeared especially insolent. Not long before the undesirables came, the town had inaugurated a much-applauded shelter and enacted new antivagrancy regulations.[41]

These mobilizations, disruptive though they were, posed no immediate threats to the state and its capacity to govern. More than with what they did, critics were concerned with what Vázquez and her followers *said* about Puerto Rico and its people. In their estimation, La Samaritana was a symptom of an ailing society that could not leave the afflictions of the past behind. Her success suggested that the goals of civilizing and modernizing the island were far from being realized. In an opinion piece titled "Irresponsibility and Superstition," Angel Archilla Cabrera voiced with unusual virulence the feelings of the learned for those they regarded as derailing progress. The text alerts us to the fact that for some, this derision was connected to the letrados' need to defend themselves from those who appeared civilized. It also makes clear that the frustration of the letrados had to do with superstition's tendency to repeat itself: "In Puerto Rico we are frequently afflicted with intense fevers of irresponsibility and superstition. It would seem as if shadows sought the gloomy abyss to produce a horrifying catastrophe, planting [the seeds of] death and desolation everywhere." In addition, Archilla Cabrera worried about "[t]hat tourist who comes here with his Kodak to contemplate our imponderable natural beauties and to observe the collective culture of the Puerto Rican people: what does he think of us when he stumbles upon these utopian, cabalistic spectacles in the mountains, the valleys or the cities?"[42]

La Samaritana Finds a Sponsor

Had it not been for Juan Jiménez García, most Spiritists would have dismissed the médica out of hand. But Jiménez García was a well-regarded leader who presided over the federation in 1919–20 and who happened to be commissioner of public works and services in Caguas at the time of the mass gatherings in barrio Hato. In 1920, Jiménez García also had presided over "La Defensa," a short-lived sugar mill that sugar growers (colonos) established in Caguas to "defend" themselves from the low prices paid at the region's dominant mill.[43] Jiménez García was also a firm believer in La Samaritana's talents and a skilled propagandist. He contacted the papers routinely to advise them of positive developments at the "Fountain of Health" and to spin stories in favor of Spiritism. Jiménez García was also an important presence at the gatherings in barrio Hato. Critics charged that he had appointed himself stage director. They noted that he addressed pilgrims before Vázquez and that he used this opportunity to attack Catholicism and urge people to embrace Spiritism.[44]

As one might expect, some sectors of the church reacted with outrage. Clergymen, who by then must have been accustomed to the anticlericalism of Spiritists, warned parishioners once again to stay away from Spiritist literature and meetings and launched a campaign to counter the Spiritist offensive. In Caguas, Redemptorist priests, along with the Knights of Columbus and the Damas Isabelinas, two conservative lay organizations identified with the elite, initiated an "oral crusade" condemning Spiritism and La Samaritana. By the end of the summer, a low-intensity leaflet war had broken out, and anonymous flyers discrediting one faith or the other and listing the names of people who had been cured or disputing such claims circulated throughout the region.[45]

Physicians and others connected to the health care business took part in these skirmishes. A man identified only as Suárez who owned Farmacia Campo Alegre in Caguas wrote to the papers to defend himself from allegations that he had circulated a flyer criticizing Jiménez García and La Samaritana. Pharmacists in Guayama complained that water from San Lorenzo had caused medicine sales to drop sharply. However, there were those who took more conciliatory approaches. Instead of issuing public denunciations, an unidentified druggist from Arroyo hung a sign on his shop that read: "I prepare prescriptions with water from San Lorenzo." After that, sales reportedly picked up.[46]

Protestant responses to La Samaritana appear muted by comparison. None of the leading critics identified themselves as such, and there were reports that Protestants could be found in the crowds in barrio Hato alongside Catholics and Spiritists. But this should not be mistaken for a Protestant endorsement of La Samaritana's ministry. Protestant leaders of multiple denominations were on the record as opponents of pilgrimages, which they regarded as spiritually bankrupt, and they were vocal critics of attempts to communicate with spirits, which some condemned for spreading superstitious beliefs and demonic influences.[47]

Although critics of Spiritism accused Jiménez García of opportunism, it is likely that he was a convinced follower of La Samaritana. Of course, interest and conviction may have coincided, too. One thing is clear, however: whether responding to principle or opportunism, La Samaritana's appeal was such that many of the Spiritist leaders charged with safeguarding the doctrine from would-be usurpers felt inclined to embrace her. It seems, then, that Spiritist practices were not as strictly divided into "high" and "low" as those who distinguished between Spiritists and spirit-mongers would lead scholars to believe. When it came to La Samaritana, differences had to be reiterated and policed, lest they collapse and leave Spiritists vulnerable to criticisms from the Catholic Church, Protestants, and scientific authorities.

A Club of Spiritist Detractors

Timely as La Samaritana's rise may have been, not all Spiritists sided with Jiménez García. Spiritists were sharply divided over La Samaritana's mediumship. For them, any final determination of the truthfulness of the cures and of the value of the spirit communications received in barrio Hato turned on the level of progress achieved by the spirit speaking through Vázquez. Was he a superior spirit of light or an ignorant spirit from a lowly sphere? As Spiritists understood it, careless contact with lowly spirits posed the risk of moral contagion and degeneration; it could even reduce Spiritists to mere spirit-mongers.

A few months after La Samaritana first came to public attention, a commission from Aguadilla's Club de Estudios Psicológicos Ramón Emeterio Betances took it upon itself to investigate the events taking place in San Lorenzo.[48] In its much-publicized report, the commission found that although the médica appeared well intentioned, and though she was under the guidance of a knowledgeable

Spiritist, she was an ignorant neophyte and possibly the victim of profit seekers. Although Kardec denied the existence of hell, the commissioners determined that "infernal influences toyed" with La Samaritana and that her "works were dangerous to [people's] health because the character of the spirit operating in the magnetization of the water was unknown." Although a few Catholic priests had embraced Spiritism publicly, and although communications from priests were familiar to Spiritists, the commission did not believe that the magnetization was the doing of Father Joaquín Saras, San Lorenzo's old parish priest, as others maintained.[49] Instead, the commissioners suggested that the spirit behaved in a manner consistent with the basest sorts described in Kardec's writings. The first evidence for this had to do with language. They noted that the spirit addressed them in a coarse way. He threatened and lashed out, saying only: "Nobody destroys the Father's work."[50]

The club's report was met with a flurry of responses. Dozens of Spiritists and other sympathetic commentators wrote to the papers and called for a dispassionate, "scientific" investigation before censures were issued. Their arguments were varied and resourceful. Some suggested that lowly spirits had duped the commission itself. Some attempted to discredit the report as mere "personal opinion." Others challenged the report and those who viewed La Samaritana as a drag on the island's progress by moving the confrontation to the terrain of comparisons. In a typical anticlerical blow, they argued that barrio Hato was superior to the Catholic complex in Lourdes, where pilgrims were exploited routinely.[51]

The most persuasive of La Samaritana's advocates were not content to pick apart the club's report; they presented counterevidence from their own readings of Kardec and from spirit communications. Among the first group, one notable was Ramón Negrón Flores, a journalist and Río Piedras politician who presided over the federation for seven years (1915–18 and 1934–37). While Negrón Flores never endorsed La Samaritana, he refused to dismiss her. Instead, he echoed Kardec's argument that "mediumship [was] a physiological condition of being that has nothing to do with the medium's mental preparation, moral culture, opinions, or beliefs."[52] Negrón Flores's reaction was especially damaging to the club's case because its commission had named him, along with Dr. Ponte Jiménez, among the very men who should judge La Samaritana scientifically.

Rosario Bellber, a suffragist leader and director of the Red Cross who succeeded Ponte Jiménez to the federation's top post, took issue with those who denied the effectiveness of barrio Hato's waters and those who impugned Vázquez, a "humble medium" elected to a "sacred mission." Besides collecting testimonies of cures, Bellber reported that her own father had taken water from barrio Hato and that it certainly had healing properties.[53]

But the most forceful endorsement of La Samaritana came by way of the spirits themselves. Dr. Ponte Jiménez, famed among Spiritists as a man of experimental science, put the question of the guide's identity to a medium. Following a series of inquiries, a spirit confirmed that La Samaritana was indeed blessed with "beautiful faculties." During those "apparent attacks," the spirit said, she was taken by a priest "who was a pastor of that parish and who now wants to be hers, so that he may guide with his advice and new lights, that part of humanity that he once led in the opposite direction."[54]

Father Joaquín Saras, or whatever spirit spoke through La Samaritana when she addressed club members, was remarkably well informed. Rather than submitting to the examination, he questioned the investigators' authority to pass judgments. Vázquez, or rather the spirit, reminded the commissioners of a scandal that had embarrassed their club in 1921, noting that, unlike them, La Samaritana did not charge for her services nor did she trick people.[55] The commission was forced to defend itself in the press.

Progress and the Color of the Soul

The debate on these matters was more than an esoteric diversion. Although La Samaritana's detractors were never explicit about the connecting line they drew between blackness and spiritual backwardness, a pronouncement on the topic was unnecessary. La Samaritana's supporters suspected that there was a racist and elitist impetus behind the allegations regarding the baseness of the guiding spirit. Leandro Sitiriche, a Spiritist who wrote frequently for newspapers, censured the critics, arguing that what preoccupied them was not the identity of the guide or the possibility of fraud. The question that truly plagued critics was: "What will be of science if it is superseded by the quackery of a black nobody?"[56]

La Samaritana brought to the surface many of the contradictions in the Spiritists' understanding of race. The doctrine of reincarnation, which proposed that spirits pass from one life and body to another in accordance with a law of perpetual progress, had a limited potential for destabilizing extant racial hierarchies. Reincarnation, as Spiritists understood it, denied the geneticist basis for racial determinism. In *The Genesis*, Kardec claimed, "Reincarnation destroys the prejudices of race and caste, since the same Spirit may be reborn in wealth or in poverty, be a great lord or a proletariat, free or a slave, a man or a woman[.]" "Men," Kardec added, "are not born inferior or subordinated except by their bodies; by their Spirits they are equal and free."[57]

On the basis of these pronouncements, Puerto Rican Spiritists nourished a vision of racial harmony well before La Samaritana began to preoccupy them. For instance, during the federation's assembly of 1908, mediums reported seeing above the stage a pair of interlocking hands, one white and the other black. Above the hands, Kardec's portrait appeared and a sun sent out its rays onto the assembly.[58]

Dramatic as it was, this vision offered an incomplete picture of Spiritists' ambivalent attitudes toward blackness. After pronouncing race epiphenomenal, Kardec took pains to limit the consequences of his doctrines. While maintaining that race itself was contingent and transitory, he espoused an evolutionist notion of racial difference that could serve as an apologia for colonialism. In *The Book of Spirits*, for instance, he cited a celestial brother who explained the peculiar bond between spirits and bodies: "In primitive peoples, as you call them, matter dominates over the Spirit; they allow brute instincts to take over. . . . Moreover, those peoples whose development is imperfect are generally under the rule of Spirits that are equally imperfect, which are sympathetic to them, until other more advanced peoples destroy or ameliorate that influence."[59]

Puerto Rican Spiritists shared Kardec's ambivalence. Although Kardec's writings predisposed them to suspect certain practitioners, neither blackness nor class disadvantage led inevitably to dismissal from the ranks of Spiritism. Spiritists were sincere when they spoke of fraternal bonds to those they aimed to uplift through their programs. Occasionally, they worked alongside black leaders, such as Simplicia Armstrong de Ramú, a member of the board of *El Iris de Paz*.[60] But such conviviality operated within limits. In a 1902 editorial for the same journal titled "Color and other social differences," Agustina Guffain reminded readers that it was "indispensable to maintain distinctions based on the better or worse fulfillment of duties and on the greater or lesser degree of dignity with which we adorn our acts." After alerting readers to their responsibility to assist less fortunate souls, Guffain proclaimed: "Let the blindfolds fall off those who hate and let the lights of love shine. Let us imitate Jesus. Pity Judas and let us never forget this sentence from the wise rationalist doctrine: 'All souls are white.'"[61]

La Samaritana illustrates how Guffain's dictum could work in practice: all souls may have been white, but dark skin remained evidence of things not seen. To heed Kardec's admonition that "broad features and thick lips . . . could never accommodate the delicate modulations of a distinguished Spirit," Spiritists could demand that La Samaritana place herself under the tutelage of her superiors to safeguard against spirit-mongering, or they could dismiss her.[62] Jiménez García and other federation leaders chose the first option, while club members opted for the second alternative.

The debate surrounding La Samaritana illustrates some uses of racial differentiation in 1920s Puerto Rico. When faced with an apparent recrudescence of backwardness, Spiritists proclaimed the universal whiteness of the soul but reasserted the distinction between proper Spiritists and spirit-mongers. That construction rested partly on a theory of racial differences that relegated black bodies and the spirits they incarnated to the lower levels of evolution. In proposing this, Spiritists removed obstacles to progress that appeared insurmountable. Superstition was not reasserting itself; it only appeared that way when those at different levels of progress to perfection were judged against one another. Distinguishing between Spiritists and so-called espiriteros served another purpose, too: it cleared Spiritists from the charge that they encouraged "superstition."

Everybody Loves Progress

Spiritist critics of La Samaritana were convinced that she knew nothing of science and was opposed to progress. However, the events in barrio Hato suggest that when it came to such things, the differences between Spiritists and spirit-mongers were far from clear-cut. Neither La Samaritana nor her supporters ever disavowed modern medicine or experimental science. On the contrary, Jiménez García and the Spiritists who defended the healer attempted to secure the prestige of scientific knowledge. They urged studies "by [unprejudiced] men of scientific orthodoxy" as the surest way to safeguard La Samaritana's ministry.[63]

Self-anointed, "scientific" Spiritists could argue that La Samaritana's treatments shared a good deal with Catholic and popular practices that were already discredited for their reportedly inherent hostility to progress. The works of the seemingly backward economy of affliction were as visible in La Samaritana's own history as they were in the careers of the island's lay preachers and prophets. Vázquez's ministry began after an illness and a long period of unconsciousness whose causes physicians could not determine. Her recovery required the assistance of a curioso, who prayed for the patient without prescribing medication. After these prayers, Vázquez regained consciousness. She sat on her bed, called for her godfather, and relayed to him a series of spirit communications. This inaugurated La Samaritana's public work and brought to her home the first seekers.

The early communications were dreamlike visions in which images of war and affliction were prominent. In one of these, Vázquez found herself on a mountain. Nearby, someone made bricks under a mango tree. Others plowed a precarious plot of land. Looking up, Vázquez saw people singing in a poorhouse. The residents were celebrating a child's baptism, but they were also mourning him. When she asked why they cried, they responded: "Because we know the end of which he was born." Soon after, Vázquez witnessed a distressing montage that she interpreted as confirmation of her calling as a healer: Soldiers marched through the hills. Angels, crowns, and a series of letters stood suspended in the sky. Meanwhile, a group of sick people waited to be healed with water from a creek in her barrio.[64]

The economy of affliction remained in evidence as La Samaritana gained fame. Most visitors described the trip to barrio Hato as a true pilgrimage. Nearly all published accounts began by listing trials and difficulties. The remoteness of the location, the difficulties with transportation, and the demanding walk to the hills followed by long periods of waiting were meaningful elements of the visit. They were more than discomfort and inconvenience; as Vázquez explained in a 1953 interview, these trials were a "necessary penance."[65]

But all this should not be confused with a rejection of progress. La Samaritana was not adverse to technology, nor did she perceive a contradiction between her hydrotherapy and modern medicine. Commission members and physicians warned that Vázquez herself continued to take patent medications, which they offered as evidence of hypocrisy. But La Samaritana's supporters did not consider the concurrent use of both therapeutic systems remarkable. Although they were not exactly empiricists, La Samaritana and her followers were pragmatists. As demand for water grew in barrio Hato, Vázquez and her supporters encased the springs in concrete and built a 2,000-gallon tank that would hold enough water to meet demand. Later, when it appeared that the owner of the property would prevent the crowds from gathering there, La Samaritana proposed moving to nearby land. That property had springs, too, and easier access to the road.[66]

La Samaritana's pragmatism was also evident in her treatments. She sought spaces and mechanisms for corrective intervention rather than the determination of first principles. To Vázquez and her followers, diagnosis was not simply an effort to determine the etiology of the illness; her aim was to set things right where they had gone awry. She intervened precisely where reputable science failed to go beyond explanations to offer solutions. The reports are emphatic on this point: La Samaritana healed those whom medical science had deemed incurable.[67]

La Samaritana never contested the benefits of technological tools; instead, she challenged implicitly the totalizing claims of a positivism that would probe only what could be seen and touched. Whether they called themselves Spiritists or they bore the label of spirit-mongers, Spiritists of all stripes imposed limits on human agency. They asserted that because "psychological" phenomena were beyond the reach of the senses, they were not susceptible to the usual methods of research. Spiritist "philosophy" was superior because it inquired into all spheres with equal rigor. In short, Spiritists placed restrictions on the very scientific rationality they sought to enshrine. One of La Samaritana's defenders urged the learned to "be brave enough to confess that you are before the presence of an effect whose cause you do not know." He then added significantly: "You do not know it all, and you never shall, because science is infinite."[68]

One might be inclined to call this approach nonmodern, but the label does not quite fit. La Samaritana's proposals emerged as an option in the conflict and dialogue with letrados and the crusade to regenerate Puerto Rico. Spiritists, spirit-mongers, and expert commentators constituted each other's practices in the context of a modernizing society. La Samaritana was not the remnant of a bygone era.

Competing Economies and the Closing of Barrio Hato

Detractors proposed a variety of solutions to the problems they believed La Samaritana epitomized. These ranged from the benign to the authoritarian. At one end, one finds calls for improvements in the education of the masses and the delivery of medical services and for investigations into the natural properties of San Lorenzo's water. Some of these calls—especially those that promised short-term returns—were heeded. For instance, following critical outcries, the government moved to fill an opening for a municipal doctor for San Lorenzo. In addition, there were imaginative countermeasures. These included the circulation of a rumor of the contamination or poisoning of the spring waters in San Lorenzo and the introduction of traffic regulations that banned the use of cargo vehicles for the transportation of passengers. The prohibition restricted the access of the poor to barrio Hato, since trucks charged the lowest transport fares. At the repressive end, one finds calls for fraud investigations, the criminalizing of La Samaritana's practice as illegal medicine, and forced closings.[69]

Ultimately, La Samaritana retreated from public view for reasons that went beyond official and Spiritist hostility. By La Samaritana's account, her public ministry in barrio Hato fell to competition from rival economies, apparently in a few years.[70] Critics and supporters shared the notion that profiteering or even the conduct of an excessive level of legitimate business could discredit religious claims. For that reason, sympathizers emphasized that La Samaritana never charged for her services. Though she was careful to avoid impropriety, La Samaritana later conceded that "*comercialismo*" had played a part in weakening barrio Hato's pull. In 1953, when a reporter sought out La Samaritana to ask for her opinion regarding a widely reported apparition of the Virgin in Sabana Grande, Vázquez explained that kiosks and souvenir peddlers and the crowds that sought such things had been responsible for the loss of fervor.[71] It was not a matter of explanations tailored after the fact to suit the situation. In 1922, there had been complaints about price-gouging by barrio Hato's "temple merchants."[72]

The domestic economy, with its gendered transactions, also played a part in barrio Hato's closing. Sometime after the crowds began to shrink, La Samaritana's spiritual guide allowed her a two-year respite from her ministry. During this sabbatical, La Samaritana married Clara Fernández, a tobacco worker she met when she moved to town to take a job at the General Cigar Company. This made her retirement from public life all but definitive. Before her wedding, Vázquez had warned those who sought her out that, according to her spiritual guides, she would lose her faculties and end her mission once she was a married woman.[73] But the prediction did not prove altogether inflexible. La Samaritana retained her talents after becoming a wife but limited her activity to a domestic arena. Until close to the time of her death in 1986, she treated patients in her home and kept a comparatively low profile. She had four children. These changes, she explained, had been preordained: "I came to earth not as a misionera but as a wife and mother." "Misionera" is a resonant term. Elenita and members of the Cheo brotherhood referred to themselves in that manner.

This statement suggests that the public and domestic roles were not fully compatible for Vázquez and points at some of the limitations to the challenge that her career posed to normative gender roles. Although this was a woman whose speech carried an unusual authority, she was also a medium who spoke with a masculine voice. A respectable man lent her legitimacy and framed her pronouncements. Her messages and actions, moreover, were restricted for the most part to healing and moral instruction, two activities often assigned to women in the dominant division of labor. Vázquez's most significant departure from customary gender roles was reminiscent of the challenges that the editors of *El Iris de Paz*, nearly all women, delivered in the first decade of the twentieth century. Like her literate predecessors, whom Herzig Shannon has recently described as "social feminists," Vázquez broke with convention partly by taking on a public role. But like Guffain and her colleagues, Vázquez aimed to perfect herself as a mother and wife.[74]

Finally, it appears that the economy of affliction was susceptible to internal contradictions. By Vázquez's own account, pragmatism got the better of barrio Hato. As La Samaritana explained in 1953, when a second set of springs was found to satisfy the thirst of the crowds, something changed. The difference was not in the efficacy of the waters or the sanctity of the location. The problem was that access to the new springs was rather effortless. A mere walk offered no genuine possibility of regeneration.

Although the crowds disappeared, the threat that La Samaritana represented did not. La Samaritana had a way of inspiring imitators and launching traditions. The memory of her ministry posed dangers of its own. Perhaps for this reason, La Samaritana's name was mentioned for decades as new campaigns to wipe out superstition were launched.[75] It is as if critics haunted by the past found it necessary to conduct regular exorcisms to rid Puerto Rico of its backward spirits.

For scholars, memory of La Samaritana should have a more salutary effect. It should serve as a reminder that faiths did not simply split, producing derivative, popular practices alongside proper doctrine. As La Samaritana shows, the very distinction between Spiritists and spirit-mongers was the result of dialogue and conflict over the route to social regeneration. La Samaritana's career reminds us that there were multiple discourses of progress in 1920s Puerto Rico. Politicians, Spiritists, and so-called spirit-mongers spoke of modernization using languages that obscured parallels and discrepancies in their utopian visions.

5

MANAGING MIRACLES IN BATISTA'S CUBA

La Estigmatizada and Clavelito

La Dolce Vita told us much of what we need to know about the making and un-
making of miracles in an era of spectacles. After following a diminutive convert-
ible conveying Marcello Rubini, his tormented fiancée, Emma, and the original Paparazzo to the site of the Madonna's apparition in the Italian countryside,
Fellini conducted a trenchant inventory of dour skeptics, assorted opportunists,
contrived emotions, and self-serving machinations. The director paused, however, to offer a counterpoint; his impish camera recorded intimate moments of
genuine fervor amid the circus acts. Immediately after a television director calls
for a break in filming preparations, a woman runs to prostrate herself and plead
for the life of the young child in her arms. Emma's desperate entreaty to the Virgin, uttered as she stands next to a studio truck, and the crowd who, consumed
by a Dyonisian fever, tears a tree apart punctuate and complete the scenes at the
"field of miracles." Religion is drama, Fellini reminds us. Miracles, like other
forms of stagecraft, can accommodate the purveyors of novelties and their recording devices. Believers may even deploy the cameras and the microphones to their
own ends. But, ultimately, miracles cannot resist entirely the interests that would
transform faith into a perishable commodity.

For all of his insights and distaste for the intrusions of commercialism, Fellini
may have underestimated the discernment of the faithful and exaggerated their
susceptibility to the media's wiles. Though it is true that relentless coverage may
fan the flames of religious fervor, it is no less the case that religious passions ex-
tinguish themselves and would-be miracles often suffocate in spite of the media's
assiduous tending. This chapter examines the case of La Estigmatizada, a visionary on a propagandizing mission, and contrasts it with two instances in which the

publicity machine fueled religious energies, becoming in effect a coparticipant in the collective enterprise of miracle-making. These two are the apparition of the Virgin in Sabana Grande, Puerto Rico, in 1953 and Clavelito's radio ministry in 1950s Cuba. As shown in Chapter 6, the apparition was the object of what is now referred to as a media blitz. Radio, television, and print journalists descended upon a small town in western Puerto Rico and reported up-to-the-minute information for several months. Clavelito, for his part, was a guajiro, or peasant, singer cum celebrity healer who employed radio broadcasts to assist listeners. This updating of Mustelier's and Manso's hydrotherapies reminds us that upon occasion, the faithful transformed spectacles into miracles, exceeding the projections of even the most calculating manipulators of public opinion.

Drawing from these examples, I argue that the miraculous, like the spectacular, ensues from processes of collective authorship with marked performative components and that spectacle, particularly in the form of media coverage, can impel as well as undermine devotion. But believers continued to adhere to discernible religious criteria and logic in determining what constituted a manifestation of the divine. The public—the media's imagined interlocutors—was seldom if ever duped as easily as its critics decried. This religious logic was far from static, however. Secularism and the interventions of the mass media did alter at times the terms of the economy of affliction. Finally, I contend that spectacle-makers and those poised to profit from their endeavors often failed in their efforts to restrict and channel the meanings of miraculous events. Fulgencio Batista and his subalterns, for instance, sought to position his dictatorial government (1952–59) as La Estigmatizada's patron in an effort to curry favor with a disaffected citizenry. The official embrace proved lethal, however, as critics heaped suggestions of politicking upon a long list of attributes that already made some Cubans doubt the trustworthiness of La Estigmatizada's claims.

A Mission in Need of Publicity

In the summer of 1956, Havana's radio and television stations, its popular magazines, and its many dailies turned their attention to a nineteen-year-old so-called guajira from Güira de Melena, a town in Havana province. Irma Izquierdo, better known as La Estigmatizada, had been suffering from stigmata, facsimiles of the wounds that Christ's Roman captors inflicted upon him. Recurrent "crises," as she called them, left her body covered in welts and often soaked in a bloody sweat that trickled from her forehead.

According to her own reports, Izquierdo's tribulations had begun during Holy Week, appropriately the time when the liturgical calendar commemorates Christ's passion and resurrection. The Monday before Easter, she awoke feeling "out of sorts" (*indispuesta*).[1] Two days later, after prolonged fasting and reclusion to her bedroom, a writhing agony ensued. Izquierdo felt a sharp pain in her left shoulder, "as if I was bearing a heavy load." Her forehead and her shoulder soon started to bleed, and wounds (*llagas*) appeared on her feet. Dark welts also formed on her back and arms. These were caused by the action of a deformed, whip-wielding hand that only Izquierdo could see, and then only in disembodied form, for her demonic tormentor never showed its face or anything beyond the aforementioned limb.

Visions of Christ himself followed these torturous episodes. According to Izquierdo, Christ appeared to her as a palpable physical presence but remained invisible to others. In response to questions from reporters, she explained how he looked in person: "His face is long, pale, with deeply sunken eyes, and he has long, very light blond hair, kind of curly."[2] Christ's appearance varied in Izquierdo's visions, however. Once she saw a panting, suffering Jesus rolling his eyes, and on another occasion she was confronted with a crucified figure who whispered a prayer to the Father. In a few especially momentous encounters, Christ addressed Izquierdo directly. In the first such instance, Christ issued a diffuse directive that echoed the pronouncements recorded in the Gospels: "Man: love yourself so that you can love God and your neighbor at the same time."[3] Izquierdo was instructed to repeat these words constantly. A few days later, however, Christ's remarks made up in specificity what they lacked in biblical loftiness. "Irma, you must publicize your case," he said.[4]

Striking as Christ's demand now appears, it was not entirely unprecedented. While it is true that noted stigmatics like Father Pio and Therese Neumann were initially inclined to hide their wounds and shun publicity, there were alternative types of behavior.[5] As William Christian Jr. has shown, Mary and other saints often demanded that seers in late medieval Castile spread the news of their visitations and often ordered that local authorities be contacted so that a shrine could be established or a procession undertaken.[6] In Izquierdo's case, however, Christ's instructions were specific. Rather than requiring action by a local corporate or ecclesiastical body, Christ instructed Izquierdo to seek a public stage. The course of action was otherwise open-ended.

Though Christ's mandate was unequivocal, Izquierdo told reporters that she had been reticent to make her story public because she had always been a "reserved" person. Christ was adamant, however, and his will prevailed in the end.

In a series of visions, he foretold that a case similar to Izquierdo's would be publicized very soon. Two days later, he reappeared to tell the young woman that the news had already been published; *Bohemia* had run a feature story on a Francisco Santoni, a young man from Sardinia whose bleeding stigmata had been making news throughout Italy.[7] Santoni, too, it should be noted, suffered whippings with an invisible instrument. The prophecy—now validated in the international reportage of a popular news and society magazine—settled the matter. Irma Izquierdo went to *El País*, a Havana daily of a populist bent. From then on, the woman the press dubbed "La Estigmatizada" thought of herself as charged with a God-given duty, and she never tired of reminding reporters for dailies and magazines that her "mission need[ed] publicity. . . . God has asked that of me."[8] In her interviews, she made a point of thanking journalists for their help, a rhetorical gesture that had the effect of pressing them into divine service in spite of their protestations of editorial autonomy and impartiality.

Izquierdo's account of her dialogues with Christ had other curious effects. In the absence of known Cuban predecessors among those afflicted with stigmata, Izquierdo's visions—and the reports that confirmed them—provided her trials with a history, an "invented tradition" by which this current manifestation of a reportedly long-standing phenomenon could be assessed and understood. In the preambles to the articles that the press wrote about her, Izquierdo learned that there had been 321 cases of stigmatization reported in the literature. She read of the late-nineteenth-century trials of a Bavarian stigmatic named Therese Neumann,[9] to whom she was compared.[10] Chances are that she also heard about the 1936 death of Rose Ferron, better known as "La Estigmatizada de Woonsocket," whose story was profiled in *Bohemia*'s "Vidas Extrañas" pages.[11] It is worth noting, however, that Izquierdo never gave any indication that she knew of Father Pio, a twentieth-century Italian stigmatic renowned throughout the world, or of the saints and mystics who had been similarly afflicted throughout the history of the church.[12] Her immediate point of reference, as she acknowledged without hesitation, was one of those articles of human interest and devotional curiosity (on Santoni) by which magazines meant to attract and entertain their readers. What had been intended for commercial consumption acquired a miraculous inflection to become the opening act in a complex religious drama that the media itself helped to further in spite of its misgivings about Izquierdo.

The divine's professed desire for publicity coincided rather fortuitously with the needs of a suspicious but nonetheless attentive press. As *Carteles* noted in an insert that ran flanked on three sides by a full page of Izquierdo's photographs, Batista had again suspended constitutional guarantees and imposed censorship measures following student demonstrations and an attack on an army garrison (Goicuría) in Matanzas by a band of insurgent Auténticos hoping to topple the government. The bloody incident, in which more than ten young men lost their lives, took place on 29 April, scarcely three weeks before the story of La Estigmatizada broke and only weeks after a series of antigovernment, army-led plots were uncovered.[13] (Fidel Castro launched a guerrilla insurgency in the Sierra Maestra mountains in November 1956.) Between 30 April and 10 June 1956, publications filled many of their pages with soft stories, the only sort certain to pass the scrutiny of the censors. In a 10 June editorial protest, *Bohemia* claimed that in the days of the media blackout, it printed no news derived from official sources and abstained from commenting on dictatorships elsewhere in Latin America, lest it indulge in acts of hypocrisy. That, of course, limited the journalistic repertoire to police chronicles, international news, and lengthy features such as "I witnessed a true miracle at Lourdes" and Samuel Feijóo's "Man's Strange Cults in Our Day," to name only two with a devotional or sensational penchant. Under the circumstances, it came as no surprise that Izquierdo received ample coverage and near-celebrity treatment. As soon as she set out on foot in a pilgrimage to the Virgin's sanctuary in El Cobre, journalists from all media joined her entourage. CMQ-TV, Cuba's leading station, went so far as to offer Izquierdo an ambulance and a nurse to assist her throughout the long journey.[14]

Though the pilgrimage was launched with only a few days of advance notice following a communication in which Christ revealed his desire to Izquierdo, this mission met with immediate, if not overwhelming, success. Curious travelers and those living along the *carretera central*, the highway that crosses the length of the island, joined Izquierdo for stretches of her fast-paced, twenty-kilometer marches. No doubt some in these congregations were simply curious to witness firsthand the comings and goings of the personage of the day. Others, however, saw this woman as a possible agent of divine grace. They assisted Izquierdo in carrying the life-size cross that she had had built for her journey, offered her shelter, and sought her prayers and advice on behalf of their ailing loved ones. Large crowds congregated near towns and made of her entrances newsworthy events. In late May, an expectant gathering of 2,000 greeted La Estigmatizada in Matanzas. A thousand others reportedly awaited her arrival in La Esperanza and Santa Clara.[15]

As she walked on, Izquierdo was asked repeatedly to restate the object of her journey. In response to the obligatory question, she replied without embellishment: "To go to El Cobre walking, so that peace might reign in the world." The goal of the pilgrimage echoed the pronouncements by seers in Fatima and Wisconsin (see below), where the faithful were also urged to pray for world peace. But peace must have certainly resonated with urgency in Cuba in 1956, a year of factional violence and political instability that augured the collapse of the *batistato*. Batista had returned to power in 1954 only by means of a transparently corrupt election in which only 40 percent of eligible voters cast a ballot.[16]

Izquierdo's expectations for her arrival in El Cobre (projected for 8 June) remained vague, however. "I suppose that something will happen," she told *Carteles*.[17] This apparent lack of clear purpose troubled the press corps but did not bother most supporters and believers. Sympathetic respondents to man-in-the-street surveys made it clear that they understood Izquierdo's project in terms of an economy of affliction; the pilgrimage was the fulfillment of a vow, a sacrifice undertaken to satisfy a promise to a saint or divine person. As young Nilda Carrillo put it, Izquierdo was doing Christ's bidding and "the miracle may take place at any moment."[18]

As shown in previous chapters, this singular attitude to affliction regulated and continues to govern many transactions between human and divine actors in the Cuban and Puerto Rican religious imaginary. This mode of relating to the divine ascribes suffering a positive value as the impetus behind moral transformation and other types of healing. Among the faithful, a measure of asceticism is regarded as a prerequisite for the manifestation of the miraculous. The trials of the flesh are themselves an offering and a way for the believers to prove their worth and commitment before the divine.

For all it did to popularize her endeavors, the press judged Izquierdo's behavior and her claims harshly, applying standards drawn from orthodox hagiographies and a general but strict code of religious propriety. The comparisons were scarcely flattering to Izquierdo. Her multiple deviations from pious ways and from the newly discovered conventions surrounding stigmata were well publicized and help account for the evanescence of her mission and the dissipation of the passions that first surrounded her. The reestablishment of the freedom of the press, of course, also had a part in Izquierdo's sudden disappearance from the public scene. After mid-July, few publications had anything to add to their prolific coverage; by the end of the summer, La Estigmatizada had returned to the obscurity whence she had come in the spring.

Izquierdo's behavior during her pilgrimage often fell short of the ascetic high mark established by her predecessors; if the press is to be credited, time and again La Estigmatizada disappointed. Early reports had claimed, for instance, that the wooden cross on Izquierdo's shoulder weighed more than fifty pounds. An anonymous, mistrustful resident of the city of Matanzas, however, got hold of the cross, placed it on a scale, and announced that it did not exceed twenty-four pounds. When confronted with this information, Izquierdo replied unconvincingly: "Well, but the arms stick out."[19]

Other news accounts reduced Izquierdo's journey to an oxymoron, dubbing it "a happy pilgrimage." And Izquierdo did blur the line between pilgrimages and road tours, two modes of travel with contrasting attitudes to consumption and the landscape that manifest their differences in highly ritualized behaviors. For an emulator of a suffering Christ, Izquierdo was too mindful of creature comforts to satisfy reporter Oscar Pino Santos and others who detected "nothing of asceticism or mysticism in her trip." Though Izquierdo walked at a remarkable pace, she took care to avoid the heat, venturing out only some late afternoons and evenings. She did not walk every day, nor did she fast or pray assiduously.[20] The stories in the press revealed also that Izquierdo carried her lighter-than-advertised cross only when entering towns. Her husband, Eladio Reyes, a friend of the family, or a devoted stranger bore Christ's burden at most other times. Indeed, if the trials of the body were expected to ready practitioners to receive a miraculous grace, Izquierdo's preparations presented a puzzling case. Far from looking emaciated, Izquierdo put on seven pounds during the first weeks of her travels. Moreover, she slept comfortably in hotels or well-appointed homes and traveled to scenic destinations along the route to El Cobre. Observant of the forms, she remarked excitedly on how well she was "getting to know Cuba" and even snapped a few pictures along the way, including one of a waterfall in which she claimed Christ's face was visible. When a day's march had been completed, Izquierdo boarded a new van that took her to her room, leaving her cross close to the road in someone else's care.[21]

Given Izquierdo's lackadaisical attitude to bodily discipline, perhaps it is fitting that she never attained the gifts that made of Mustelier, Manso, and Antoñica Izquierdo such revered figures. As a "disconcerted" journalist pointed out, La Estigmatizada was neither the preacher nor the healer that experience had taught Cubans would rise amid miraculous happenings. Though patients were brought before her, Izquierdo's only reported successful cures were known through secondhand testimonies: an elderly woman had claimed to feel better after touching the cross, and the pain ailing a bus driver had reportedly disappeared after he carried the cross for a kilometer.[22] Izquierdo confessed, however, that she was no better equipped to attend to the sick than any other person. She acknowledged her discomfort and pity at seeing a hydrocephalic child, and when a woman seeking a cure for her daughters approached her, Izquierdo asked if the children had been taken to a doctor. Upon hearing that medical treatment had failed,

Izquierdo stated simply that she had heard it said that an infusion of *cundiamor* might be good.[23]

Gender expectations also played a part in intensifying the doubts that had begun to enshroud La Estigmatizada and her mission. Initially described as a small-town, and perhaps excessively devoted guajira, Izquierdo proved neither a shy, conservative, country bumpkin nor an especially pious woman. In most interviews she came across as more of an aspiring starlet than a visionary; she smoked, polished her nails, and obliged photographers and journalists by posing for staged pictures and answering vacuous queries about her likes and dislikes. The list of her favorite activities included listening to piano music and cha-cha-cha, hardly the beat of choice among churchgoing matrons.

There was also something risqué about some of Izquierdo's wounds. Besides the lacerations in her arms and feet, a scratched inscription unlike any of Christ's stigmata appeared on Izquierdo's body. INRI, the acronym that crowned many crucifixes, could be read in dark letters on La Estigmatizada's legs, a syllable clinging to each one of her thighs. Several magazines published photographs of Izquierdo with her skirt gathered at her lap to display the writing on her body or submitting to a physician's examination while sitting on a bed. Though hardly salacious, such images were not part of the habitual devotional repertoire, which usually emphasized Marian chastity and piety.

Care should be taken not to exaggerate the formality and asceticism demanded by the Cuban and Puerto Rican economies of affliction. Not everything that struck journalists as discrediting struck believers as sacrilegious. When reporters related the story of how Christ had revealed a lottery number to Izquierdo during one of her visions, they meant to expose her as frivolous and disrespectful. Supporters, however, found the incident unremarkable and appear to have taken Izquierdo at her word. The vision had been a lesson in faith: Izquierdo had doubted Christ and had not played what turned out to be the winning number. Had she believed, she would have been rewarded. Interventions of the divine in such areas were common in both Cuba and Puerto Rico, where saints were regularly invoked for assistance in finances, finding lost objects, avoiding legal troubles, and other concerns of ordinary living. This does not mean, of course, that believers did not regard greed and self-interest with disapproval. Some people were perturbed when Clavelito began foretelling lottery numbers and made statements against the practice. And in Puerto Rico, a pilgrim reported that the Virgin of Sabana Grande punished her when she sought help in a lottery drawing.[24]

Izquierdo's lack of decorum was compounded by a perceived want in devotion. *Bohemia*'s report, the first to break the story, spoke of Izquierdo's excesses

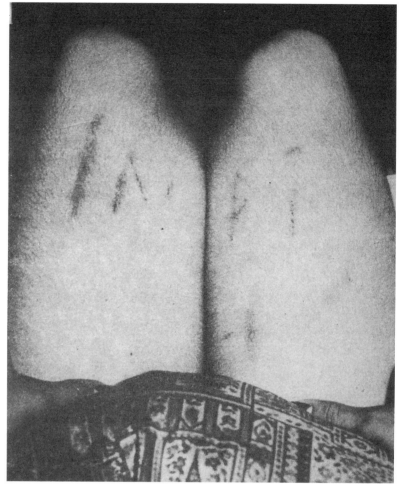

Irma Izquierdo's thighs. From *Carteles*, 15 July 1956. (Universidad de la Habana)

during previous Easters, her membership in various church organizations, and the altars found in every room of her rather well-equipped home. In response, Izquierdo insisted that she was no "fanatic," by which she meant that she was a practicing Catholic who attended mass occasionally but no more frequently than other women.[25] This explanation may have contributed to the subsequent impression of laxity, but again, it was her behavior during the pilgrimage that raised eyebrows. Baffling expectations, Izquierdo did not pray much or dwell on the subject of religion. The only evidence of prayers that reporters could find took the form of printed flyers asking for peace and love for mankind that the visionary distributed. Further, Izquierdo was headed for a sanctuary, but her first stop upon arriving in a new town was seldom the local church. Instead, she often headed for the police station, where officers, journalists, and curious crowds greeted her.

The press noted these habits and repeatedly portrayed Izquierdo in the company of men in uniform, hinting in veiled tones that efforts were under way to profit politically from the peripatetic mission. In a typical instance, a reporter inquired about the provenance of the pilgrims' new van and suggested that it might have been an "official donation."[26] Izquierdo denied the charge, saying only that it belonged to her family. Unable to produce a smoking gun, journalists underlined those signs that lent themselves to pointed readings. For instance, they noted that Izquierdo—the daughter of an army corporal—traveled in the company of a permanent army escort whose members handled crowds and traffic and doubled up as cross-bearers if called upon. Izquierdo had also been known to spend a few nights at police headquarters when no suitable rooms could be found to accommodate her and Eladio. Reports of "ample," albeit unspecified, government aid also circulated in the press.

There is little doubt that officials in Batista's government took an active interest in the pilgrimage and aimed to ensure that it unfolded smoothly. But circumstances were such that, regardless of their schemes or inclinations, government officers could not pronounce themselves in support of La Estigmatizada. After all, Batista had been cultivating an alliance with the Catholic hierarchy for some years, and in the late 1950s he went so far as to direct $1.6 million dollars in lottery revenues into church coffers.[27] The rapprochement strategy was nowhere as evident as in the celebrations of the fiftieth anniversary of the republic, during which Batista and the church hierarchy presided over the imposing ceremonies that welcomed the image of El Cobre's Virgin to Havana.[28] Any public utterance in Izquierdo's favor, whether sincere or cynical, would have put the government at odds with the church at a moment when it needed all the support that it could muster. As discussed below, when faced with Izquierdo, the church chose silence at first. Its denial of the young woman's claims to stigmatization and private revelations was unambiguous, however.

God Needs Publicity, Too

While the press generated ample doubts about Izquierdo and pushed forth the notion that she was sincere but self-deluding, her placement in the spotlight ensured that a new bout would take place in the long-standing struggle between

Irma Izquierdo en route to El Cobre. From *Carteles*, 27 May 1956.
(Universidad de la Habana)

defenders of rationality and orthodoxy and independent-minded believers. Certainly a few supporters made themselves heard. But it was the by now customary set of critics—physicians, rationalists, and church officials—who carried the day. Their victory was scarcely surprising; Izquierdo was something of a crippled champion. What is remarkable about the conflict is that for the first time the debate surrounding a religious leader elicited a persistent desire to reaffirm the existence of God himself. This time the faithful confronted their usual adversaries alongside of secularism, a force that had been gaining strength in Spain and its Caribbean colonies since the liberal reforms of the nineteenth century first began to curb ecclesiastical prerogatives.

The state and its allies applied no special correctives on this occasion; they did not incarcerate Izquierdo, nor did they confine her to a medical facility or castigate her with vitriol. As shown in the preceding chapters, this was not the first time that a visionary had met with such a reaction from the authorities. But the context for the apparent inactivity of church and state officials was new. Faced with political violence and clinging desperately to power, Batista and his lieutenants seem to have opted for a populist solution, a laissez-faire strategy tempered with intermittent, albeit fairly discreet, efforts to assist the stigmatic. The ecclesiastical establishment, for its part, considered its response with care. Such eruptions of religious sentiment were inherently disruptive and even embarrassing, since they promoted less-than-orthodox practices and superstitions. But they did serve to arrest perceived threats to religious sentiment stemming from secularism and from a crippled but ideologically potent Communist Party. For some conservatives in the church, professed atheism came to play a part akin to that of witchcraft and superstition at the beginning of the century. According to proponents of this notion, godlessness eroded civilization, threatened order, and diminished the cultural heritage of the nation just as surely as superstition did. The *Diario de la Marina*, an old pro-Spanish daily that also espoused prochurch views, frequently sounded such warnings in its sections titled "Catholic News" and "Spanish Societies." The paper also gave ample publicity to the campaigns of "the worker's Pope," Pious XII, against international Communism, as well as the Cuban government's efforts in this area. On occasion it also sought to promote Catholic devotion with news of miraculous occurrences abroad.[29] Shortly after Izquierdo first came to public attention, for instance, the *Diario* reported on the Second Inter-American Meeting of Education Ministers in Lima, where the U.S. representatives congratulated the Cuban delegation for its advocacy of greater "spirituality" in schools. The proposal, submitted by Dr. Evelio Pentón, was meant to counter "the dangers of communist infiltration in the schools." The very next day, the paper announced that Havana's Cardinal Manuel Arteaga was conducting a collection in honor of the pope's eightieth birthday to benefit the "working class."[30]

Conservatives in the Cuban church were not entirely alone, of course. Fear of Communism had impelled state, ecclesiastical, and miraculous interventions for decades. In 1929, soon after a socialist government ascended to power in Portugal, the main visionary at Fatima revealed that the Virgin had appeared in 1917 to ask the faithful to pray for Russia's conversion.[31] A similar message was repeated on U.S. soil even before the House Un-American Activities Committee held its infamous hearings. In 1950, thousands (as many as 100,000, according to the *New York Times*) gathered in Necedah, Wisconsin, to listen to Ann Van Hoof. Van Hoof, whose visions of the Virgin continued until the 1970s, reported that Mary wanted the faithful to pray the Rosary for the rebirth of the Christian faith in Russia so as to avoid an impending war with the United States. According to the revelations, the recently launched Korean War was only the beginning of a conflict that threatened to escalate and spread onto North American shores.[32]

But circumstances in 1950s Cuba were different from those that prevailed in the United States and Portugal. Here there was little of the government-sponsored "red scare" that framed the apparitions of the Virgin in the other two countries. (Nor was Izquierdo acceptable to most conservatives Catholics as a counter to Communism.) This is in great measure because Cuban Communists had gradually lost much of their vigor, and hence their capacity to threaten Batista's regime.

Following World War II, the *auténticos*, who were Batista's political adversaries, expelled their Communist allies in the Partido Socialista Popular (PSP) from the Congreso de Trabajadores Cubanos (CTC), an organization that represented unions and gave them a good deal of influence in the ruling Auténtico coalition. At the time of the Batista coup in 1952, the PSP held no more than nine seats in the lower house of parliament.[33] And by 1956, Communists and their supporters controlled only 15 percent of the 2,000 labor unions in the island.[34] While the PSP continued to agitate against Batista in the 1950s, calling for strikes and even sending guerrillas into the Escambray Mountains, its position remained morally strong but tactically weak.[35] Although Batista proscribed the Communist Party during the 1950s, the neutralization of the threat it posed had begun a decade earlier when Communists joined Batista in a coalition with the most conservative parties to broker the deal that had made possible the *pax batistiana* of 1940.[36]

For all of the official tolerance of Izquierdo's enterprise, laissez-faire strategies did not prevail in every case in the 1950s. As recently as 1952, several leading intellectuals and various trade organizations had found "superstition" noxious enough to demand that the government take action against Clavelito. As I show below, the growing cadre of secular humanists sometimes defeated the advocates of pragmatic populism and staid, anti-Communist theism.

Even in Izquierdo's case, the Cold War, Batista's populist strategies, and the church's fears of godlessness were insufficient to guarantee the stigmatic a warm reception. Many Catholics and conservatives viewed La Estigmatizada's mission as a base spectacle and as an affront to the sanctity of Christian salvation and its symbols. Writing in the same *Diario de la Marina*, César García Pons charged that Christ's cross was far too serious a matter for anybody—especially an unstable and ignorant person—to claim a right to bear it. In Izquierdo's pilgrimage, García Pons argued, "the majesty" of the Christian foundations of Cuban society was compromised by the use of the cross in "sudden popular growths in which everything has a part—curiosity, ignorance, unreflecting enthusiasm, and the following of spectacle." True to a formula favored by critics since the turn of the century, García Pons's objections transcended the purely doctrinal to propose broad-ranging considerations about the meaning of such displays and the risks they posed to the nation as a political and cultural entity. According to García Pons, La Estigmatizada deserved attention because, in her case,

> the common good, which should derive its inspiration from clean, well-defined, noble and rational beliefs, taking these last two adjectives in their strictest sense, suffers from the confusionism [*sic*] to which all of this

gives cause because it mocks and vulgarizes ideas, moral influences, and symbols that, *regardless of the degree of commitment they inspire*, nobody denies are the stuff of [our] national tradition. . . . Finally, let us say that even if some refuse to admit that . . . a people cannot toy with certain values without running risks, and that happenings such as this are, at the very least, wrong-headed temptations against its historical unity, made possible by cheap popular sympathies.[37]

Though rather typical of this type of writing, García Pons's statement had an unusual twist (see phrase in italics). In the 1950s, conservative Catholics perceived that the commitment to churchly Christianity had diminished. Whether one accepts the proposition that commitments ran deeper in the days of old, García Pons's phrase is worth noting because it suggests that when faced with both official support and the growth of secular mores, some Catholics turned to culture and "tradition" to make their stands. By 1956, it was no longer possible to take faith for granted or to act under the presumption that all Cubans were prepared to grant the existence of a sphere of divine activity or the existence of the divine itself. This was a predicament for the church and for La Estigmatizada's supporters as well.

At first the church maintained a "discreet" and pregnant silence regarding Izquierdo. After some cajoling by the press, however, Cardinal Arteaga allowed his private secretary, Monsignor Raúl del Valle, to address the matter publicly in the church-friendly *Diario de la Marina*, albeit in an "unofficial" capacity. Del Valle judged Izquierdo according to six criteria derived from the study of those exceptional cases in which the church had found evidence of supernatural intervention in stigmatized men and women, most notably saints of the stature of St. Francis of Assisi. "Genuine stigmatization," the priest maintained, must meet the following criteria: "(1) exercise of Christian virtues to an eminent degree; (2) true stigmata or lesions to fleshy tissue; (3) a sudden appearance of the wounds; (4) permanence and immutability of the lesions, in spite of the remedies of medical science; (5) hemorrhaging; (6) absence of scaring or suppuration." Though the priest refused to speculate as to Izquierdo's performance on the first count, there was scarcely a need to reaffirm the failure. Izquierdo's less than eminent devotion was already a matter of record. As to the other factors, del Valle deferred to the medical establishment, which had already pronounced itself on the etiology of Izquierdo's ailments and which had shown that the visionary's wounds—shallow, superficial, and healing—had "external causes."

Del Valle argued in effect that the supernatural should be invoked as an explanation only where science had failed to provide an adequate, natural explanation. He denied any "preternatural" factors and argued instead that Izquierdo's "hallucinations" and "hysteria" were "matter[s] for scientists" rather than theologians. "Christian neuropsychiatry, which does not deny the supernatural order," the priest argued, "is capable of distinguishing between genuine stigmatization" and phenomena produced "as a result of psychoneurotic ailments."[38]

Physician after physician examined Izquierdo or the descriptions of her symptoms to arrive at the same conclusion: a naturally occurring pathology could account for the welts and lacerations and for her "delusional" episodes. Dr. Margarita Villaverde, Izquierdo's gynecologist, analyzed a handkerchief with blood from Izquierdo's forehead wounds and proposed that the stigmata were the result of "hemographism," a condition found in a small number of women that reportedly made their skin hypersensitive, especially around the time of menstruation. Others reached similar conclusions, thinking the physical manifestations evidence of "hysterical trophism." Dr. Villaverde also revealed to reporters that Izquierdo had been coming to her clinic because she was having difficulty conceiving even after two years of marriage due to an inflammation of the womb.[39] In the course of early-twentieth-century witchcraft scares in Cuba, infertility had been counted as a prototypical motivation for the ritual killing of white children. Now, however, Izquierdo's gynecological diagnosis was thought to indicate that she suffered from "hysteria."

After some weeks of self-restraint, Dr. René Vega-Vega, Izquierdo's psychiatrist, joined the public debate to reiterate the medical consensus. In the course of a published statement on Izquierdo's "*histerismo*," he, too, remarked on the state of Cuban culture after pausing briefly to carry out a series of contortions by which he meant to appease his scruples about breaching his confidentiality obligations. Dr. Vega-Vega opened his column in *Carteles* with commentary about the failed promise of the twentieth century and the persistence of the past: "Even though the twentieth century is at its peak, the events [surrounding Izquierdo] have unfolded in the same way as if we were in the Middle Ages, when mental illnesses were considered disruptions of the soul rather than the body and [were] attributed a divine origin." In addition, the doctor made some unexpected disclosures. Izquierdo, he reminded readers, had endured other difficulties prior to her supposed stigmatization. This was common knowledge, for *Bohemia* had reported in early May that young Irma's behavior during Easter had bordered on the fanatical; as a child she had fasted during those days, consuming only bread and wine. The doctor, however, added a significant footnote. Only a year earlier, Izquierdo understood her Holy Week tribulations in ways that deviated from Catholic orthodoxy.

According to the psychiatrist, Izquierdo first came to his office on 29 July 1955, when her mother brought her after treatment efforts at various "spiritist centers" had caused the patient to deteriorate. At the time, Izquierdo reportedly claimed that she was a "medium" and that she was "possessed" by spirits—especially *negros congos* (Kongo blacks, usually slaves of Central African origin)—who had been conveying messages from beyond. Dr. Vega-Vega referred Izquierdo to another physician for treatment of a glandular disorder and took charge of her psychiatric therapy. After only two months in an anticipated year of treatment, Izquierdo no longer communicated with spirits or believed that there was a supernatural cause for her condition. But in October 1955, the patient stopped keeping her appointments with the doctor and suffered what Vega-Vega regarded as a relapse. Her family, the physician inferred, was now exploiting the young woman "to parade her ridiculously across the island."[40]

Izquierdo's crises were a thorough reenactment of the passion. During episodes when stigmata appeared on her body, Izquierdo also complained of the weight of the cross, requested water only to refuse it for tasting like vinegar, and recounted the correspondences between her pains and Christ's own. But in spite of the seeming orthodoxy, evidence of Spiritism remained, which was not lost to all witnesses. Izquierdo, for instance, continued to refer to her visions as "communications" and persisted in describing her "crises" in terms similar to those of mediumship. During these episodes, Izquierdo explained, she sang in Latin. She also spoke, preached, and recited using words unknown to her and in unfamiliar voices, "as if someone had taken over me." This someone, Izquierdo hinted, was Christ himself rather than the Holy Ghost usually invoked in cases of glossolalia.[41] There was also the story of Izquierdo's fainting spell en route to Jatibonico. After the visionary fell, a woman had run to kiss her feet. A soldier in the escort, however, put an end to this act of veneration and lifted Izquierdo's limp body onto a motorcycle. There he administered Spiritist passes, after which Izquierdo recovered, only to say that she had not eaten that day.[42]

Aniceto Díaz, a noted musician and a practitioner of Spiritism, offered a rejoinder to the physicians and the church on the basis of his "own investigations with a freed spirit." In a column that also appeared in *Carteles*, Díaz reported his findings. "Mrs. Irma Izquierdo," he wrote, "is a magnificent medium, and . . . the spirit of Jesus Christ, the martyr from Galilee[,] manifests himself through her and . . . all the phenomena appearing in her body is [*sic*] to give proof that it is the very Jesus Christ, the son of God." Díaz's claims, however, went largely unheeded. Spiritists did not embrace Izquierdo as they had Manso, a man who proved more adept in his handling of the press and the rhetoric of positive reason than this woman, who sought publicity by Christ's command but "did not care about surveys," as one reporter put it.[43]

The limitation of the miraculous to a purely pathological state satisfied physicians, rationalists, and even the official church. Those who continued to believe in La Estigmatizada, however, subscribed to competing views. They accepted the medical diagnosis but contested its ultimate explanatory value, choosing instead to subject scientific etiology to a logic derived from an intimate understanding of the economy of affliction. Izquierdo might be ill, but her sickness was a station along her personal *via crucis* (way of the cross). The ailment had put her on the path to El Cobre, which was simultaneously the route to recovery. Izquierdo's mission, then, was also a quest for healing. Fe Sánchez, a young woman whose opinion was recorded, summarized the believer's reasoning succinctly. "I believe," Sánchez said, "that what she has is a disease. . . . But she will be cured of that disease when she has finished her mission." Yet others reasoned in the manner of Manuel de Jesús, a man the press described as an "honest shoeshine." De Jesús explained the matter thus: "She was born healthy . . . and now she is sick. Why? Because God has sent her that disease. It is a supernatural disease."[44]

These testimonies made manifest the resilience of an orientation to the divine and to knowledge that was often capable of outmaneuvering science and the enforcers of its discipline. The imaginary, however embattled, could usually seek refuge in spaces beyond the reach of positive knowledge: that is, in the terrain of first causes. Only the religious imaginary could provide a satisfactory answer to the ultimate question: why?

However, in spite of its remarkable ability to resist attacks, the religious imaginary was neither unassailable nor unchanging. Believers' remarks about Izquierdo also demonstrate that secularism had had an impact. Early in the century, proponents of the imaginary had faced charges of superstition and quackery. These accusations questioned specific beliefs and practices but presumed that legitimate faiths were possible without questioning the existence of the divine as such. By the 1950s, circumstances had changed; secularism had caused a fundamental questioning of all faith. This questioning, of course, resulted from multiple and complex factors but was rooted in part in the continuing sway of Social Darwinism, a framework that placed beliefs along an evolutionary scale ranging from primitive superstition to rational belief, but reserved the topmost rung of the ladder for positive reason unaided by theological crutches. Such ideas reached their most influential formulations in the writings of Fernando Ortiz, who made it his life's work to reveal both "Afro-Cuban" and "white" religions as more or less sophisticated iterations of the same deficiencies in ratiocination.[45]

In a few telling instances, Izquierdo's supporters appear to have acknowledged and confronted secular presumptions head-on. In a comment regarding La Estigmatizada that struck reporters as "unmathematical," an accountant suggested that hers was "a phenomenon that demonstrat[ed] that there is something superior to man in this world." In a similar vein, another man argued that Izquierdo's miraculous stigmatization and visions were "warning[s] from Jesus to make the world see that God exists." A third maintained that Izquierdo's wounds were "something that God sen[t] her to convince people that he exists."[46] Unremarkable when considered in isolation, such statements are striking if one recalls that the supporters of Mustelier and Manso, and even those accused of practicing witchcraft, never gave any indication of believing that humanity was in need of evidence for God's existence. La Estigmatizada's supporters were unusual for thinking God himself was in need of publicity.

In the course of the summer of 1956, the publicity surrounding La Estigmatizada was debated a few times. Was this campaign a contrived effort to gratify the delusional ego of a sick woman? Part of a divinely sanctioned mission, as the protagonist of the miracles claimed? Proof of God's power, or evidence of sinister forces at work? The Baptist Church, speaking through Baptist seminary professor Rev. Domingo Fernández Suárez, suspected it was the latter case. Fernández Suárez accepted *Bohemia*'s reports as truthful and acknowledged the supernatural character of the events described there. He proposed, however, that far from being evidence of divine activity, "all stigmatized [were] victims of a plan of diabolical action." "If the Redeemer," he asked, "wanted to give the world a special message, would he choose a person who does not live according to the Gospel? Impossible."[47]

Some physicians, for their part, echoed the sentiments of the Catholic Church, sensing that Izquierdo had been the object of too much attention already. In a curt statement, Dr. Joaquín Pascual Gispert asserted that there was nothing noteworthy or newsworthy about Izquierdo, who was afflicted with a rather common disease such as hysteria or schizophrenia. All the attention, the doctor argued, had likely exacerbated the patient's condition: "I find all of the publicity of which she has been an object undue and prejudicial."[48]

At bottom, critics suggested—then as today—that there was something about this kind of publicity and its tactics that diminished the sacred, stripping it of its far-off dignity. Believers, on the other hand, have often taken more forgiving stances. The thousands of Cubans who listened to Clavelito's radio broadcasts and those who followed the news about the apparition of the Virgin in Puerto Rico came to depend on the media for spiritual sustenance and even involved spectacle-makers in the staging of religious drama.

The Guajiro King of All Media

Manuel Alfonso Pozo, better known as Clavelito, was precisely the sort of man who horrified sociologist Roger Bastide, a leading scholar alarmed by the rise of "tourist *candomblés*" and religiopolitical opportunists in 1950s Brazil. From the vantage point of those who would safeguard authentic religion from ideological pandering and the ravages of market-driven "degeneration," Clavelito was an abomination. This self-promoting guajiro singer rose to dizzying popularity as a radio healer, licensed his life story to a soap opera producer, accepted commissions to write astrology pamphlets after a month of "sleepless study," and topped it all off with a run for public office. And yet this seemingly cynical figure captured the public imagination and commanded an intense faith, at least for a while. He attracted hundreds to his broadcasting studio and received thousands of letters daily, and tens of thousands more tuned in to his show, taking care to place a glass of water over the receiver so that it would be "magnetized" by Clavelito's recitation of a trademark décima. By some estimates (though not all), the short-lived "El Buzón de Clavelito" was the most popular show ever on Cuban radio.[49]

Clavelito, whose 1952 heyday predated La Estigmatizada's by four years, offers a dramatic counterpoint to Izquierdo's story. Rather than a troubled visionary seeking a public outlet, Clavelito was a performer who took on a religious significance. His trajectory shows that spectacles could be rendered into miracles just as a miraculous pilgrimage could be transformed into news and entertainment. This alchemy, I argue below, entailed a significant reworking of the compact between humans and the divine. Moreover, Clavelito demonstrated anew that the reportedly ancient regime that Ortiz called hydrotherapy was more than a vestige of the past; techniques derived from the imaginary could adapt to present circumstances and incorporate innovations. With Clavelito on the air, it was now possible to heal without direct application of compresses, as the Virgin of Jiquiabo had advocated, or without visiting La Loma de San Juan, as Manso had called for. The imaginary and its therapeutics could be broadcast; they could take part in the dynamics of the marketplace with its need for instant deliveries. If this adaptation entailed a loss, most notably an alteration to the terms that usually regulated the economy of affliction, few beyond the customary naysayers expressed any regret. The faithful, a group that one might suppose to be constituted of "traditionalists," proved remarkably unsentimental when confronted with these changes. Finally, the controversies surrounding Clavelito speak to the rise of secular mores and the redefinition of the threat of superstition, now understood as an unwitting ally to Batista's illegitimate power rather than as an obstacle to the establishment of republican concord.

Clavelito got his start on CMHI in Santa Clara, not far from Ranchuelo (Las Villas), where he was born to a poor family in 1908. Later, however, he followed the trail of other guajiro performers to the capital. Clavelito and his partner of the mid-1940s, La Calandria, gained an audience in Havana when their humorous show debating the merits of blondes versus brunettes rose on the charts. Clavelito's transition from the hair-color controversies into radiotherapy took place with greater ease than one would anticipate today. Ascetic to an extent, the Cuban imaginary was far from sanctimonious; the comedian did not disqualify the healer. The singer, in any case, moved on alone to Havana's CMQ, where he sang his usual repertoire. "El Buzón de Clavelito" ("Clavelito's Mailbox"), however, was first heard on Gaspar Pumarejo's Radio Unión, then ranked fourth among Cuba's stations.[50] Historian Oscar Luis López claims that the show's format was Pumarejo's idea to improve ratings. Clavelito himself, however, offered an account that made his new direction appear a vagary of fortune. In an interview with *Bohemia*, he explained that his was to be a write-in show in which he would improvise replies to queries about love and current events. The transformation of the broadcasts into public healing sessions had been unplanned; it reportedly occurred when Clavelito responded to a listener's call for a remedy and later read a thank-you note from the healed man.[51] Encouraged by this evidence of Clavelito's healing talent, countless others wrote in, turning the show into a grand success, or so the story went.

Some contemporaries, however, questioned Clavelito's account. They pointed out that he had been moving in this ministerial direction prior to his arrival on Radio Unión.[52] Clavelito conceded that he had been thinking of sharing his talents for some time, and had indeed tried his hand at it for a week before managers at another station (CMQ) put an end to his trial run. "Don't go getting me in trouble with the priests," Clavelito was told; "they will never abide by a guajiro performer curing people by simply proposing it over a microphone."[53] As it turns out, the manager's prediction was incorrect. Though Clavelito's show did prove polemical, the church remained quiet throughout. For reasons that remain unclear to me, the priests never intervened.

Regardless of the initial impetus, Clavelito's subsequent moves at Radio Unión were carefully orchestrated. After the exchange with his patient listener, Clavelito called upon his audience, whom he addressed as "brothers," to come to the station's recording studios. There he would "magnetize" the water they were to bring, which could then be used to heal any corporal or spiritual ailments, provided it was consumed "with faith" in Clavelito. To his amazement, 150—mostly women—responded and had their water bottles treated with the beam of Clavelito's handheld flashlight.[54] Those who were unable to come were advised to place a glass of water over the radio so that the water could be magnetized when the singer's voice rang with the words: "Think of me / [and] you will make it so / that the strength of my thoughts / will work wonders on you."[55]

The response was overwhelming: Clavelito received thousands of letters daily (3,000 to 4,000, according to his count) in addition to hundreds of telegrams. The show itself had to move locations in order to accommodate the crowds. Ratings skyrocketed. Newspapers and magazines ran daily features on Clavelito, and spin-off radio shows soon appeared.

Clavelito, however, denied he was a healer, a brujo, or even a religious figure. Though his show inspired hundreds of testimonials to his curative powers, he insisted that he was simply "a man of the people," someone blessed by "Providence" with a "supernatural power."[56] While dismissing any association with Spiritism, curanderismo, or witchcraft, he did not shy away from grandiose pronouncements. In a moment of nearly messianic hubris he went so far as to say that he intended to do good until *after* his death. He asserted rather cryptically that he was "the man of destiny," a man in whom "the impossible became possible."[57] It is unclear whether his followers concurred, but they do not appear to have found such statements objectionable. Some even saw an image of Clavelito in their glasses of magnetized water, a sort of vision more often associated with disembodied beings than with ordinary, living mortals.

Clavelito's fans left outrage to others. Some critics wrote columns and pressed for legal action. But many others chose humor—Clavelito's old forte—as a way of paring the man to ordinary size. They parroted and parodied the guajiro's verses, evidently to a perturbing effect. At the closing of one of his interviews, Clavelito warned writers and jokesters alike that ever since he had been a child those who had wronged him had met with misfortune. This time, however, Clavelito's retributive power proved an insufficient safeguard.[58] For instance, a resident of Jiguaní (Oriente) who forgot the singer's trademark jingle long ago still remembers a parody of the healing décima. It began circulating when a man named Olegario was mutilated by his own fiancée, whom he refused to marry. The punch lines to this irreverent version went like this: "Put your thoughts in me / and place your hand on the radio / and you will see Olegario / how your peter grows back."[59]

"A tempest in a glass of water"

As Clavelito rose in prominence, so did the voices of his detractors. In this case, the intervention of a state agency and the failed disciplinary measures of an association of broadcasters whose own authority was hotly contested accompanied the by-now- familiar din of rationalists and law-and-order advocates. Some of the most prominent figures in Cuban public life also made themselves heard in the controversies surrounding the guajiro singer, charging, as they did many others before him, with profiting at the expense of the superstitious and the ignorant. Speaking of Clavelito, Jorge Mañach, Nicolás Guillén, and a few lesser-known intellectuals sought to give the debate a sociological and political dimension; that is, they aimed to move the conversation from the healing of individuals to the treatment of a body politic afflicted with the trauma of Batista's dictatorial regime. Clavelito, nonetheless, harbored political ambitions of his own.

The Commission for Ethics in Radio, a trade group composed of radio announcers, producers, writers, and publicity agents, had had run-ins with the management of Radio Unión before taking on the man some derided as a "tropical oracle." After a protracted dispute that lasted until March 1952, the month when Clavelito's new program first aired, Dr. Juan J. Tarajano, the commission's director, finally persuaded the station to retire one of its popular features. At issue was whether the show violated a provision in place since 1947, the year of the commission's founding, banning broadcasters from issuing "predictions, prognostications or warnings that could cause alarm or fears or generate superstitions or excite interest or faith in such practices."[60] Not surprisingly, the station reacted to the loss by seeking a suitable replacement, which appears to have been Clavelito, with his newly publicized talent for healing. The commission, for its part, waited a few days for the new show's format to become clear—a pause that has led Oscar Luis López to assert incorrectly that capitalist contradictions had paralyzed state and trade agencies and kept them from silencing Clavelito's shameful voice— only to relaunch its offensive. In an inspired turn of phrase, *Bohemia* referred to the ensuing tussle as "a tempest in a glass of water."[61]

On 25 July 1952 the commission published Circular No. 47. The document, which was reprinted in most major newspapers, restated the norms governing the contents of commercial broadcasts and declared several shows in violation of the code. Professor Baruff's astrology program on CCO, CMQ's soap opera "María, la Iluminada," and especially "Clavelito's Mailbox" were singled out for immediate muzzling, upon penalty of suspension of the violators. Clavelito and Radio Unión assumed a defiant posture; the show went on, and the station managers upped the ante, playing clips of their star in between shows throughout the day. It should be noted parenthetically that this strategy dispensed such ratings that even a member of the commission succumbed to temptation: He bought several spots to advertise his products during the sanctioned program. Such a public humiliation, coupled with the station's defiance, led Dr. Tarajano to submit his resignation, which was not accepted.

Aware of the impasse, the radio directorship of the communications ministry stepped in to enforce the commission's determination. The state office banned all broadcasts based on divination and interpretation of dreams, those that stimulated beliefs opposed to "civilization," and those that disturbed the moral and social orders. Clavelito's and Professor Baruff's shows were ordered off the air immediately. But Unión Radio did not lose it all; its biographical soap opera, "Clavelito, el Hombre del Destino," survived.[62] And soon enough, Clavelito was back on the air with a new show, albeit one that omitted predictions, lottery numbers, and therapeutic guidance; this one was called "Clavelito and His People." But Clavelito did not abandon the ethereal realms altogether; he continued to publish, adding several esoteric volumes on astrology and the afterlife to his collections of décimas and a verse novel.[63] Immediately following the ban, he also made his views known with a set of songs whose lyrics were published in the press. In one of these, Clavelito gave public demand a decidedly guajiro twist: "I don't know why it is, that the people never get it [what they want] . . . / That they won't even let them have / a little bit of hope." In yet another décima Clavelito complained that any foreigner in his place, who only did good, would receive applause and wealth. But because he was no more than a guajiro, he was the victim of an injustice.[64]

It is fitting that the task of disciplining superstition's latest promoter fell first to a trade organization rather than to the initiative of physicians, police officers, journalists, or the church. After all, in Clavelito's hands, magnetized water had become a promotional item allowing other commodities to be peddled over the airwaves. Clavelito's success could be measured in surveys and ratings as much as in the number of patients who claimed that they had been cured. Although no money passed from the hands of patients into the pockets of the station owners or the performer, the connection between the faithful and Clavelito was unlike that between Manso or Mustelier and their followers. Pecuniary interests and the laws of supply and demand mediated and partly governed the patient-healer relationship. Advertisements for Ace Detergent and other products interrupted Clavelito's songs and advice. But believers remained untroubled. The healer's services remained free and accessible to them, and whatever transactions were taking place occurred offstage. Moreover, for all of his antics, Clavelito operated within the confines of an established medical genre. Like several of his predecessors, he healed using only water that had been transformed by the influence of what Spiritists called a "magnetic fluid" or "current." His proposal that such forces could propagate like radio waves to reach far-off places was well within the realm of reason, particularly for Spiritists who already believed that their healing influence could transcend physical distance. Clavelito's only other evident innovation was that he did not hold consultations or, rather, that he held his consultations in a public forum instead of in a back room or hospital-like rural compound.

In the telling of his own life story, Clavelito appealed to Cubanness and tradition, as he aimed to counter the notion that he might be insincere or that the disclosure of his talents may have been motivated by self-interest. In a series of articles he wrote for *Bohemia*, he told the story of how he discovered his talent as a child and spoke of his guajiro and *mambí* (proindependence insurgents) roots, all the while extolling somewhat immodestly his own virtues as a son and husband.[65] He was insistent on his poverty and maintained that his family's indigence was such that his mother resorted to water cures as a free alternative to professional medical care. Following the maternal model, Clavelito came to realize that the water he left out overnight (*agua serenada*) was more powerful than most because of some inexplicable influence emanating from him. His family recognized the talent and had him cure a handicapped elderly woman when he was only twelve years old.[66]

Clavelito was far from a traditionalist, however. He signaled a significant alteration to the terms of the economy of affliction, a fact lost upon many of his critics who persisted in regarding him as typical. Accusations of profiteering had been customary since the days of the Virgin of Jiquiabo in the 1880s, and they had been reiterated routinely whenever a new religious figure rose to prominence. Because Clavelito, who was something of an aberration among major figures, was just like the rest as far as most critics were concerned, many failed to notice that commodification on this scale truly was unusual.

It should be noted, however, that the critics' indiscriminate charges of avarice, though unwarranted when it came to most of the figures discussed in this book, did have reasonable foundations in some cases. Their chariness was grounded in experience and common sense. Cuban cities had been teeming for decades with palm readers, diviners, hypnotists, self-appointed gurus, and proponents of dozens of unorthodox therapies. Many advertised in newspapers, magazines, and storefronts and sold "magic" powders, aphrodisiacs, and remedies by mail. A few were known unequivocally as frauds, and a number were believed to be extortionists or instigators of other crimes, including widely publicized crimes of passion. Though Clavelito did not commit or promote such acts, there was no denying that his was a commercial enterprise as well as a phenomenon of faith.

In their haste to condemn Clavelito as a promoter of superstition, critics also failed to see that there was more than a hint of secularism and even of today's New Age sensibilities to this man and to the activity surrounding him. Clavelito did Izquierdo one better; rather than denying his fanaticism, as Izquierdo would later, he insisted that he was not even religious.[67] In fact, Clavelito seemed to propose nearly secular miracles, appeals to an unspecified supernatural rather than to divinity as such. Clavelito rarely spoke of God or any other divine force except to claim that he had been privy to God's "deepest secrets," which he revealed in turn through his songs.[68] In a telling omission of a fundamental of the economy of affliction, Clavelito's regime required little of patients. There were no pilgrimages, no sacrifices, no protracted prayers, and in fact no cultic activity as such. As Clavelito put it, he required only a glass of water, faith, and respectful silence, the latter presumably to prevent difficulties with the broadcast. Clavelito's faith demanded nothing; it was unrehearsed and actualized only in the cure itself rather than in ritual preparations.

Instead of moral transformation and social regeneration, Clavelito promised his listeners that he would heal their afflictions without necessarily transforming the existing social order. "All problems have a solution," he preached. But Clavelito's promises of individual satisfaction prefigured contemporary discourse; one might find similar words in today's gospels of self-realization: "We all have a right to succeed in business, in study, in sports, in gambling, in love, and we all have a right to enjoy the good things in life. If you are not happy, if you have a problem, if you have bad health, if you are unemployed, if you don't have enough money. . . . Listen to Clavelito in silence. . . . In silence, please."[69]

Insinuating Secularism and Politics

Clavelito studiously avoided entanglements in the webs of politics and religion. He insisted on his nondenominationalism and was adamant that he harbored no political ambitions; that is, until he ran for office. Generally, he pursued a strategy of rhetorical detachment, repeating tirelessly that his therapeutics did not recognize social cleavages of any sort. Clavelito summarized his reasoning thus: "Mankind has faith in me because I am a man isolated from others."[70] Some of the guajiro's critics, however, injected the debates surrounding the radio show with precisely the sort of polemics that Clavelito wanted to avoid. They dragged the singer back into the company of his fellow men and their contentious frays. In their commentaries, Mañach, Guillén, and other less well known intellectuals took advantage of the opportunity to put forth a critique of Batista's regime, at times couched as a sociological theory of the origins of superstitious outbreaks. They proposed that political corruption had begun to corrode the very soul of the Cuban people as witnessed in Clavelito's popularity. In the course of condemning superstition and its newfound political consequences, some of these commentators also revealed, or, more precisely, intimated, the secularist convictions that had come to dominate the island's leading intellectual circles.

Though Clavelito refused to talk politics, M. Velilla de Solorzano, an adjunct professor of social psychology at the University of Havana, could pinpoint precisely when Cubans had lost trust in their own capacity to shape the future. That day had been 10 March 1952, the day of the coup that returned Batista to the presidential office. Velilla de Solorzano argued that the general's forced reentry had generated profound fissures, the very cracks in collective reason through which Clavelito had slipped into the public sphere. As democratic mores lost out,

> [t]he faith that was ours [in the party or new government], the faith we could count on, had to be deposited somewhere. Impulsive, radical and liberal we refused to turn to the traditional Faith. At such a time, another people would have crowded into churches to discharge their impotence and frustration in Pater Nosters and Hail Marys. But it was not so. . . . Most of the people, especially the poorest classes, the class that is almost without culture, were left alone, reduced, abandoned to their sorrows and without any hope. . . . That faction of the people awaited a true strongman to direct them and infuse them with enough strength to overcome their weakness. But there has been none. Not knowing what to do with that faith, they have given it to the first to claim it: "Clavelito."[71]

Jorge Mañach agreed; though he did not name Batista specifically, he also defended the notion that superstition—as crystallized in Clavelito and people of his ilk—threatened the nation's progress and political maturation because it diminished self-reliance, the motor force of social advancement. Cuba, Mañach argued, was suffering through a stage of "incipient *babalaísmo*" and was beginning to despair of its capacity to extricate itself from the present circumstances.[72] Citing Bertrand Russell and others, he suggested that this ailment was a particularly acute manifestation of a "universal epidemic": a worldwide increase in irrationality that had reached major proportions after World War II, when many had grown weary of the failed promise of rationality. Mañach argued that "what [made] superstition so deplorable and noxious to the conscience of a people is that it tends not only to supernaturalize experience irrationally, but also to sap mankind's moral strength, making him [man] believe that his destiny or his prosperity in life do not depend on his intelligence and will but rather in the convergence of stars in the sky, or some magical ritual or another."[73]

In spite of his misgivings about superstition, Mañach was scarcely an advocate of what Velilla de Solorzano called "traditional Faith." Like the psychologist, he distinguished between superstition and religion. If he tolerated the latter it was mostly because he thought the human need to believe in some form of the supernatural was nearly irresistible. A secularist at heart, Mañach was, as he acknowledged, "insinuating very 'heretical' things": only history and the expenditure of intellectual energies had redeemed some faiths and lifted them above the level of mere absurdities. Religion was a distinguished variant of supernaturalism, which, while remaining inferior to scientific reason, retained the virtue of satisfying man's greater moral aspirations rather than the baser desires to which superstition catered. Nonetheless, all irrationality remained a menace to society. Returning to 10 March as if it had been day of reckoning, Mañach argued that the public's lassitude, their failure to rise up, had had much to do with "the predictions of the so-called Professor Barú, [which] contributed a good deal to disconcerting the people and contaminating them with false notions and inert resignation." Clavelito, Mañach continued, who never went so far as to credit the conspirators in the coup with great virtues or an auspicious future, was likewise charged with feeding the "passive hopes of a people who are truly in need in of lucidity and courage."[74]

The argument that adversity gave rise to new faiths, rejuvenated devotions, and false hopes had a distinguished pedigree by 1952. Countless others, including luminaries of Freud's stature, had long suggested that wish fulfillment was a major, perhaps even the main, component of religion. But in the Cuban context, there was something ironic in Mañach's and Velilla de Solorzano's suggestions. So-called brujos, diviners, and quacks had been condemned habitually for their debasing and destabilizing impact. Their very presence in the island, it was often said, threatened public order, the republic, and civilization. Now, however, the latest incarnations of this evil force of the past were denounced for their soporific effects, for helping quell the passions needed to overthrow conspirators who had shown themselves to be true enemies of the republic. From instigators of chaos, the brujos and their newer colleagues had become unwitting stewards of the status quo.

Guillén dispensed with the sweeping theorizing, but he, too, castigated Clavelito for his sins of omission, for his silences and his quiet acquiescence. In the eighth stanza of his justly lauded "Coplas de Juan Descalzo," Cuba's national poet charged that Clavelito's panacea, his magnetized water, fell far short of what was required to contend with hunger, unemployment, and a political regime founded on a "stick and rope" approach to the people. He urged Clavelito to speak out, to let Cuba see him fighting, and suggested that his stance amounted to collusion: "You think that Batista is cool / because he has let you perform, / but if you wanted to speak / to the people as you should, / then you would surely hear / another rooster's crow."[75]

It is difficult to say whether Clavelito listened to Guillén's exhortations or if they fell on deaf ears. It is clear, however, that after losing out to the Radio Ethics Commission, Clavelito overcame his vaunted reluctance to enter the political arena. But far from turning his broadcast studio into a pulpit for denunciation, as one might expect from a professedly "isolated man," Clavelito sought instead the office of representative to the legislature for Havana, a decision he soon grew to lament. Clavelito's popularity may well have failed him, or he may have been robbed, as he claimed in a décima. However, his participation in the notoriously corrupt election-year charades of the 1950s batistato—even as an opposition candidate affiliated with Ramón Grau San Martín—does cast some doubt as to his prophetic commitment to the cause of the downtrodden. After all, when Grau San Martín called for a last-minute boycott of the elections, Clavelito persevered. He claimed that the peasantry had elected him but that powerful interests had relegated him to second place after Morales Gómez. In this injustice, and in the added insult of being denied again when Morales Gómez resigned, the performer found an analogy to Christ's fate: "Clavelito promised, / to give his salary to the hospitals, / and those suffering diseases / and that put him on the cross. / Clavelito promised / we would know who is who. / And the same happened / with Jesus of Nazareth too / being good and preaching it got him crucified."[76]

Christlike or not, there was no resurrection for Clavelito. After his failed candidacy, he was gone from the public stage. He died in 1975 never having attained office and with his show long gone from the air. Middle-aged and elderly Cubans, however, remember his décimas fondly, and many can still recite a few of his verses.

⋅ • ⋅

Publicity works miracles; Izquierdo and Clavelito offer abundant proof of that. If Izquierdo is to be credited, Christ himself could demand the deployment of the media in the effort to save humankind. Once launched, however, miracles are often beyond controlling; neither paparazzi, nor media moguls, nor politicians can predict or manage the ultimate outcomes. Izquierdo and Clavelito succeeded in recruiting the assistance of journals, newspapers, and radio and television stations. But it was ultimately the faithful who determined where and when the divine was manifest. Izquierdo's deviation from the conventions of a religious genre largely accounts for her wilting under the limelight. Clavelito, on the contrary, prospered in spite of suspicions of profiteering because what he proposed was in accord with religious logic. Religious criteria rather than media-imposed measures continued to regulate miracles and the faith and practices they called forth.

Religious logic is not beyond history, however. While they overestimated the power of spectacle-makers and the erosion of "tradition," Fellini and Bastide were correct to perceive secularism and the media as forces capable of effecting powerful changes. The very terms of the economy of affliction were renegotiated as miracles entered into a market dominated by commodity exchanges on a mass scale. Though observant of the forms, Clavelito revealed that the need for instant resolutions could outweigh ritual and devotional life, that present wants could be satisfied without much sacrifice, and indeed without demanding a transformed future.

The criticisms of Clavelito and Izquierdo share a similar susceptibility to historical change. It is true that the critics agreed on the fundamentals; from the turn of the century to the 1950s, they denounced practitioners of heterodox religions as misplaced vestiges of primitive faith and magic. In perverse echoes of Melville J. Herskovits's assertions, physicians, intellectuals, and church officials depicted La Estigmatizada and Clavelito as "survivals" from a distant past, just as had been said of the brujos and others. However, if "superstition" remained a repository of cultural debris, the menace it stood for mutated over time. In the 1900s, critics charged that superstitious practices threatened the survival of a would-be modern republic. But by the 1950s, tumultuous misbelievers had lapsed into listlessness; superstition remained a threat, but now it was because it allegedly prolonged an unendurable state of affairs. While still treasonous, Clavelito and Izquierdo lacked the unbridled energy of their "cannibal" predecessors.

Politics, self-interest, and circumstance divided critics, who never formed as monolithic a group as their statements seem to suggest. The debates surrounding La Estigmatizada and Clavelito reveal that there were at least two factions. A first group, present in some form since the late nineteenth century, harbored secularist values and often advocated law-and-order measures to deal with superstition and attendant problems. Other critics, particularly those with strategic interests to defend, were at times more willing to allow questionable devotions to subsist. This, I have argued, was the case with government officials during La Estigmatizada's pilgrimage and with candidates courting Afro-Cuban votes during the early republic. A similar, uneasy tolerance can be discerned in the attitudes of those who were more preoccupied with godlessness than with the supposed gullibility of the superstitious masses.

In spite of their divisions, or perhaps because of them, by the 1950s, opponents of superstition had come to an understanding and had developed a practicable division of labor in the struggle against superstition. In the face of an increasingly secular regime of knowledge and governance, the church had retreated and laid claim to a reduced area of expertise. When confronted with Izquierdo, for instance, the cardinal's secretary declared that the matter was one for scientists rather than theologians. Rationalists with secular humanist leanings, for their part, were often restrained. Only a few dared go beyond insinuating that religion, while useful, might not be superior to superstition in the end.

6

MANAGING MIRACLES IN THE COMMONWEALTH

The Virgin Visits Sabana Grande

Journalists and publicists had a hand in some of the most salient religious dramas that unfolded in Cuba and Puerto Rico in the last century. In 1953, thousands of Puerto Ricans tuned in to WKAQ's live broadcasts and kept up with the newspapers to learn about a new round of Marian apparitions unfolding in the southwestern corner of the island. This public recruited the media industry in the performance of miracles and depended on its production for spiritual sustenance. The supernatural events taking place in barrio Rincón, a poor, sugar-growing community three kilometers outside of the town of Sabana Grande, represented, according to some versions, an imposing return to a type of religious performance with deep roots in Puerto Rico's past. Early reports that children had seen a heavenly lady appear near the spring in their schoolyard exploded into a mass event that attracted droves and disrupted daily routines. Traffic jammed as tens of thousands of pilgrims made their way to the incipient shrine. Courts in San Juan were forced to postpone trials to allow jurors to make the trying journey west.[1] Even naming patterns were altered for a time. Government record keepers remarked on the dramatic increase in the popularity of the name Milagros (literally, miracle) in the wake of the visions.[2]

Believers in the apparitions, however, were not simply repairing to tried-and-true forms reheated by propaganda; the visions owed a debt to the legendary apparitions of southern Europe as well as to the no less celebrated miracle of Hollywood cinema. The Puerto Rican faithful "made something" of their own, to speak with Michel de Certeau, of devotional accounts favored by the church as proper and traditional, and also of the products of the global entertainment industry.[3] These sources, so often associated with the Americanization and deculturation of Puerto Ricans, appear partly domesticated here, serving the purposes of the sacred. If the visions were a return to tradition, the faithful followed a tortuous route. Believers showed that they retained what Arcadio Díaz-Quiñones has called "another memory" and that this memory held at bay the state-sponsored erasure of the past.[4] This other memory, however, went beyond mere recollection; it possessed generative force and adaptive capacities. And it was surely as modern as those favored by sectors that viewed the visions with suspicion.

While some of the issues examined here are addressed in Chapter 5, too, new issues bear highlighting. This chapter examines consumption-production processes that made use of exogenous inputs and addressed themselves to local, islandwide, and international audiences simultaneously; the previous chapter focuses on the role of the national print and broadcast media in publicizing and shaping miracles within Cuba. Now, my main concerns are with the faithful and their search for models and meanings, an effort that led them to far-flung destinations. The miracles in Sabana Grande's dusty barrio projected Puerto Rico onto an international stage where a divine plan for the globe would play itself out.

In addition to the concerns outlined above, this chapter reconsiders the complex relationship between suspect religious practices and the state. I show below that the recently inaugurated commonwealth did not institute most of the familiar repressive measures, nor did it grant believers uncontested autonomy of action. Instead, the authorities attempted to manage the shrine, transforming what Díaz-Quiñones might call a "place of memory" into a showcase of good administration. At the discursive level, a parallel effort was afoot to reinterpret a seemingly premodern devotion. Talk of "folk" and "traditional" spirituality at times outweighed invectives like "primitive" and "superstitious." In so doing, the authorities redefined the standards for judging Puerto Rico's progress.

European Models for a Puerto Rican Lady

In early May 1953, when the visions in barrio Rincón were still in their formative stages and the question of the Virgin's identity had yet to be settled, contradictory descriptions of the lady and her attire circulated in newspapers and by word of mouth. This contributed to the church's skepticism and led critics to discount the apparition as little more than a fanciful fabrication. Those inclined to believe, however, eventually crafted a hard-fought consensus: the Virgin known variously by toponymous designations such as "La Virgen del Pozo" and "La Virgen de Sabana Grande" was the celebrated Lady of Fatima. The confusion and the contests surrounding the Virgin's identity are worth investigating in some detail, for they offer a look at the sorts of proposals and counterproposals that characterize the fractious process of miracle-making. This process involved partisans and critics of the visions and drew broadly from canonical, legendary, and even Hollywood models. The tidy narratives found in devotional accounts tend to obscure these disputes because they are committed to the notion that a divine plan was in operation from the start.

Daily reports from 1953 reveal dissention within the ranks of barrio Rincón's child visionaries. Several girls, including Santía Martínez Lugo, a seer who was subsequently excluded from the devotional roster, told reporters that the Virgin she saw was Our Lady of Miracles (*La Milagrosa*) rather than the one who had appeared in Portugal, as some papers claimed.[5] The very next day, however, Ramonita Belén, a seer now included among the three *principales*, asserted that the Virgin she had been seeing was indeed Fatima's. A simple experiment lent some credence to Ramonita's position. When presented with a sampling of icons that a reporter provided for the purpose of identification, Ramonita selected the image of the Portuguese Virgin from among those of her competitors.[6] The test proved insufficient to settle the matter, however. Many others had a hand in the debate.

The Virgin's initial silence during her apparitions contributed to the doubts plaguing barrio Rincón. In the course of a month of daily apparitions, the lady never stated her name though she did indicate her celestial origin and referred to Christ as her son. Such difficulties, it should be noted, seldom perturbed visionaries in early modern Spain. There the irruption of saints into the countryside served precisely to identify a town's most effective divine intercessors and to fix the honors due them for their assistance. In these early cases, saints generally demanded that the seers report their experiences to local dignitaries so that the town could enter into a corporate compact with a divine person.[7] In 1953, however, the Virgin made no such demands of Sabana Grande's residents.

Attempts to link the events in barrio Rincón to an apparition that the church had recognized as legitimate did little to mollify the hierarchy in Puerto Rico. While most pilgrims settled on one of several well-known Marian advocations, the church assumed an unlikely posture: It argued that barrio Rincón's children had not seen a saint, but a ghost. The rationale for this seemingly specious claim went as follows. The evidence at hand suggested that extraordinary events were taking place. But the behavior of the visions' protagonist—whomever she might be—deviated too far from the hierarchy's notions of decorum and propriety to permit identification with Mary. As Bishop James Edward McManus put it, the

Virgin would never ride on a jeep, sit on a motorcycle, or rest by a storm drain, as the seers described. Nor would the Virgin keep company with children so frequently and in so casual a manner. In a statement explaining his refusal to notify the Vatican of the visions, McManus averred that the children had been influenced by adults in such a way that they believed their misguided assertions to be true. Though what they had seen was in fact "a ghost" or "a dead person," ignorance had led them to believe it was the Virgin.[8]

Significantly, the ghostly theory did not originate with the bishop of Ponce, but with the seers' early understanding of the visions. Clergymen like McManus and Monsignor Murga, the bishop's man on the field, picked up on the notion of a specter in barrio Rincón, where evidently a variety of meanings were essayed in a brief period. As El Mundo reported, a seer's grandfather claimed that when the boy first told him of the visions he said that he had seen a dead person. According to Domingo Collado, his grandson Juan Angel spoke of the Virgin for the first time a full day later.[9]

As it turns out, there was an abundance of candidates for the position of barrio Rincón's ghost. Several residents had died in the sorts of circumstances that made for restless souls. There was, for instance, a man who had died of stab wounds on the very grounds of the school-cum-shrine. A cross that many pilgrims mistook for a memorial to the Virgin marked the spot of this man's violent demise.[10] Although some people were already convinced that the children had seen the Virgin on 2 May, there were also those who related the apparitions to the premature death of a devout fifteen-year-old named María Inocencia. The girl, described as blonde, blue-eyed (just as the Virgin was first characterized), and very dedicated to the church, had lived in a house built where the school stood in 1953. Given these associations, some reasoned that "what the children have seen could be the materialization of the spirit of this youth." María Inocencia's claim was weakened, however, when other seers revealed that the lady was dark-haired and of relatively dark complexion, or, as Juan Angel Collado recently put it, "like most Puerto Rican women, not too white and not too dark."[11]

Doubts regarding the Virgin's identity found concrete expression in the devotions practiced at the makeshift shrine in Sabana Grande. Only a week away from 25 May, a day that the visionaries had designated as the occasion for a great miracle, seers and pilgrims were still debating the lady's identity.[12] Meanwhile, saints proliferated. The altar installed where the first visions occurred was soon crowded with a montage of images. A generic, nameless Virgin stood as a silent mediator between Santía's Milagrosa and the French Virgin of Lourdes, who also had partisans in Sabana Grande.[13] For their part, the peddlers who plied their trade at the shrine seem to have sided with Ramonita; they favored the Virgin of Fatima, whose icons they sold along with rosaries, décimas, novenas, pictures of the seers, empty bottles, drinking water, meals, and other reportedly overpriced goods.[14]

In spite of the Virgin's early reserve, a working consensus emerged. While today's devotees refer to the Virgin of the visions as Our Lady of the Rosary, it is clear that this was not the saint in most peoples' minds in the 1950s. In the early years, it was Fatima and, to a lesser extent, Lourdes who provided the models and narrative forms for the miracles unfolding in barrio Rincón. And it was the Lady of Fatima whom most visionaries saw and whom most pilgrims sought out in their visits to the shrine.

Although other historical precedents—some of them local—were well known, Fatima's sway over barrio Rincón's supernatural theater was perceptible from the very first moments. Rather than appearing as a blinding, luminous figure, as she had in sixteenth-century Spain, or as a figure capable of taming beasts, as she had of old in the Puerto Rican town of Hormigueros, the Virgin appeared in Sabana Grande as a young woman suspended above a cloud among the trees.[15] This is precisely the way she was seen in Fatima, Portugal, in 1917.

Fatima's best-known miracles found multiple and enthusiastic reenactments in Puerto Rico. By 20 May 1953, vague rumors of Fatima-like celestial prodigies had begun to circulate: a daily cited two young seers who claimed that solar marvels were no more than preparation for the great miracles that would occur on 25 May.[16] Though in the end the awaited miracles did not satisfy the expectations of all those who gathered in barrio Rincón on the appointed day, reports of unusual solar phenomena persisted. According to some, around eleven o'clock in the morning of 25 May, a patch of colors broke out from a strip of the horizon framed by mountaintops and thick clouds. The sun, for its part, turned a light shade of "copper." After this, anonymous seers observed the genuflection of a lady clad in a black veil, just above the treetops. But by the time they reached the spot, the lady had dissipated into the gray clouds. Her arrival, however, coincided with the miraculous cure of Georgina Politis de Rivera, a paradigmatic beneficiary of barrio Rincón's healing waters.[17] This suggested to believers that the barrio had been graced once more with the Virgin's presence, this time in the form of the lady in black.

Days later, hundreds of Puerto Ricans related seeing a "dancing," "moving," and "colored" sun at various points throughout the island. These events struck some reporters and most witnesses as signs evoking Fatima's celestial spectacle.

In Caguas, where an editorial claimed "that disillusionment had burdened every heart when the announced time [11:00 A.M., 25 May 1953] passed without any portents," thousands reportedly took to the streets around 6:00 P.M. on 27 May to stare at an extraordinary sunset. In the words of a witness, "a warm sun moved like a disc of color and the clouds surrounding it were dyed in a prodigious combination of colors. Many fell on their knees and uttered a prayer to the Almighty." According to a news account, others looked at the sky and screamed: "the miracle, the miracle . . . just like Fatima." Similar incidents were registered at Fort Buchanan, a U.S. military base outside of the capital, in Manatí and Coamo, and in three locales where the Virgin appeared following the visions in barrio Rincón: Santurce, Ponce, and Vega Baja.[18]

Facundo Bueso, dean of the Faculty of Natural Sciences at the University of Puerto Rico, led the search for natural, scientific alternatives to the supernatural explanations that devotees favored. He hypothesized that salt crystals and dust particles suspended in the atmosphere had caused sunlight to refract, thus creating the illusion of a moving sun and of changes in color.[19] Though his contention was plausible, Facundo Bueso dissuaded few believers. Perhaps it was for that reason that most scientists and physicians affected what the press called a "scientific attitude" of detachment; that is, they ignored barrio Rincón. Dr. Luis A. Sanjurjo, president of the Medical Association, told reporters that his organization would not investigate any allegations of miraculous cures. He explained that such investigations required access to all medical records and were only carried out at a physician's request. He took care to note, however, that if an investigation were conducted, one would have to take into account that some of the patients suffered from psychosomatic and emotional ailments.[20]

But there were exceptions even among rationalists. Dr. Manuel Quevedo Báez, the noted physician who had denounced La Samaritana in her day, struck an open-minded pose in 1953. In a column on the subject of the new apparitions, Quevedo Báez reviewed the literature regarding the psychological development of children and adolescents. He argued rather disingenuously that youth were unaware of the problems of the social order and thus immune to factors that might lead them to make false claims. The doctor then went on to conclude that children might well serve as God's instruments. "Scientific orthodoxy," he said, should "pause" for faith. "What is so strange," he pondered, "about visions of a heavenly Angel or a Virgin that awaken or revive the dormant faith of this sinful and irreverent humanity?"[21] Quevedo Báez's change of heart, if indeed it was that, is difficult to explain. One could cite the wisdom of old age and the uncertainties of confronting human mortality. One might also observe that this rapprochement between science and faith took place precisely when Catholicism and "tradition"—as opposed to quackery and superstition—appeared to be at odds with cold reason.

For all of her popularity, believers did not come to Fatima's Virgin entirely unaided; the press, the movies, and even a skeptical church did their part to connect the apparitions in Fatima and Sabana Grande in a persuasive fashion. Both supportive and critical dailies insisted on tallying and accounting for similarities and differences between the events in Portugal and Puerto Rico. Fatima emerged as the measure of the visions in Sabana Grande with little debate. The sympathetic *El Imparcial* noted, for instance, that the Virgin had appeared in Portugal on the Sunday before the holiday commemorating Mary's ascent to heaven (Fiesta de la Asunción). The paper then went on to remind its readers that in 1953 the feast would fall on 29 May, only four days after what many called "the day of the miracle." In addition, reporters referred to Fatima habitually whenever it was necessary to offer context for ongoing events. Boosters like journalist Jacobo Córdova Chirino took pleasure in calling attention to the fact that the 100,000 to 150,000 pilgrims congregated in Sabana Grande's barrio on 25 May exceeded the size of the multitude in the Portuguese village, where only 70,000 souls had gathered.[22]

Believers in barrio Rincón's visions also relied on the press for the sorts of details from Fatima's pious narratives that found daily restatement at the Puerto Rican shrine. Like other papers, *El Imparcial* ran a special feature titled "What Happened in Fatima" in its weekend magazine. The article described the Virgin's suspension above a tree and miracles involving the sun and rain and identified the Virgin of Fatima as Our Lady of the Rosary. Although it is impossible to ascertain precisely what the young seers made of this information and the accompanying photographs, there can be little doubt that at least some of them became familiar with it. Reporter F. González Alberty made a point of presenting seer Milagros Borreli with a copy of the magazine.[23]

Those who had not participated in church missions or read about Fatima in the papers could always catch one of the movies. As chance would have it, John Brahm's *The Miracle of Our Lady of Fatima* (Warner Brothers, 1952) played on Puerto Rican screens in the spring of 1953 around the time when news of barrio Rincón's visions began to spread. The timing could not have been better; cinema owners had an immediate blockbuster in their hands. The activity in barrio Rincón generated tremendous interest in the film, and, as social scientists noted, the cinematic representation itself helped to promote the shrine.[24]

Extended engagements became commonplace as the publicity campaign began to draw explicit connections between Hollywood's account of Fatima and Puerto Rican events. An ad for the film's screening at the Teatro Fox Delicias in Ponce described the production as the most "topical film in Puerto Rico." But the publicists for the Riera Theater in Mayagüez were more explicit: "First in Portugal. Now in Sabana Grande. See how the Virgin appeared to small children." Such was the success of *The Miracle* that theaters soon attempted to extend their bonanza. Other Mary-inspired features were revived to great acclaim. Cobián's Holiday, a popular San Juan theater, replayed Franz Werfel's *The Song of Bernadette*. The film had won four Academy Awards in 1943. A decade later, however, its claim to public attention resided elsewhere. According to the advertising, "The events in Sabana Grande seem[ed] like a replica of this film."[25]

Echoes of both films were perceptible in some of the miracles following the visions in Sabana Grande. For instance, the descriptions of the solar phenomena in Caguas and of the colored rains in Sabana Grande bear a striking resemblance to the climactic scenes of *The Miracle of Our Lady of Fatima*. Countless details, some of them known only through recent devotional accounts of Sabana Grande's miracles, evoke cinematic touches. In a 1980s retelling of her experiences, the seers' schoolteacher Josefa Ríos revealed something of what the Virgin had told her. Like Bernadette, Josefa was promised happiness. This guarantee, however, was followed by an important admonition: "not in this life." The phrase has a familiar ring to anyone familiar with the 1943 film. In two separate scenes, Bernadette reports that the Virgin had made a similar commitment to her.

For all of its influence, it is important to note that Fatima did not dictate all that occurred in Sabana Grande. Government officials, critics, and other models helped to shape the miracle, too. Lourdes' influence is plainly evident in the physical transformation of the shrine in barrio Rincón. Although the source of the healing waters there was a natural spring, following local usage, the seers referred to the spring as a *pozo*, or well. The appellation caught on and was soon extended to the site in general and to the Virgin who appeared there, whence "La Virgen del Pozo." But as the shrine developed, the faithful transformed the sanctified landscape in conformity with the Virgin's directions, or to make it resemble places of recognized sanctity. As a result, the spring began a slow metamorphosis and emerged years later as a grotto modeled after the one that the Virgin had shown Bernadette. According to witness testimonies, those who built the concrete hollow examined dozens of photographs of the Lourdes shrine.[26] In addition, it is likely that they recalled scenes from *The Song of Bernadette*.

Although the impact of these movies is palpable, it would be ill-advised to

The encased spring. The sign reads: "Please, do not sit down." From photo file 5442, Proyecto de Digitalización de la Colección de Fotos del Periódico *El Mundo*. (Universidad de Puerto Rico)

reduce the visions in barrio Rincón to a simple case of life imitating art. Other sources and a good many innovations helped to shape the miracles of 1953. The seers, in any event, seem not to have known the film prior to seeing the apparitions, though the expectations of those pilgrims who had seen the movies may have influenced them indirectly. According to *El Mundo*, "the movie about the Virgin of Fatima" was not shown in Sabana Grande in time to exert a direct influence.[27]

The Church and Korea Lend a Hand

Our Ladies of Fatima and Lourdes achieved ecclesiastical recognition and enormous popularity among the laity early on. Both were commonly adored in Puerto Rico well before 1953. Fatima's rise to prominence, however, was more than a matter of diffusion; it owed a good deal to the church and its evangelizing campaigns. In 1950, only three years before the first visions in Sabana Grande, the southern dioceses of Ponce had celebrated its silver jubilee with a series of revival missions. Led by Jesuit Saturnino Junquera, these missions featured processions headed by an image of Our Lady of Fatima that was also put on display in parish churches throughout the see.[28]

The evidence suggests that the church hierarchy sought to promote the cult of Our Lady of Fatima alongside that of Our Lady of Providence in an effort to stave off devotions of the sort burgeoning in barrio Rincón. In early May, just as the news of the apparition touched off a rash of secondary miracles and apparitions throughout the island,[29] Father Junquera returned from Mexico to lead "a vast program of missions" scheduled in celebration of Our Lady of Providence's 100th anniversary. On this occasion, Junquera declared the comparatively unpopular Virgin of Providence "patroness of Puerto Rico," fulfilling the hierarchy's long-held wishes.[30] Later that month, Bishop James P. Davis of San Juan also consecrated a chapel to Our Lady of Fatima in Santurce's barrio Obrero. A few weeks afterward, in June 1953, Davis blessed another chapel honoring this Virgin. The second chapel was located in the northeastern town of Rio Grande where residents concerned with the plight of relatives fighting in Korea had pressed the church for consolation in the form of their own house of worship.[31]

The push for these orthodox Virgins precisely at this point appears to be more than accidental. After all, May and June 1953 were months of unprecedented visionary activity that more than suggested the appropriation of Fatima's Virgin for purposes that the church did not sanction. Regardless of their intent, it is safe to say that the church's missions did not discourage believers from seeking their own communion. Scarcely a day after multitudes descended upon barrio Rincón to witness a miracle, and only a week after the opening of the chapel in Santurce's barrio Obrero, the Virgin appeared in a private home on Labra Street, also in Santurce.[32]

Preoccupations surrounding warfare were not limited to Rio Grande. Wartime anxieties served in and of themselves to connect the Puerto Rican visions to Fatima. As anyone who had seen the popular movie knew, the seers there had assured Portuguese pilgrims that World War I would soon end. They had it on the Virgin's word that their children would return safely from the front. Like Fatima's and Rio Grande's residents, pilgrims who came to barrio Rincón were often worried for relatives serving abroad. According to reports, they asked after them regularly through the children seers. While expectations varied, many among the faithful believed that the Virgin would perform a preliminary miracle on 15 May; on that day, she would reveal if a Puerto Rican prisoner of war would be repatriated. Given the saint's concern with Puerto Rico's sons, water from the miraculous well in Sabana Grande also found its way to Korean battlefields. Puerto Rican soldiers from Company C of the famed 65th Infantry Regiment wrote *El Imparcial* from their post. The soldiers reported that after taking a few sips of the sanctified water they felt safer and more confident, as if they enjoyed "the divine protection of the Holy Virgin."[33]

Ironically, in its efforts to discredit what they regarded as a suspect claim, the church hierarchy in Puerto Rico upheld Fatima and Lourdes as genuine apparitions offering legitimate standards of comparison. Church officials were quick to point out wherever happenings in barrio Rincón deviated from these two models. In so doing they assisted those engaged in the performance of the miracles, contributing to the expectation that newspapers, missions, and movies had helped to promote.

The Virgin seemed to have a parry for every one of the church's attacks. In a piece published in *El Mundo*, a daily that had been suspicious of the apparition in Sabana Grande from the start, Monsignor Vicente Murga, vicar general of Ponce, rector of Santa María University, and historian, reiterated the official version of the miracles in Fatima. Pastor of a see that then included Sabana Grande, Monsignor Murga hoped that his account would give pause to the pilgrims. He reminded the Catholic flock that Fatima had been under review for thirteen years before it gained the Vatican's sanction; he pointed out that the European visions took place over a six-month period and that they never lasted more than ten minutes. The children in barrio Rincón, he noted, claimed to see the Virgin for extended periods every day, and this without the benefit of the ecstatic states. Murga concluded by pointing out that when the public miracle occurred in Fatima, it was visible to all in a multitude that included believers as well as scientists and nonbelievers. Finally, he highlighted that the apparitions there had been accompanied by three messages from the Virgin.[34]

Local clergy and high-church officials echoed Murga's last remarks. In early May, Father Pinto, a parish priest from the nearby town of Lajas, made some discreet inquiries when he visited barrio Rincón. While insisting that he was there only as an unofficial observer, he interviewed one of the girl seers and asked point-

Sgt. Ismael Trabal carries his son. From *El Mundo*, 26 May 1953.
(Universidad de Puerto Rico)

edly if the Virgin did not have a special communication to convey. At this early date, the girl said simply that the Virgin did not.[35] On 27 May, Bishop James E. McManus announced that he would not inform the Vatican of the miracles that had allegedly taken place in Sabana Grande. He cited a number of reasons that tended to discredit the pilgrim's claims before the church's eyes; notable among these was the lack of proper, credible messages. The bishop's expectations in this regard were especially exacting. After all, even in Fatima there had been no talk of messages of the kind that he demanded—well-composed, public statements— until years after the first apparition.

Some of the omissions that the clergymen pointed out in their remarks to the press soon were rendered moot by corrective developments at the shrine. Reports of messages proliferated at a prodigious rate following the church's criticisms. On 30 April, only a week after the first visions, a man called José López turned to a crowd that had just prayed the rosary to report that on 23 April he had received "certain messages." Addressing the gathering in a loud voice, he said: "Many things are happening. Children attack their parents, brothers fight brothers, wives are unfaithful to their husbands, and many things [like this]. That is why the Virgin comes. So that we join each other as brethren, as God's true children and we live filled with joy."[36] Nearly a month later, on 18 May, several pilgrims reported with evident elation that the Virgin had visited the home of one of the seers, where she had issued "messages" as well as "prescriptions." The impact of this news, however, was dampened by simultaneous reports of the Virgin's calls to three other homes in the barrio.[37]

Finally, the leading devotional account claims that the Virgin gave the seers a set of written messages inscribed in seven scrolls in 1953. According to this version, the Virgin later took away the secret documents because Ramonita, the youngest seer, disclosed their existence to the press. Although I have found no evidence in the coverage from 1953, the seers claim that several headlines proclaimed that they, that is the young visionaries, had in their possession documents "written on flesh," a confusion stemming from the children's lack of familiarity with parchment. Mercifully, the content of these messages was not lost. Before reclaiming the scrolls, the Virgin imprinted them in Juan Angel's memory, asking him to read the entire set every night for the rest of his life. Four of the seven messages have been made public. The texts can be found in Noelle Méndez de Guzmán's *La verdadera historia: Aparición de la Virgen del Rosario.*[38]

The Miracle of Order

Puerto Rico's central government adopted a curious policy in its dealings with the thousands of pilgrims gathering in barrio Rincón. Rather than condemn Mary's apparition as an expression of ignorance or backwardness, the authorities chose instead to remain noncommittal in regard to specific claims of miracles and to take on the mass mobilization of believers as a test of the government's administrative mettle. In this instance, Puerto Rico's standing among cultured and civilized nations would not be measured by the content of its faiths but by the orderliness and civility of its public behaviors. This strategy enjoyed the support of the press, who thought it proper for the government to play the role of arbiter. *El Mundo*, while weary of the talk of apparitions, described the rationale behind this tolerant-but-vigilant approach in one of its editorials; it was a "test" of Puerto Rico's civilizational mettle: "He who believes should act with all the respect that his beliefs demand. He who does not believe should act with all the tolerance of a democratic spirit and with all the respect that he would wish for his own ideas and beliefs. Circumstances like these test the culture of a people."[39]

If the events unfolding at barrio Rincón can be described as a performance, government officials were decidedly its most conscientious stage managers. The scale of this intervention far surpassed what Cuban officials had done to assist Izquierdo's pilgrimage to El Cobre. Once 25 May had been destined for miracles, the commonwealth government moved in to administer nearly everything except the devotions. Indeed, the government was quietly, but nonetheless doggedly, committed to contesting the jurisdiction of the divine and reclaiming the holy site as a public space.

Sabana Grande's city hall launched some of the earliest ad hoc efforts to regulate conduct at the shrine. Mayor Juan Arroyo Ortiz led a campaign to rid barrio Rincón of beggars, dozens of whom arrived in town as news of the apparition spread. To avert this public nuisance, the mayor prohibited handouts, as well as panhandling. Though effective, such piecemeal measures were soon superseded. Specialists and bureaucrats of all sorts stepped in to put in place what can only be described as a centralized management plan.[40]

By the end of May, the detachment of police assigned to the shrine and its vicinity had grown to 300 officers.[41] They directed traffic along the access routes to Sabana Grande; patrolled the town, the shrine, and the road between the two; and ensured that the interminable, gender-segregated lines of pilgrims waiting to collect water from the well remained orderly. They issued exhortations and directives through a public address system installed with crowd control in mind. Officers were also assigned to an escort detail and charged with accompanying the seers wherever they went. One of these officers—Eladio García of San Germán—became such a fixture that pilgrims referred to him as "the children's policeman."

In addition to the police, another 300 civil defense volunteers were deployed. These officials saw pilgrims through their sojourns in tents and makeshift shelters nearby, carried patients to an emergency clinic established by the Department of Health, and installed the portable generators, latrines, and other conveniences that lent barrio Rincón the appearance of a boomtown.

Though rather tolerant and deliberate, the central government attempted to safeguard "public order," a pursuit that encompassed matters of property, propriety, and scientific reason. The faithful applauded some of these measures and met others with indifference. With the nodding approval of the majority of the Virgin's devotees, the police banned alcohol sales in barrio Rincón and sent away anyone who appeared drunk. They also prevented price-gouging and maintained

The spring at the time of the first apparitions. From photo file 5524, Proyecto de
Digitalización de la Colección de Fotos del Periódico *El Mundo*.
(Universidad de Puerto Rico)

a strict watch over queues to prevent latecomers from cutting in line. All of this
was to the liking of the faithful, who denounced impious activities like drinking
and profiteering and who kept a watchful eye for disruptive practices such as
"favoritism" in the lines.

Punctiliousness of this sort commonly accompanied the irruption of the divine in the Puerto Rican landscape. Pilgrims to La Samaritana's well in 1922, for
instance, reported that bottles that had held liquor shattered upon contact with

magnetized water. It is also apposite that La Samaritana, who later abandoned the site and moved to town, claimed that she had done so because commercial interests had taken over and desecrated the spot outside San Lorenzo.

Other regulatory steps were met with less enthusiasm. In its efforts to reestablish the state's jurisdiction, government officials posted signs throughout barrio Rincón. One of these notices, tacked to the wall of the school dining hall where pilgrims were sure to see it, proclaimed in solemn administrative language that "the fluvial waters of Puerto Rico that have not been treated in water plants controlled by the Health Department should not be drunk without being boiled." According to reporters, the sign never failed to generate comments among pilgrims, one of whom retorted: "What they should do is put water from the well in the aqueduct."[42]

The sign was a small part of a broader practice of government-sponsored prophylaxis. Before 25 May, the authorities launched a comprehensive campaign to ready barrio Rincón for the influx of pilgrims. Besides the security arrangements mentioned above, Health Department personnel fumigated the cane fields surrounding the well with DDT, installed portable potties, and brought in germicide-treated water to supply the pilgrims at reasonable prices (five cents per six-ounce cup). Inspectors monitored food kiosks and instructed vendors to employ a chlorine solution when cleaning their pots.[43]

The health authorities' concern with germs, vermin, and hygiene was connected to a long-standing preoccupation with the crowd as a disease vector. In 1922, for instance, La Samaritana reactivated fears of an insalubrious countryside, as critics of the gatherings in San Lorenzo warned that the congregation of sick people—mostly jíbaros—constituted a health hazard and posed a risk of epidemics. Similar fears resurfaced in 1953 in a somewhat muted form; that is, without citing jíbaros specifically. *El Mundo*, for instance, used its editorial pages to dissuade its readers from gathering in barrio Rincón. Among the horrors to be encountered at the site, the editorial cautioned that there would be "thousands upon thousands of beings shoving one another in a river of sweat, bad odors, and a rush [*afluvio*] of disease and misery."[44]

While this and other editorials from 1953 never mentioned peasants in particular, it was known that jíbaros constituted the "immense majority" of the gathering. Social scientists who canvassed the crowd during the apparition sightings confirmed this impression without explaining why jíbaros might be so "predisposed" to believe in the visions.[45] Journalists, however, could not resist hypothesizing; *El Imparcial* cited "intellectuals" and "cultured people" who explained the overrepresentation of poor country folk rather nostalgically in terms of a rural attachment to traditional spirituality: "The explanation that is offered . . . is that peasants are closer to nature [and] to God than those of us who live in the cities tied to the violent hustle of working life." "The man of the country," the writer mused, "looks to the heavens[.] They know how to approach God with greater religious fervor because they have to ask him for what they need for their crops and harvests. The man of the country looks to heaven with imploring eyes. The man of the city looks at his neighbors with greedy eyes."[46]

Some of the measures the government introduced at the shrine generated neither applause nor derision; in fact, the faithful met these with indifference. For instance, when the Health Department established a first aid and emergency clinic at the shrine, no one seems to have remarked on the irony of erecting a temporary medical facility at a site where the Virgin herself was healing those whom physicians had declared beyond hope. Remarkably, there were no hints of animosity. According to the medical staff stationed in barrio Rincón, the patients treated there were mostly elderly and infant pilgrims overcome by exhaustion or sunstroke. Water from the well was seldom used in these cases, which were left to ordinary medicine in a curious division of labor that assigned the easily tractable to physicians and the chronic cases to the Virgin.

Nevertheless, the outpouring of grace in barrio Rincón had a perceptible impact upon health care providers outside of the shrine. Pharmacists complained of a drastic reduction in sales (45 percent), and drugstore owners from San Germán, Yauco, and Sabana Grande reported that their daily receipts had dropped from $100 to $15. During the last week of May, several state-run health care centers in the southwestern region reported that they had delivered no services because of a lack of demand.[47] None of this, however, amounted to a rejection of medicine as such. Indeed, many pilgrims returned to their doctors after being healed at the shrine to seek scientific confirmation that a miracle had occurred.[48]

Whether the authorities' measures or piety are to be credited, an exemplary order was maintained at the shrine and its surroundings. Early headlines described the site as a threat to public order. But these warnings were soon replaced by pronouncements praising the conduct of the pilgrims and the government's organizing efforts. Early on, *El Mundo* reported that a number of persons had suffered dislocated or broken limbs in their haste to reach the well in barrio Rincón and that another had been hurt in a car accident while en route. In response, they said, the police handed out sixteen speeding tickets to pilgrims in only a few days. As time passed, however, the shrine grew in solemnity, and for a while even such minor disruptions seem to have become infrequent, at least according to *El Imparcial*. Although there were early concerns about pickpockets, three weeks into the apparition cycle only two thefts had been reported to police. Sabana Grande's justice of the peace, Quintín Hernández, reported that nearly 200 cases involving "common offenses" were usually heard before his court each month. By 24 May, however, only twenty-five cases had been brought before him. None of those were felonies, he added.[49]

Politicians were among the first to celebrate the pilgrims' comportment and, implicitly, the government's administrative success: order appeared as something of a miracle in a society that seemed so prone to chaotic displays. Senators Luis A. Negrón López and Ernesto Carrasquillo visited the shrine along with Juan A. Irizarry, an attorney for the police. When they were denied access to the well ahead of the patient pilgrims waiting in line, Senator Carrasquillo and Mr. Irizarry made the best of a potentially embarrassing situation. They declared the checks put in place at the shrine "the most perfect organization they had ever witnessed in Puerto Rico." Other commentators argued that in retrospect the most miraculous event of 25 May was "the miracle of order."[50]

The most serious infractions committed at the shrine were acts of sacrilegious unseemliness. According to a paper, only a week before the day of the miracle, a group of incredulous, jeering men carrying rum bottles gathered near the entrance to the well, where they poked fun at the devotees and cast obscenities their way. Mercifully, the journalist assured readers, the police acted "strongly and rapidly," and for a few nights the jail was filled with these "types."[51] Nevertheless, incarceration remained exceptional; as far as I have been able to establish, no pilgrims or seers were arrested in Sabana Grande.

In Sabana Grande, impiety was the exception; both authorities and the faithful looked upon it as a trespass. According to the press, even the most clownish rogues generally felt compelled to behave well while in barrio Rincón. The Virgin would not countenance turning pilgrimage into carnival. In fact, while the visions lasted, the appeal of permissible amusements waned, too. The feast of San Isidro Labrador, Sabana Grande's patron saint, was poorly attended. The revelries in the town's square, which generally included gambling and heavy drinking, were reportedly subdued because of the events at the spring. Even the procession in the saint's honor was canceled.[52]

This turn toward hypernomian behavior took effect without complaints of excessive use of force. Dealings between police officers and pilgrims can scarcely be described as antagonistic. Police were mindful of the pilgrims' values, many of which they shared, and appealed to them frequently in the effort to keep the order in barrio Rincón. Some individual officers were among believers who took part in the devotions at the shrine. Throughout the morning of 25 May, for instance, officers used the newly installed loudspeakers to ask for "divine protection" and to urge pilgrims to cooperate by remaining "calm" and "serene" at all times.[53]

There can be little doubt that some officers were sincere in their entreaties. A pilgrim waiting outside the seer's home for the opportunity to speak to María Milagros Borreli, who briefly emerged as a healer and blesser, reported that three police officers had come to ask the girl to bless their shields.[54] Milagros Borreli even delivered a private message from the Virgin to one of them. Yet other police officers made public statements of faith in the apparition or in the miraculous properties of barrio Rincón's waters. Lt. José M. Rosario told reporters that he borrowed water from a pilgrim who had just returned from Sabana Grande as a remedy for his tired eyesight and a stomachache. The effect of this treatment left him convinced that something supernatural was afoot.[55]

In some respects, accounting for tolerance is just as puzzling as accounting for moments of repression. One might begin to explain the authorities' patience with the apparition and its believers in terms of self-interest. The central government's management of the crowds in barrio Rincón was certainly in keeping with the populist strategies that Luis Muñoz Marín and the ruling Popular Democratic Party (PPD) employed with great success throughout the 1950s.[56] At the local level of government, mayors were also attuned to the opportunities for political profit that the apparition in Sabana Grande offered. But the willingness of politicians to exploit the miraculous offers only a partial explanation for the relatively harmonious relationship between the authorities and the faithful. After all, politicians managed to profit from persecuted faiths quite well. During election periods in the early Cuban republic, seemingly sympathetic candidates addressed so-called brujos and ñáñigos in their sacred languages, holding out promises of protection. Circumstances, of course, could also frustrate schemes for political profit. Batista, I have suggested, was unable to capitalize on Izquierdo's popularity because he could not risk alienating the church. Political opportunism alone cannot explain the rather tolerant atmosphere in barrio Rincón.

Even with such caveats in mind, there is no denying that politicians were among the most influential promoters of the apparition. Manuel García, the mayor of the northwestern town of Rincón, played an important role in shaping the shrine and its devotions. García served both as on-site organizer and as self-appointed spokesman for the believers. Shortly after seer Bertita Pinto revealed that the Virgin wanted a sanctuary and altar built, Mayor García took on the task of publicizing the saint's wishes. He organized a collection to fund the project, an initiative that put him at odds with Sabana Grande's mayor and the church. Regardless of the opposition, García decided to donate the money for the construction of an altar and a stage near the spring. Subsequently, seers gathered there, with García himself claiming a spot on center stage. Standing on this platform, the mayor led rosaries and prayers, relayed the seers' instructions and comments to the pilgrims, and delivered speeches in favor of the apparition.[57]

Mayor García also emerged as a zealous public defender of the apparition. He stepped in whenever criticisms or inconsistencies threatened to discredit the shrine. At one point, when some of the seers claimed that the devil had appeared in the school, while other seers denied it, the press turned to García. The mayor adjudicated the dispute putting questions to the Virgin through Bertita Pinto, who claimed that no demonic apparition had occurred. According to García, the Virgin herself assured him that Bertita's version was correct: the devil had not been there. Some weeks later, faced with the disappointment of those who had witnessed no miracles on 25 May, the mayor spoke on several radio shows to answer criticisms. The leaders of the faithful rewarded Mayor García for his efforts by electing him honorary president of the newly formed Committee for the Shrine and Religious Acts in Barrio Rincón.[58]

The misgivings of Sabana Grande's mayor regarding the apparition and the activism of his colleague from Rincón did not prevent him from promoting himself once he resolved to work in the Virgin's favor. At first, Mayor Arroyo Ortiz was suspicious. As late as 13 May, he told a reporter that he had never visited the shrine and that all correspondence about it should be directed elsewhere. Only three days later, however, Arroyo relented, apparently overcome by the publicity, if not by heartfelt devotion. On 16 May, the mayor asked Sabana Grande's business owners to close their shops at noon so that everyone could attend prayer sessions celebrated in barrio Rincón on nine consecutive afternoons. Shortly after, Arroyo had signs welcoming the pilgrims planted on all entrances to the shrine. By the end of May, his early reserve was gone. With the press at hand, he declared himself "the happiest mayor because I have had the pleasure of having all of Puerto Rico in my town."[59]

Although the central government agencies involved in the shrine helped to popularize the new devotion, their strategy was one of compromise and conciliation. The government agencies and their experts instituted such measures as were required to reclaim authority, while being careful not to rouse the pilgrims' hostility. Such tact, even if motivated only by political savvy, appears surprising in retrospect. One would expect that the authorities' spirited advocacy of modernization during these years would have predisposed them to harsher measures.

The effort to modernize Puerto Rico and to transform it into a showcase for democracy and industrial progress required, among other things, that the masses leave behind their attachments to seemingly premodern practices.[60] The Populares, still basking in the glow of the 1952 vote that instituted the new commonwealth formula, sought to attain the modernization of hearts and minds through education. In order to reach the public, now conceived as "*el pueblo*," the populist government relied on pamphlets and films produced by the newly created División de Educación de la Comunidad (DIVEDCO) of the Department of Education. Representatives of this organization found their way to barrio Rincón, where they assisted researchers in filming interviews with the pilgrims.[61] The authorities also counted on the assistance of an intelligentsia and a professional cadre then emerging out of the University of Puerto Rico in Río Piedras. In 1949, only a year after the Popular victory that made Muñoz Marín president of the senate, Rosa M. Ordoñez, a specialist in health and hygiene affiliated with the university's Servicio de Extensión Agrícola, published a column in *El Mundo*. There she argued that the widespread belief in witchcraft and spirits in the countryside was similar to the beliefs of "savage tribes" of the South Pacific. She warned that even if rooted in ignorance rather than perversity, such superstitions were harmful, for they could prevent people from seeking appropriate care. In a phrase that reveals the will to produce a "broken memory," Ordoñez marked the space that such faiths were to occupy in modern Puerto Rico: "As fairy tales, as mythological legends, they are very fine. But to accord these stories the character of reality is outside of the civilized minds of the twentieth century."[62]

The latter-day extirpation effort went further, of course. According to instruction commissioner Mariano Villaronga, superstition and quackery—especially the kinds that promoted miraculous cures or "certain products"—were among "the social problems that had to be attacked in Puerto Rico."[63] Following such directives, in 1951 the Department of Instruction distributed among the rural population 300,000 copies of a new book titled *La ciencia contra la superstición*. This was the third volume in a series called "Books for the people." The text contained "simple explanations" of what citizens should do to protect themselves from disease and to procure adequate care. The message delivered in these publications was reinforced by film productions like Jack Delano's *Una gota de agua* (1949), about the need to boil water, and Skip Faust's *Doña Julia* (1955). The second film tells the story of a jíbara's effort to put her trust in a new rural hospital once a healer's failure to cure her sick child has put her at fatal risk.

Given this history, it is difficult to say precisely why the government behaved as it did in barrio Rincón, especially if one accepts Díaz-Quiñones contention that the events there stood for the peasantry's effort to assert "memories" that the state went about burying systematically. Several possibilities suggest themselves. First, government officials were careful to exclude Catholicism and other respectable religions from the category of "superstition." Although the apparition in Sabana Grande ushered in healing practices and miraculous cures of various sorts, it would have been impolitic to denounce barrio Rincón's Virgin as non-Catholic fakery before the church had determined to do so itself. So long as doubt remained, the miracles there may have been given the benefit. Second, it is also possible that the threat of allowing the devotional movement to go on was preferable to the danger of alienating such a vast constituency. The Virgin's messages and her followers were menacing only as proponents of a competing utopian project. With that threat arrested by means of "softer" disciplinary measures of the sort put in place at the shrine, government officials may have found it preferable to let matters take their course. With professional knowledge safeguarded and the state's role reclaimed, there was little for functionaries to fear. Talk of uprisings or violent millennial expectations was unheard of at the shrine in 1953.

Finally, the commonwealth government may have had an interest in nurturing a religious mobilization that put the faithful at odds with the Catholic hierarchy. During the elections of 1960 the bishops opposed Muñoz Marín and urged their flock not to vote for the Popular Democratic Party. From the pulpit and by means of public pastoral letters, they tarred the PPD and even threatened the excommunication of Catholics who supported it. Muñoz Marín defended himself and won the elections, arguing that the hierarchy threatened to violate the separation of church and state with their political intervention and thus risked destabilizing democratic order. In his pronouncements, he also suggested that there was a distinction to be drawn between the faith of the people and the clergy's pretension to command them and their beliefs. The events in Sabana Grande offered the governor an opportunity to measure the distance between believers and their pastors as the relationship between his administration and the church deteriorated.[64]

The Virgin, Puerto Rico, and Beyond

The measures intended to service and supervise the apparition site so as to keep it in good order had the added effect of furthering the shrine's claim to a national status. While dailies and broadcasts had already made the apparition common knowledge throughout the island, in the absence of government intervention many of the faithful may have been forced to remain a listening and reading public. The introduction of special bus services and the reopening of railroad routes allowed thousands of Puerto Ricans to see for themselves and drink from the Virgin's well. The buses of the Autoridad de Transportación, a government agency, carried an astonishing 33,238 passengers to the town on the weekend of 23–24 May 1953 alone.[65] Though no passenger counts are available, thousands of others are known to have traveled on foot and by truck, hired cars, and railroads. Between 17 May and 25 May, the Train Company responded to petitions with the introduction of a special rail service from the northwestern town of Aguadilla to Sabana Grande. On the evening of 24 May, the company also operated a night express with service from San Juan to Sabana Grande in order to meet demand from the San Juan area.[66]

As in Limpias and Eskioga, which sat along important rail lines and regional routes, the availability of mass transportation to barrio Rincón was a factor in the development of a local apparition site into a cultic center capable of attracting pilgrims from the entire country. It should be emphasized, however, that mass transport never made travel to Sabana Grande effortless. Trains and buses were slow and overcrowded, and country roads were narrow and severely congested. Moreover, the last three kilometers between Sabana Grande and barrio Rincón had to be traversed on foot. Once at the shrine, pilgrims faced long waits in line (as long as eighteen hours) often followed by a night spent in a cane field before they could collect water or view the well.

These very difficulties made a pilgrimage out of the journey. Time and again, the faithful emphasized the value of their travails and of the hardships they endured. This can be seen most succinctly in an exchange between pilgrims and an exhausted elderly woman who had commandeered a bed at the emergency clinic after traveling for a day and vainly standing in line all evening. When passersby took up a collection to pay for her return fare, she objected, saying, "But I want to drink of the water. But I want to get it myself, because if I don't make the sacrifice it doesn't count and there's no miracle."[67] Other pilgrims described their standing waits similarly, as the "penance" that ensured that they would "deserve the miracle." In spite of the interventions by agents of order and the ongoing media circus, an economy of affliction continued to function. There was no evidence of the sorts of concessions and evasions that Clavelito promoted in his radio show.

The press, of course, also played a part in ensuring that the influence of the shrine transcended Sabana Grande's immediate environs. Broadcasts reached the entire island, as did most major dailies.[68] Moreover, the reports emphasized the presence of people from every corner of Puerto Rico, giving readers the sense that this was a mobilization in which all Puerto Ricans participated.

Barrio Rincón's Virgin was more than simply national, however. Although international coverage of the visions taking place in Puerto Rico was insignificant when compared to Fatima's high mark, or to the international media frenzy that would surround the infamous chupacabras during the 1990s, believers outside of the island were well informed of events at the shrine. In the absence of Univisión, it appears that the Virgin relied on word-of-mouth networks and "ethnic" newspapers abroad. It bears pointing out that the Puerto Rican diaspora began to grow massive in the 1950s and by 1953 it already displayed a notable plasticity. Migrants and island residents recirculated between Puerto Rico and cities in the United States, participating in most aspects of life in these multiple locales. The visions were no exception; pilgrims there asked seers to consult the Virgin regarding the fate of relatives who had migrated, as was the case with a man who wanted to know if his son had found work in New York. For their part, Puerto Ricans in the United States participated actively in the events of Sabana Grande. Blas Reyes was probably typical; though in New York, he read about the visions less than a week after they began. Soon Reyes and, according to his testimony, "many" others began to make travel arrangements, hastening to arrive before 25 May.[69]

The appeal of the visions was not limited to Puerto Ricans. Since early May, critics and boosters had noted the presence of foreign nationals at the site. On 25 May, *El Mundo* pointed out that the crowd included people from every town in the island, Puerto Ricans from New York and Miami, and pilgrims from Cuba, Panama, Mexico, the Dominican Republic, the Virgin Islands, and other unspecified countries. *El Imparcial* added Jamaicans to the list and noted that many of the foreign pilgrims had bought excursion packages.[70]

The international presence was not lost on devotees. Only hours after the day of miracles, plans were in place to solicit contributions from abroad for the construction of the chapel at the shrine.[71] More than money was at stake, however. Both the press and the faithful seem to have valued the internationalization of the shrine as an indication of Puerto Rico's standing on the world stage. Some publications gushed at the sight of the crowd congregated in barrio Rincón. *El Imparcial* noted, for example, "In point of fact this is perhaps the greatest outdoor mass celebrated not only in Puerto Rico, but in the entire world because never before have close to 100,000 persons congregated in a religious act of this kind against the advice of church dignitaries."[72]

As years passed, the sense that the visions taking place in barrio Rincón were aimed at a global audience grew from a vague impression into explicit statements of divine will. The most explicit formulation of this tendency can be found in the words of Juan Angel Collado, the boy seer of 1953 who grew to become the leader of the Virgin's devotees. Collado, who like Fatima's main seer has continued to receive and reveal messages from Mary, states in a video distributed by his organization that the Virgin appeared for "the entire world" and not for Puerto Rico alone. It is for this reason that Collado has felt called upon to proselytize abroad, taking his apostolate to Mexico and the Dominican Republic, among other places.

One might mention in passing that the concern with the international significance of barrio Rincón's visions grew more prominent as the Virgin's revealed messages became more eschatological in scope and millenarian in tone. William Christian has remarked upon a similar tendency in the visions that took place in Eskioga after the 1930s. He explains the turn to end-of-the-world imagery of the sort that concerns the entire world more or less equally as a response to the decrease in enthusiasm at the local level and the relative increase in the presence and influence of non-Basques at the vision site.[73] A similar process might be at play in Puerto Rico, where one would expect that internationalization would require messages capable of addressing concerns other than those of Puerto Ricans.

Contested Meanings and Competing Expectations

Like the Virgin's identity, the meaning of the visions and the significance of the miracles in barrio Rincón were matters of dispute. Pilgrims, government officials, politicians, journalists, and clergymen offered widely divergent interpretations that could claim some foundation in one of hundreds of natural and supernatural events taking place at the shrine and its satellites. This time, however, no clear consensus emerged from the debate. It is only in recent decades that organized devotees have managed to quiet the din of competing explanations to propose a single purpose and meaning for the events of 1953. They have accomplished this by means of a devotional account that reveals some of the Virgin's secret messages. Among other things, the Virgin's statements and the seers' glosses elucidate the saint's motivation for intervening in Puerto Rico.

A sector among the faithful understood the significance of the Virgin's 1953 apparition in terms reminiscent of the Cheos's prophetic campaign of the early 1900s. They reasoned that the Holy Mother had manifested herself in Sabana Grande's outskirts as a countermeasure against the continuing spread of Protestantism. The visions were for them an urgent call for the revival of the Catholic faith and its devotions, which were being threatened by the expansion of Evangelical religions. Ramonita Belén, the seer who articulated this position most clearly, singled out Sabana Grande's Adventist congregation as the object of divine wrath. At a moment when seers were facing pressure to produce some evidence of the Virgin's presence in the field near the school, Ramonita told the press that the Virgin would perform a miracle. An earthquake would shake barrio Rincón at 11:00 A.M. on 25 May that only Adventists would perceive. Catholics would be spared and the seers themselves would be protected. As she assured reporters, Ramonita had no concern for her own safety; the Virgin, she said, had given her and the other seers the garb of angels.[74]

Ramonita's words did nothing to temper the animus between Sabana Grande's Catholics and Protestants, but they were certainly not the first shots fired between the two camps. According to the papers, even before there was talk of miracles, the visions themselves were cause for a small-scale "holy war." As the visionaries' story spread, the shrine was transformed into a contested zone where "opposing religious groups wage[d] true verbal battles defending or attacking in their own way the idea of miraculous apparitions." Catholics, Evangelical Protestants, Adventists, Pentecostals, and Presbyterians were reportedly so "entrenched" in their positions that for a while the atmosphere at the shrine was as tense as it was hallowed.[75]

Mayor Manuel García played a prominent role in the interfaith scuffle. Because he had the attention of journalists and access to broadcasters, his salvos received a good deal of attention. For instance, after going on a radio show to defend the events of 25 May as miraculous, the mayor took care to deny Protestants any credit for the country's magnificent outpouring of faith. García's statements motivated a number of rejoinders, including a letter to the editor that condemned the alleged apparitions on religious grounds. According to a Jesús Olivo of Río Piedras, the mayor was quite right; there had been no Pentecostals at the shrine on 25 May because "Pentecostals believe in a living God who manifests himself with power before everyone and not in fraudulent apparitions and false miracles [milagrerías] that only deceive fools."[76]

Common as the Catholic-Protestant animosities appear to have been at the shrine, they never monopolized the meanings of the visions. In this regard, the circumstances surrounding the apparition were unlike those in which the Cheos labored. The ethos of the Cheos's prophetic enterprise was that of a militant Catholic revival that sought showdowns with its adversaries in the faith. Instead of demarcating an exclusively Catholic zone, early on the shrine emerged as a locale of ecumenical activity. Evidently, the Virgin did not require denominational segregation. Regardless of what Olivo and García asserted, there was a Protestant and non-Catholic presence in barrio Rincón in 1953 and beyond. Time and again, journalists remarked on the diversity of the crowds. As El Imparcial put it, it was not uncommon to see "Catholics and Protestants, the humble and great personalities" rubbing elbows around the well.[77] Evidently, the Virgin recompensed some of these non-Catholics without regard for their formal affiliations. Juan Rodríguez, the father of a child healed of paralysis with water from barrio Rincón, admitted readily that he was a Spiritist. This circumstance impressed *El Mundo* as a strike against the credibility of the visions as a genuine miracle.[78]

Although organized Spiritists remained hostile to the Catholic Church and its devotional practices, there were scattered, albeit unsuccessful, attempts to claim barrio Rincón for the science-religion. La Samaritana, for instance, likened the events in San Lorenzo to those in Sabana Grande. While she never pronounced the new well a Spiritist center, her comments blurred distinctions between events that Catholics regarded as legitimate and those Spiritists claimed for themselves.[79] In early June, a Leocadio Medina wrote *El Imparcial* with a more explicit statement. He argued that the visionaries were no more and no less than "seeing mediums." As the letter writer would have it, "cases" such as Sabana Grande's were common in Puerto Rico. There were other places where spiritual action had "magnetized" waters in a so-called Well of Miracles. The children believed that they had encountered the spirit of Mary, "mother of our Great Spiritual Guide, Jesus of Nazareth." But this had yet to be confirmed. Medina promised that Spiritists would "continue to investigate until it is known for certain that it is not another of the many spirits of light that inhabit space."[80]

Even if it ran counter to the Virgin's apparent catholicity, some among barrio Rincón's faithful attempted to exclude other religious groups. María Reyes Camacho de Pinto, Bertita's mother and grandmother of Juan Angel Collado, told the press that the Virgin visited her home on the night of 19 May. The Virgin came to the house along with seven angels to request that she go to the well right then. According to Mrs. Pinto, the saint honored the house with her visit because the Pintos's was the "most Catholic home in the barrio." The call took place in the presence of some visitors, including a lady from Mayagüez who asked Mrs. Pinto if her own history of visions and "attacks" in church might not mean that she was a Spiritist. Mrs. Pinto became indignant at the very thought and asked her guest to leave. The Virgin, she said, had instructed her not to allow in her home anyone who spoke of Spiritism.[81]

Though it has dissipated in recent decades, a relatively ecumenical sense of collective ownership prevailed at the site of the visions in the early years. Such sentiments even survived the first stages of formalization of the Virgin's cult. Newspaper reports of the celebration of the second anniversary of the apparitions in 1955 speak of a lingering Protestant influence. Speakers installed around the newly built chapel played recorded testimonials of cures as well as liturgical music. Catholic songs could be heard, followed by Protestant hymns like "The Old Rugged Cross."[82]

The origins of this rather tolerant arrangement are difficult to pinpoint. In spite of the Virgin's identification with Catholicism, early on most pilgrims appear to have shared a commonsense understanding of the visions in Sabana Grande as public rather than exclusively Catholic events. Moreover, it is clear that the pilgrims' notion of what was public could take on antiauthoritarian inflections capable of contesting not just denominational segregation but also the supremacy of the church over the shrine and even over its own parish churches. Given this climate that emphasized the rights of the citizenry, it is likely that Protestants gained a foothold in barrio Rincón simply as members of a heterogeneous Puerto Rican public rather than as representatives of competing faiths.

Nowhere is the pilgrims' sense of entitlement as members of the public more apparent than in their outrage at being denied access to Sabana Grande's parish church when they came to it in processions. On one such occasion, the police had to intervene to prevent pilgrims from breaking down the doors to the church. A spokesman for Father Ortiz, the parish priest, then addressed the crowd from a balcony. He asked the pilgrims to remain calm and said that the priest had gone to Ponce to meet with the bishop. The crowd was incensed, and some retorted that "the church is a public property of which no one person can dispose." Others complained that "if the parish priest is under orders not to participate . . . what he should have done is to go, but leaving the church open."[83]

Journalists were divided in their opinions, too. Editorial policies wavered, as did the reporters' way of representing the apparitions. A first interpretation saw the events in Sabana Grande as evidence of Puerto Ricans' puerility as a people. A second variety of criticism more in keeping with an emerging scholarly regard for Puerto Rican folklore portrayed the visions as evidence of a return to the island's traditional faith. The first approach was less prevalent in *El Imparcial* than in *El Mundo*, a paper that felt compelled to guard science and reason against threats from blind faith. As an editorial explained: "We have the conviction that miracles are not commonplace and that we should not employ the term incorrectly, lest we apply to occurrences without merit and [thus] confuse superstition with religion, [and] witchcraft with science. That is the grave danger that every believer and every civilized being must avoid."[84]

But even *El Mundo* wavered in its convictions. Its editorial of 26 May declared that the episodes of the previous day "might endure as a monument to credulity, fantasy, and the excitability of our people when they are bent on the supernatural." An article appearing in the same issue of this paper, however, praised Puerto Ricans' faith instead of castigating them: "Through this long and difficult trial, the pilgrims—men, women, and children—are giving proof of their faithful devotion to the virgin and the traditional religious spirit of our people."

The talk of traditional values and faith was more than a contrivance. Believers in the apparition and its miracles endorsed it, and some even deployed this kind of discourse against those who would use the apparitions as evidence of Puerto Rican infantilism. To this group of the faithful, the Virgin's visit was evidence of a kind of progress. In a letter to *El Imparcial*, Juanita González Bouillerce proposed that "the apparition of the Holy Mother of God [was] recognition of our great faith as a Christian people." According to González Bouillerce, Puerto Ricans had "reached spiritual maturity, becoming genuinely deserving of the visitation of the Holy Virgin Mary."[85]

Some of the apparition's boosters also seized upon this second discourse, though they now gave it a populist, partisan inflection. Speaking to reporters, Mayor García expressed the conviction that miracles would take place to save souls and to "unify the Puerto Rican family, which is so divided."[86] In the days of the PPD rule, few phrases were as redolent with Muñoz Marín's brand of politics as *la gran familia puertorriqueña*. To like-minded politicians, the allusion to the family became a way of speaking of the alleged homogeneity of Puerto Rican people under the leadership of a patriarchal figure, a way of opposing those who would divide the kin group with the introduction of radical ideas.

While believers proposed a number of interpretations, miraculous claims tended to emphasize two themes that had been prominent in the religious imaginary at least since the turn of the century: regeneration and healing. The Virgin herself signaled that her intervention was therapeutic. Besides the miraculous cures effected with water from the well, the Virgin intervened in person to cure believers of a variety of afflictions. Juan Angel, for instance, fell ill from exhaustion in early May and was unable to participate in the processions and activities at the shrine. According to the boy, the Virgin soon visited his room in the company of two angels and two seers, Bertita and Isidra. He reported that one of these angels administered a series of shots under his ear, in his right arm, and in other body parts. Following this treatment, the boy recovered quickly. A few days later the seers reported that the Virgin also had visited the home of Dolores Pinto, where she "gave messages and issued prescriptions."[87] In this regard, Sabana Grande's saint was an innovator. The Virgin had not gone to such lengths in Lourdes or Fatima.

The significance of these cures was not lost upon the faithful. Even as many believers speculated as to the nature of the awaited miracle and went on to propose earthquakes, celestial phenomena, and other such marvels, La Samaritana told reporters that the event of 25 May would be a cure. She suggested that the mother of Sabana Grande's parish priest would be healed so that this man who was not a believer would believe in the apparition.[88] Although the miracle never occurred, the most celebrated prodigies of the appointed day were in fact cures. When Georgina Politis shed her steel corset by the well, many thought that the Virgin's promise had been redeemed. News of the "miracle of the Greek woman" spread far and wide, as did word that painter Nora Freyre had abandoned her wheelchair on the same date.[89]

The concern with regeneration was articulated clearly even though believers seldom employed that loaded term, perhaps because of a lingering identification with the vocabulary of Spiritist reformism. In April 1953, a journalist for *El Mundo* reported that barrio Rincón's neighbors believed that the apparitions were a sign of the Virgin's pleasure at their return to the church, "which they had abandoned." The Virgin, they believed, wanted to reward them for "adoring God" once again.[90] José López, whose message from the Virgin is cited above, struck a similar note. When he addressed those gathering at the incipient shrine, he spoke of the need to strengthen fraternal bonds in a society torn asunder by violence. Finally, there was the testimony of Dolores Pinto, a shopkeeper, a practicing Catholic, and the father of seer Bertita Pinto.[91] Although Pinto doubted his daughter's claims at first, he later remembered a prayer he had made earlier. As he told the press, several months before the first apparition sighting he had walked by a shop in barrio Rincón on his way to church. As he passed, someone said: "There goes Pinto. He thinks he will become a saint going to church." When he got home that evening, Pinto recalled, he prayed to the Virgin. He asked her to perform a miracle so that everyone would believe in God and go back to church. Bertita's encounter with the Virgin and the cures at the well struck Pinto as a response to his prayer. After all, the barrio's lackluster devotion had been revitalized beyond all expectations. Processions, rosaries, and church visits began immediately, even before the multitude of pilgrims began to arrive.[92]

Familiar as the call for regeneration was, the miracles in Sabana Grande suggested a new, didactic approach to the country's rehabilitation that had more in common with state-led efforts than with prior "Catholic" mobilizations. Instead of inspiring an army of preachers to rise up, the Virgin herself took over the education of her followers at the Lola Rodríguez de Tió elementary school. She assumed the duties of the rural teacher and gave a literal inflection to the clichéd custom of referring to schools as "temples of learning." In fact, the Virgin made a habit of visiting the young seers' classroom. In her first visit, which took place soon after the children were forbidden to go to the nearby well, the Virgin walked into the classroom, rang the school bell, and sat down at the teacher's desk. In the next minutes, she touched the teacher's medal of La Milagrosa, led the children in singing "*Los ángeles cantan*," and asked that flowers be brought to her. The flowers wilted as soon as the saint handled them. The incident brought hundreds of pilgrims to the shrine and the school itself in the first week of May.[93]

All indications are that Josefa Ríos and other teachers did not resent the saint's intrusion. After only a few days, the young doña Josefa emerged as an important presence at the shrine. She crowned an image of *La Inmaculada* when it was installed on the altar by the well, led the children in the rosary, granted interviews, and graciously stepped aside whenever the Virgin walked from the well to her classroom. Elsewhere, schoolteachers shared in the seers' spotlight at satellite apparition sites. Teachers José Resto Vélez, Daisy Coello, and Laura Alvarez, for example, were among those who witnessed the Virgin's apparition in Cerro Gordo, Vega Alta, on 26 May 1953.[94] Given the respectability of such professionals, the press made sure to highlight their testimonies.

Officials from the Department of Education kept themselves at arm's length from the Virgin, but they did not oppose the visionaries. Instead of ordering an immediate school closure, as journalists expected, officials asked only that pilgrims refrain from interrupting ongoing classes. Juan A. Nazario, the school superintendent for the region that included Sabana Grande, visited the school shortly after news of the apparition broke but made few public statements. He explained that barrio Rincón's school had indeed closed for a few days in early May because its only teacher, Josefa Ríos, had been ill. But he denied any punitive intent behind the measure. Nazario did reveal, however, that he was drafting a report on the situation in barrio Rincón for the secretary of education. Secretary Mariano Villaronga, for his part, told journalists that he had not ordered an investigation. Deferring to a by-now-familiar division of labor, he said matter-of-factly that any determinations regarding the alleged apparition were the responsibility of the ecclesiastical authorities.

A few days after Nazario's comments to the press, the school was closed again. Officials acknowledged that their pleas had gone unanswered; pilgrims continued to gather around the school, disrupting instruction. Schoolwork, of course, had been compromised even before the superintendent canceled classes. The

Virgin's visits, frequent prayers, and the children's distraction made teaching difficult. But the press did not blame Superintendent Nazario, a devout Presbyterian, for the closure. On the contrary, they assured readers that the Protestant official was "a man of liberal ideas."[95]

If believers agreed that the Virgin's message was a call to regeneration and healing, this did not preclude disputes over other interpretations. A minority of believers anticipated a grand, albeit unspecified, show of celestial force on 25 May, and some seem to have harbored millennial expectations.[96] They were disappointed, but their misgivings did not go unnoticed. The seers and others close to them intervened to deny one of the possible meanings of the apparitions; they assured critics that the Virgin had not come to announce the advent of a catastrophe, let alone of final judgment. Bertita's mother quipped that it seemed that "people wanted for the Virgin to come and devastate the world."[97] Bertita, for her part, confronted publicly those who felt the miracles lacked vigor. She asked rhetorically: "What did they want? For the earth to open up?"[98]

A Return of Sorts

Scholars as disparate as Arcadio Díaz-Quiñones and Luis Zayas Micheli would seem to agree; the visions in Sabana Grande marked something of a return to religious traditions that persisted in spite of the designs of the modernizing state sectors and the opposition of a no less modernizing church hierarchy. Díaz-Quiñones's poetic pen writes that while the commonwealth government sought to bury the past and to render the island a tabula rasa, "the inflamed past refused to disappear, and sometimes erupted in ways that could not be hidden." In 1953, he adds, the past "came back dramatically, revealing the contradictory rhythms of the [erasure and modernization] process."[99] In an apparent echo of this position, Zayas Micheli also has observed that "what the return that the Virgin of Sabana Grande's Well created was a kind of restoration, from religion, of the traditional life of the towns."[100] By way of conclusion to this winding account, I submit that the two statements are far from equivalent. They suggest two distinct sorts of "returns" and contrasting understandings of "tradition" and the dynamics of memory. I take issue with Zayas Micheli's notion of a restoration to argue with Díaz-Quiñones that what the Virgin proposed was not a reestablishment of a historical past. Rather, her irruption into barrio Rincón amounted to a reiteration of memories wrought amid present-day struggles. These memories were vital and under frequent reworking, fueled in part with glimpses of the divine originating with the newly quotidian experiences (like cinema) rather than in unidentified repositories of immemorial traditions.

A cursory review should suffice to highlight the shortcomings of interpretations that equate the quest for regeneration with restoration. First, there is little evidence of traditionalism in the visions of Sabana Grande. It is clear that in performing the miraculous, the visionaries and the faithful referred to late-nineteenth-century (Lourdes) and early-twentieth-century (Fatima) European models and even to cinematic accounts, favoring these above models from the immediate environs. Second, there is little to support Zayas Micheli's argument that Protestantism tended to "homogenize" the island to produce a sense of belonging to a broader Puerto Rico whereas "popular Catholicism" tended to reassert the primacy of the town (pueblo) over the spiritual life. On the contrary, the events of 1953 point to the integration of the country in its devotions. Media coverage and transportation networks evidently assisted pilgrims from all over the map in making their way to the shrine. Moreover, the Virgin manifested herself throughout the island, in effect diffusing the sense of expectation that reigned in Sabana Grande. At the shrine itself, it was not the town and its corporate representatives that carried the day. Central government, mayors from other towns, and others played important roles in shaping the events that unfolded there. Finally, there is ample evidence to suggest that the faithful sought and were well aware of the international projection of the saint's mission. The Virgin and her followers may have chosen Puerto Rico, but theirs was a plan of global proportions.

If what the Virgin proposed was not a restoration, then what sort of return was this? Díaz-Quiñones's few lines on this subject sketch out a convincing case. The will to rub out all vestiges of superstition was evident in the actions of state officials and in the discourse of many critics. But the management of barrio Rincón and the crowds it attracted also sounded out the "contradictory rhythms" of which Díaz-Quiñones writes. Rather than resorting to outright repression, modernizers transformed the shrine—a blight in a landscape of improvements—into a testing ground of administrative skill, of good order, of properly regulated "traditional" faith. Barrio Rincón's story, however, also reveals the limitations of the new regime. The faithful asserted their independence from the church and accepted many of the measures that state officials introduced. But they remained critical of both church and state and resisted the temptation to buy entirely into either the modernizing or the orthodox visions of the future. Theirs was an assertion of autonomy. Of course, their mended and resilient memory, complete with its own educational program, harbored inequities of its own. Some of today's faithful, now grouped in a formal organization under the guidance of seer Juan Angel Collado, display a remarkable tolerance of authoritarian practices and at times appear to adhere to rigidly held histories as they advocate the country's moral transformation.

EPILOGUE: THE CHUPACABRAS

Discourses and Social Action

A few years ago, the renowned anthropologists Jean and John Comaroff called attention to the rise of a new "planetary species" of monstrous beings given to conflating "the virtual with the veritable, the cinematic with the scientific, gods with godzillas, the prophetic with the profitable."[1] The Comaroffs proposed that the sightings of uncanny fauna reported around the world in the last decade are linked to the conquests of neoliberalism, an economic arrangement that many have experienced as paradoxical. Under this post-Fordist dispensation, consumption itself can appear to generate wealth more readily than manufacturing and trade, the mainstays of nineteenth-century capitalism. The new breeds, the Comaroffs maintain, have come to fill the epistemic voids that crop up where globalizing designs find their local articulations. To postapartheid South Africans and those who have experienced the new world order as deprivation and post-revolutionary disillusionment, these beasts have revealed the inner works of the new economy: magical transactions account for fortunes that seem to come out of nowhere. The newly enriched are even said to resort to witchcraft to siphon off the productive vitality of their victims.

More than bearing witness, today's monsters attest to these macabre machinations as coconspirators. As the Comaroffs portray them, the creatures themselves are symptoms of the growth of "occult economies." They point out that recent decades have seen the emergence of generative consumerism and the proliferation of hidden avenues to wealth accumulation that include pyramid schemes, a gruesome traffic in human organs, and the alleged exploitation of zombie labor. The Howick Monster, a twenty-five-foot creature said to inhabit the Howick Falls in South Africa, speaks to the role that monstrous beings play in the occult trades;

the beast has helped a lucky few to amass "monster money," largely the proceeds of commerce with tourists who visit the falls hoping to catch a glimpse.

Puerto Rico's infamous chupacabras bears a family resemblance to the South African leviathan. Like others in the contemporary bestiary, the gargoylelike "goatsucker" made news in the 1990s. By then, the contradictions between the "promise of late capitalism" and "post modern pessimism" had become plain enough to herald the consolidation of what the Comaroffs dub "the Age of Futilitarianism."[2] A shadowy predator of uncertain origin, the chupacabras left goats (*cabras*) and thousands of backyard animals drained of their blood; the remains appeared as if they had been sucked dry (*chupar*). Although the headlines detailed losses to farmers and animal owners, the chupacabras brought a good deal of monster money, too. Lacking a fixed habitation, the attacker did not stimulate a boom in tourism. But impresarios made quick returns selling novelties to memorialize the killings, which soon spread beyond Puerto Rico to reach hemispheric proportions. From Tijuana to Miami to Santiago de Chile, entrepreneurs stamped likenesses of the chupacabras on shampoo bottles, Halloween masks, and T-shirts. Media concerns ranging from local newspapers to international broadcasting networks made a lively trade in chupacabras stories as well.

Such similarities notwithstanding, there are reasons for questioning the usefulness of the Comaroffs' model for understanding the chupacabras and the specters that prowled about Cuba and Puerto Rico in the first half of the twentieth century. It is true that scholars have not proposed a taxonomical scheme that would group man-gods, brujos, and bloodsuckers within a single class. Nevertheless, the rise of all of these figures has long invited neofunctionalist analyses.[3] Accounts that would explain the popularization of nonrational propositions in terms of shifts in economic and political structures are common and often very insightful. My aim is not to deny the significance of political economies to the ecologies of representations discussed in this book. Nor is it my intent to contest the rise of the economies of the occult, as such. Instead, I want to begin by echoing Isak Niehaus's recent call to recognize that the zombies and witches of the South African Lowveld—and one might add Puerto Rico's chupacabras to the list of denizens of the occult—"derive their broad appeal from indeterminacy that defies interpretive control."[4]

In seizing upon a single meaning among a profusion of possibilities, analysts risk obscuring contradictions and dissonances between narratives of preternatural depredations and the social actions that accompany those narratives. As Niehaus has observed, the generic stories that late-twentieth-century South Africans tell of zombie-making witches do point at the illegitimate enrichment of some people at the expense of others. These stories also recall the history of dislocations, including the creation of ethnic homelands and schemes that promoted labor migration, which helped bring those inequalities about. Niehaus cautions, however, that when witchcraft accusations are voiced in the Lowveld, they are not aimed at the wealthy, as the stories lead one to expect. Instead, the denunciations point at impoverished persons who are singled out by more prosperous neighbors convinced that those in desperate straits must resort to witchcraft to subsist.[5] In other words, social actions may defy and even contradict the meanings that narratives of occult dealings put forth.

In accounting for the chupacabras, it is useful to differentiate between the discourses of attacks and sightings, which are multivocal in their own right, and the social actions that Puerto Ricans have pursued in connection to those accounts. This approach reveals that chupacabras narratives are often diagnostic of the excesses of the government of the United States in Puerto Rico, an unincorporated "commonwealth" that is neither independent nor a state of the American union. Social actions, however, do not pit witnesses and victims of the chupacabras against imperious agents of American neocolonialism. In searching for the chupacabras and its kin, Puerto Ricans have engaged commonwealth politicians, state functionaries, and even journalists, goading them into exchanges that dramatize the fractious relationship between the island's government and the citizenry it claims to serve. As I proceed, I am mindful that the distinction between discourse and social action, though useful, should not be reified. Like the figures discussed in the preceding chapters, the chupacabras shows that the circulation of stories, news, and rumors is a kind of social intervention with varied effects on conduct and politics.[6]

The analysis I offer below calls attention to satirical elements in the chupacabras episode. In doing this, I want to highlight a tendency that Niehaus has observed also, namely that the dominant takes on the occult discount satire, forcing conclusions on discourses that do not always offer closure.[7] The Comaroffs have dismissed out of hand the "lurid" and "salacious" appearance of the new breeds. They affirm that only from the "cool distance" of the academy could one think of the Howick Monster in terms of satire and ignore the extent to which fantastical beings resonate with the experiences of ordinary people living in postcolonial societies. To this, the anthropologists add a necessary reminder: occult transactions should not be dismissed as laughing matters, especially when they can be seen to generate quotidian and extraordinary forms of violence, including mob justice for those accused of dealing in the occult.[8]

The Comaroffs are not the only influential scholars to dismiss the vulgar on the grounds that rumors of unspeakable ravages give metaphorical expression to real experiences. The literature on organ-theft rumors shares this tendency, too. Nancy Scheper-Hughes has argued that Latin Americans' persistent talk of people kidnapped for their body parts voices anxieties generated by an all too real global trade in organs for transplants. Such assertions have their critics, but few have attempted to recover the lurid for analysis. Stephan Palmié, for example, has argued that rumors that speak of threats to bodily integrity are better understood as analytical devices that allow those who experience commodification in their own bodies to produce "spontaneous historiographies." Luise White, for her part, has aimed to subvert the logic of Scheper-Hughes's interpretation. She argues that one might see instances of a literal traffic in organs as lending credibility to the rumors, rather than as a reason for their demythification.[9]

Interpreting specters only as explanations and glosses on intensely experienced depredations may oversimplify the processes through which witches, wizards, and monsters have come to life in Puerto Rico. One might object on empirical grounds that by the 1990s Puerto Ricans were well acquainted with neoliberalism and with such occult dealings as drug trafficking and government corruption.[10] In that sense, there is limited evidence for the existence of an epistemic void that the chupacabras might be said to fill. My concern, however, is that the chupacabras and its predecessors may be better seen as resulting from collective engagements in shifting ecologies of representations. The narratives about the chupacabras are not only attempts by the victims of history to make sense of their plight; they are also manifestations of an evolving political rationality that has conjured allegedly irrational practices only to dispose of them. These tasks, which Talal Asad has declared essential to modern statecraft, have helped to constitute "the secular" and "the sacred" into distinct domains susceptible to management.[11] More to the point, these efforts have required the intervention of journalists, politicians, and experts who have, in effect, coauthored the discourses of the occult while insisting on the existence of credulous misbelievers.

Rather than ask how those who encountered the chupacabras came to believe in its existence, I am interested in exploring how the notion of a credulous population was sustained and put into circulation. I argue that the allegedly credulous upset the usual "hierarchies of credibility" to reveal state officials and journalists as the most literal-minded parties involved in the constitution of the occult.[12] Framing the matter in this fashion, I part company with Niehaus, whose essay attempts to ascertain the subjective conditions that explain why so many South Africans experience witchcraft narratives as plausible and indeed as real.[13]

Satire in Action

In the beginning there was the word; "chupacabras" begged for commentary and satire. Before the bloodsucking predator acquired its proper name, its attacks gave rise to tentative explanations and a good deal of disquiet. The name, however, added another dimension; it transformed the killer of farm and domestic animals into what Puerto Ricans call a *vacilón*, an exchange of sardonic comments, off-color jokes, and inventive twists of the vernacular tongue.[14] "Chupar," a verb rich in connotations of all sorts of oral pleasures, got the revelry off to a promising start. Cabras gave it lasting power. The noun invoked simultaneously the dead goats found scattered throughout the island since late 1994, the devil in his caprine form, the witches said to consort with him, the sacrificial offerings of Afro-Caribbean religions, and a large dose of innuendo. It was difficult to speak of cabras without also bringing to mind *cabrones*, an expletive with uses and undertones that the English word "cuckold" does not quite match. It is fitting, then, that at least one account credits satirist Silverio Pérez with coining the celebrated moniker.[15]

As one might expect, there were objections to the name, which proved instantly popular. Jorge Martín, a UFO investigator with his own magazine and radio show who was a leading source for the international media, proposed to rename the mysterious predator(s) EBAs, a Spanish-language acronym for "Alien Biological Entities." Martín favored the scientific-sounding neologism because it linked the chupacabras to a global coterie of cryptozoological entities such as Big Foot. According to Martín, the federal government, the military establishment of the United States, and Puerto Rican authorities had orchestrated a broad-ranging conspiracy to suppress signs of these creatures and their off-world origins. The host of Univisión's television show *Ocurrió Así* also expressed regret about the name. The broadcaster cautioned that its crassness contributed to the reluctance of Puerto Rican and federal governments to investigate the attacks.

The record suggests that Univisión's man was not far off the mark. Canóvanas's mayor, José Ramón "Chemo" Soto, and Representatives Juan E. Sánchez and José Núñez González were the only politicians to call for an official inquiry. But Soto and the legislators, both of whom sat on the Agriculture Committee of Puerto Rico's House of Representatives, were circumspect about their understanding of the attacks. They did not speak of aliens who mutilated their prey or genetic experiments gone awry, nor did they refer to Satanism or vampires, as others did. Instead, the politicians spoke dutifully of gauging the extent of the losses to small farmers and assuaging the concerns of the citizenry. Soto, who was running for reelection in a northeastern town where numerous attacks were reported, was mindful of appeals coming from evangelical Protestants who had spotted the chupacabras. As Robin Derby has noted, Pentecostals constituted an important voting block in Canóvanas.[16] Eager to take advantage of a populist opening as they were, Soto, Sánchez, and Núñez González worried about being associated too closely with the improbable rumors and tawdry jokes that the chupacabras inspired. In calling for an investigation, they took care to distance themselves from the irreverent moniker. They prefaced all allusions to goatsuckers with the judicious disclaimer "so-called."[17] Few things trumpeted the start of vacilón as loudly as the word "chupacabras" issuing from the mouths of broadcasters and elected officials.[18]

But there was more than political opportunism and bawdiness to the chupacabras episode; the elusive creature, so skilled at evading repeated capture attempts, laid down a trap of its own. The predator dug a discursive pit that caught more than one officious politician and many of the experts who sought to dismiss the rumors by means of rational-sounding explanations. Puerto Rico's reportedly superstitious populace feasted on the pretensions of the reasonable and the decorous. Witnesses to the chupacabras's movements redeployed reports that seemed to confirm their irrational bent to needle government officials who failed to act and experts who failed to explain; in the process, the latter were revealed as unwilling interlocutors who sought silence while professing a desire for open dialogues.

The chupacabras exposed to ridicule those whose interest in the attacks seemed overly zealous. Tabloids and call-in shows echoed calls for the government to deliver adequate protection and a persuasive accounting of the killings. But the politicians who heeded such pleas risked mockery and unmasking. When Soto organized a series of expeditions that aimed to capture the chupacabras using a live, caged goat as bait, Arturo Yépez penned an editorial cartoon that christened him "Canóvanas Jones." The identification of the mayor with Indiana Jones was acclaimed widely. Even Soto took it in stride.[19] But Puerto Rico's police superintendent, Pedro Toledo, criticized him for promoting "collective hysteria" and endangering the public. Melba Rivera, Soto's opponent in the upcoming race for Canóvanas's mayoral seat, called for an investigation to determine if her rival had diverted municipal funds to finance his "safaris."[20] Even would-be beneficiaries of Soto's efforts questioned his motives. When the mayor visited Rita Franceschini, the owner of a dog that had fallen victim to the predator, she asked what he would do if he captured the chupacabras. Soto replied that he would call the media. But Franceschini's husband cut the mayor off, saying: "What you will do is run for governor." Soto and the Franceschinis laughed aloud as journalists looked on.[21]

In making outlandish rumors cause for official actions, Soto and the legislators upset what Ann Stoler called the state's "hierarchies of credibility."[22] Although the mayor cited reasons of state, his initiatives and remarks flouted the rules of the political game. In some interviews, Soto entertained the possibility that the chupacabras might be of extraterrestrial origin. Moreover, while hunting for the creature, Soto supplemented his arsenal with a large crucifix, a plea for supernatural assistance so redolent with pop culture references that it bordered on a parody of piety. As far as most rationalists were concerned, Soto's excursions were exercises in futility, nothing less than invitations to multiple rounds of hide-and-seek. A search of the Canóvanas countryside would never provide answers to the sorts of questions that science and good government should pose: Were the killings the acts of local or exotic predators, or the work of human hands? What should be done about those who were vulnerable to fear due to their ignorance? What should be done about those that imported dangerous animals, perpetrated hoaxes, or threatened the public order with their meddling?

The notion that Soto's activities could have discomfiting consequences found some validation during the mayor's first expedition. In addition to a large contingent of Puerto Rican and international reporters, more than 200 volunteers, including off-duty police officers, joined the search party on the evening of 29 October 1995. The date itself suggested a certain lack of decorum; this was the last weekend night before Halloween. Because the majority of the participants were uninvited civilians who turned up armed and dressed in camouflage, they came to be known as "los Rambos." The tag harmonized with Soto's movie-inspired nickname. It also sounded a jovial note amid the din of paramilitary activity. The reference to Sylvester Stallone's overwrought Vietnam veteran repositioned Soto's bushwhacking foray; already reminiscent of the African hunting parties and jungle patrols of American cinema, the search for the chupacabras became a costumed romp. To the consternation of police brass, the Rambos even managed to fire a few shots at the shadows.[23]

Episodes of this sort took place elsewhere. Wherever the chupacabras or its victims were spotted, curious people gathered to search and to engage in what Puerto Ricans call *novelerear*, the leisurely pursuit of the latest. Because many of these unsanctioned searches took place at night in the semirural periphery of towns, many came equipped with night vision gear and other pieces of military surplus. UFO investigators arrived loaded with equipment and their own agendas, but their calls for seriousness were not always heeded. Though some gatherings were staid, others were carnivalesque affairs. Teenagers congregated by the road-side, hamming it up for television cameras and pausing sporadically to search the brush. Taunts and the noise of traffic punctuated the late nights.

The chupacabras played the part of a carnival *diablito*, leading revelers in performances that amounted to biting satires of well-governed citizenship.[24] Eyewitnesses and those willing to credit them pitted their own stories and the rumors they had overheard against the versions that officials put forth. Hearsay and what passed for facts circulated in tit-for-tat exchanges quite unlike the hermetic monologues described in many sociological studies of "conspiracy thinking."[25] These performances dramatized the absurdity of the prescribed modes of communication between citizens, politicians, and civil servants. Functionaries faced with the uncanniest of reports referred those who required assistance from one branch of the bureaucracy to the next, reminding citizens that the Department of Agriculture handled complaints related to the death of domestic animals while the Department of Natural Resources was responsible for wildlife, unless, of course, the event had occurred on federal land. In such cases, the Park Service or the military would have to be contacted.

Much of the exchange between citizens and the government concerned the historical record, or, put more trenchantly, what historian Luise White calls "the usable past."[26] Those eager to discount the stories called attention to Puerto Rico's folklore and the islanders' penchant for superstition. They concerned themselves with questions of origins and reminded the public that the chupacabras was the latest in a series of preternatural predators. It was generally agreed that the most recent flare-up had occurred in 1975. At that time, a flying, bloodsucking creature similar to the chupacabras had gone on a killing spree that claimed hundreds of animals. *El Vocero*, a daily that specializes in crime chronicles, which was then in its first year of circulation, had called the perpetrator "el Vampiro de Moca" after the western town where the attacks began.[27] Those who were persuaded that something was amiss did not deny the parallels between the chupacabras and the vampiro, but they made a different use of the past. In the historical record they found evidence of unsolved mysteries that demanded resolution. Rather than explaining the chupacabras, history suggested to them that the rumors, with their talk of government cover-ups, made plausible claims. In their review, they had occasion to recall many moments when the relationship between officials and citizens had shown itself to be grotesque.

Action and inaction suggested that the authorities had something to hide. The official response to the chupacabras called into question the government's interest in fact-finding and exposed its efforts to drape a "veil of transparency" over a pile of carcasses that grew to enormous proportions in a matter of months.[28] By April 1996, the chupacabras had claimed more than 2,000 victims in Puerto Rico alone. Although politicians claimed to seek the truth, they were quick to offer explanations that failed to account for the countless details that eyewitnesses put before them. If feral dogs or imported predators had killed the animals, as the government's experts insisted, why had no blood been spilled in the attacks? What about the surgical precision of the wounds? What about the missing genitalia? If human beings had done this, why did the remains not exhibit rigor mortis? And what about the UFO sightings that accompanied attacks? Confronted with a surfeit of information that could not be accepted as evidence, government officials ceased collecting the carcasses that animal owners saved in the name of science and good citizenship. On those occasions when remains and testimonials were collected, the authorities failed to disclose their findings. If the legislature ever produced the report that Soto and his colleagues requested, it was never made public. Nor were the results of necropsies performed on the victims of the chupacabras ever released. Veterinarians with Puerto Rico's Department of Agriculture spoke to the press, but they held on to their records.[29]

The absence of sanctioned data did not pose an impediment to the revelry or to private investigations. UFOlogists and the tabloid press found their own veterinarian in Dr. Carlos Soto, a private practitioner with offices in Toa Alta. His necropsies, some of which were videotaped for broadcast, concluded that no known predator could be blamed for the mounting death toll.[30] The vacilón, however, moved on without need of titled experts. With a bit of perverse wit, even an empty cage could be made to speak of a monstrous presence. In November of 1995 it was said that a couple had managed to capture a goatsucker and had kept it for six days in their home in San Lorenzo's barrio Hato. Regrettably, by the time researchers and reporters made their way to the house, the creature was gone. Still, the story did not disappoint partisans of the chupacabras. The vacant cage was discussed avidly. In many ways, it was the very point of the narrative. This is because, according to the couple, a group of police officers and unidentified government agents, Puerto Ricans by their reckoning, had seized their captive, which had turned out to be a surprisingly small and tame animal. True to their image, police officers warned the couple to remain silent, adding that if they spoke out, they would suffer financial losses. Inspectors would declare the couple's rental property "contaminated" and the government would break its lease.[31]

Because this and other rumors traced a clear line of demarcation between salt-of-the-earth eyewitnesses and abusive naysayers in government, it bears underscoring that the vacilón—as discourse and as social action—often bridged that divide. One need only recall that mayors, legislators, and police officers took part in the revelry and contributed to the rumors. Their participation was not always unwitting.

The Lurid, the Salacious, and the Dreadful

Journalists, like scholars, found it difficult to account for the ribald exchanges that accompanied the chupacabras. In Puerto Rico and abroad, mainline reportage muffled the bawdy elements of the stories and denied Joneses and Rambos the leading parts. Instead, journalists constructed sensible but fragile distinctions between that which belonged to dread and that which could be discounted as mere play. Elisions and occasional fabrications were necessary to segregate true believers—the protagonists of journalistic and scholarly narratives—from those who played irreverent games. In packaging rumors and testimonials for consumption as news, the press rendered unintelligible the actions discussed above. Provocation and vacilón became the pleas of a population in the grip of panic.

Journalistic reports offered an ambivalent accounting of Puerto Ricans' encounters with bloodsuckers. Some news noted the satirical performances that both the chupacabras and the vampiro had inspired. Most, however, rendered salacious images in faint colors to paint panic in a sharp palette. In 1975, the editors of the island's leading dailies refused to cover the Vampiro de Moca precisely because they found the material unfit for publication. *El Vocero* was the only paper to report the attacks regularly. When the Puerto Rico Association of Journalists censured that paper's Moca correspondent, Augusto R. Vale Salinas, for reporting "tasteless" stories that verged on "obscurantism," most reporters applauded the decision.[32] After all, Vale Salinas and his daily had clearly contributed to the spectacle. The tabloid had published numerous cartoons, sardonic verses, and several photographs of dubious newsworthiness. Besides signature images of blood and gore, the latter included a picture of a man who posed by a Moca roadside sign in a Count Dracula costume complete with prosthetic fangs. Vale Salinas insisted, however, that the fright was real and newsworthy. Moca's rural people, its *campesinos*, were truly frightened. The town square was empty. Windows had been nailed shut in many homes. Barrio Cruz's residents had even organized a posse.[33] In Vale Salinas's reportage, the vacilón was an appendix to the narrative; satire deserved a nod of acknowledgment, but it remained outside of the plot.

By the 1990s, when bloodsuckers were spotted again, editorial policies had loosened. *El Vocero*, by then the best-selling newspaper on the island, covered the attacks assiduously, as did other dailies. (Some critics saw this as evidence of a decline in journalistic standards, but the declension narrative does not stand up to scrutiny.)[34] Although *El Vocero* editor Germán Negroni acknowledged that he initially regarded the attacks as pranks, the coverage in his paper did not always reflect this. Instead, *El Vocero* and other dailies tended to replicate narrative strategies pioneered in the 1970s: the reports distinguished between scared believers and those who got the joke. Though journalists and editors aligned themselves with the second group, they cited the concerns of the first to justify the coverage.[35]

By the time the goatsucker's story hit the international press, evidence of vacilón had receded even further from view. Most correspondents referred to a panic in Puerto Rico without noting the extent of the satire. The *Washington Post's* Karl Ross, for instance, criticized *El Vocero* for spreading fear and faulted the Puerto Rican government for launching an investigation that lent credibility to the chupacabras. Ross, however, felt no need to question the tabloid's assertions that the chupacabras had unleashed a wave of "hysteria."[36] Ironically, reports such as Ross's gave rise to a lewd brand of bloodsucker nationalism that found its way to the Puerto Rican press and even the *Boston Globe*.[37] The international visibility of the chupacabras and its attacks abroad, notably in Mexico and the United States, led some to claim ownership of the creature and assert its Puerto Ricanness emphatically, albeit in terms that politicians could not appropriate. Chauvinism and satire combined concisely in one of countless jokes: "Question: What do you get when you cross a chupacabras and a coquí? Answer: A chupaquí."[38]

Startling omissions were required to arrange the chupacabras episode into a narrative of spreading panic. The following instance underscores the point: *El Vocero* and Puerto Rico's electronic media reported that late on the night of 23 December 1995 a mysterious assailant attacked Osvaldo Claudio as he washed his car at home. The story went that the chupacabras grabbed Claudio from behind as he turned to shut off a garden hose. In the fight that ensued, the creature dug its claws deep into the man's abdomen. It then fled the scene. Shortly after this incident, similar attacks were reported in other locations.[39] The news that human lives were at risk fueled the demand for government action and confirmed the wisdom of Soto's preemptive actions.

Sensational as the reports were, they masked much of the vacilón that the news also unleashed. Claudio's interview with Jorge Martín, the UFO investigator, revealed that a strong current of eroticism had been suppressed in the newspaper reports. It appears that Claudio had first mistaken his assailant for his wife because rather than grabbing him, the creature had embraced him from behind, caressing his sides and stomach. Claudio responded by asking his wife to "quit it," and only then did he realize that "an enormous apelike creature, some seven or eight feet tall" was handling him. Claudio's wounds were the result of his efforts to escape the embrace. Moreover, Claudio charged that no journalist had interviewed him. Reporters assumed that the chupacabras had inflicted his wounds, when the attack had been perpetrated by a creature that resembled Big Foot.[40]

The tendency of the press to purge its accounts of sexual content may have been part of a halfhearted effort to stay a course of propriety. The omissions, however, maintained distinctions that obscured the satirical elements of the chupacabras genre. To distinguish between revelers and earnest witnesses, these accounts ignored the fact that many who stood face-to-face with bloodsuckers could have been persuaded to join in the revelry. Dread and vacilón were of a piece. Madeline Tolentino, a Canóvanas resident who had seen the chupacabras, remarked in an interview that a young boy—one of the many innocents that the press paraded alongside so-called peasants—had misled reporters and investigators about what he had seen. The boy's testimony had produced a sketch in which the chupacabras appeared to have a "pointy tail" and "vulgar genitals." When Tolentino was shown the sketch, she urged the boy to tell the truth: the chupacabras did not have an outsize penis.[41] Instead, it looked like the creatures in Species, a sci-fi thriller she rented soon after her encounters. Tolentino's husband did note, however, that the chupacabras was not unconcerned with sexual matters, as sometimes it removed the genitalia of its victims.[42] Several commentators and scholars, including Derby, have taken notice of the predator's preoccupation with reproductive organs. But here, too, seriousness trumps satire, as the chupacabras is said to recall U.S.-sponsored programs to control the fertility of Puerto Rican women.[43]

In highlighting the religious affiliations of eyewitnesses, journalistic narratives of the chupacabras erected a wall between believers and nonbelievers. The reports suggested that the sightings and the dread they inspired were ultimately matters of faith. They also implied that satire belonged in the nonbelievers' camp.[44] Although it is true that some leading witnesses looked upon the bloodsuckers through religious lenses, it is difficult to accept a distinction between believers and nonbelievers with full confidence. When one looks beyond the reports of the mainstream media, one finds that vacilón was not reserved for miscreants, nor did the circulation of rumors depend entirely on those who professed to believe.

In 1975, witnesses described the vampiro as a large, foul-smelling, winged animal. Judging by the countermeasures they deployed, some must have been convinced that the vampiro was demonic. In a well-publicized instance, a man described as a campesino painted large crosses on the hindquarters of his only cow in an effort to ward off the devil. Rumors linking the killings to a group of alleged Satan worshippers also circulated at the time. Satanism was invoked again in 1995. Witnesses referred to the "sulphurous" smell of the chupacabras, and there were stories regarding Santería and Haitian "sects." Luis Angel Guadalupe and his brother-in-law, who were chased by the predator while they fished in Rio Canóvanas in 1995, described their pursuer as "the devil himself." In December of the same year, Eliezer Rivera, a Pentecostal minister who is also a police detective, reported seeing the bloodsucker hovering in the middle of a dark Canóvanas road. Although Rivera did not say that he had seen Lucifer, others interpreted the incident as a demonic visitation.

The press, however, seldom remarked on the involvement of those who might be described as people of little faith. The deaths of two chicks and a hen were added to the tally of the vampiro's victims on 11 March 1975. What the papers did not mention was that the owner of the birds, Juana Arocho Soto, quickly withdrew the complaint she had filed with the police. In an interview with the investigating officer, Arocho explained that she had reported the incident at her neighbors' insistence. She had no doubt that an ordinary predator had killed her birds.[45] The police closed the case without calling the media. And the vampiro went on.

If such stories proved difficult to discredit, it was largely because many participants did not strive for facticity.[46] Eliezer Rivera, who was indeed concerned with proving that his account was truthful, prefaced his narrative with the assertion that he had not credited reports about the chupacabras until encountering it himself. (In this regard, his account followed the structure of a conversion story.) The minister's concern with verisimilitude was not shared throughout Puerto Rico, however. When Rivera failed a polygraph test administered on a television talk show, reports of attacks continued unabated.[47]

Vital Discourses, Dead Issues

The depredations of Puerto Rico's bloodsuckers covered the map of the island. Although the vampiro was associated with Moca and the chupacabras was linked largely with Canóvanas, attacks and sightings were reported in nearly every corner, including the island municipality of Vieques. No area was wholly exempt. The bloodsuckers appeared in mountain roads, commercial farms, suburbs (*ur-*

banizaciones), and junkyards, as well as in the middle of Santurce's commercial district, where the chupacabras perched itself on the building of the Water and Sewerage Authority to consume a dead rat.[48]

Although there were no fixed rules, there were identifiable patterns. The vampiro and the chupacabras both favored backyards and small plots in the outlying barrios of peripheral towns, where disquiet and vacilón merged. The recurrent outbreaks of animal deaths were simultaneously tragic and comical; they spoke of a countryside that had reverted to a feral state after suffering urban sprawl, environmental degradation, and the near collapse of small-scale agriculture. Rumors and reports asserted the wildness of what remained and rendered this wilderness unnatural. The news called for the intervention of experts in the arcane and exotic. Zoologists shared the limelight with parapsychologists, UFO investigators, and a few explorers of the Amazon River.[49] What remained of Puerto Rico's rural landscape was relocated to the edge of the jungle.

The depredations called attention to other menacing places, too. The chupacabras's attacks illuminated the guarded perimeters of lands and facilities under the control of the U.S. federal government, rendering these zones mysterious when not downright sinister.[50] The rumors seemed to suggest that the American presence in the island had farcical qualities, too. Witnesses in Canóvanas insisted that if the chupacabras had managed to avoid capture, it was because it made escapes into El Yunque, a subtropical rainforest managed by the U.S. Department of Agriculture Forest Service.[51] They asserted that Forest Service agents colluded with the creature or its handlers. Citing the closing of a road due to hurricane damage, agents of the U.S. Department of Agriculture, along with unidentified federal officials, turned away people in hot pursuit of the chupacabras. A few environment-minded commentators theorized flippantly that the predator itself was an endangered species of the sort El Yunque had been intended to protect.[52] The chupacabras, they explained, had sought refuge in El Yunque and Toro Negro, a rainforest located in the west, fleeing deforestation and pollution in the rest of Puerto Rico. Evidently, not even the noblest justifications for government actions were off-limits to the vacilón. Federal agents had failed to live up to the responsibilities that legitimated the use of power but had not given up coercive authority. Enforcers whose presence was seldom noticed came into view precisely as these failures became evident.

Those who inferred a connection between the dead animals and an increase in the number of sightings of unidentified flying objects noted that UFOs often appeared in or near places like a controversial radar installation in Lajas, managed by the U.S. Navy, the National Guard's Camp Santiago in Salinas, and

Roosevelt Roads Naval Station in Ceiba. A Puerto Rican janitor employed at Fort Buchanan, an army base in the heart of San Juan's metropolitan area, maintained that the frozen body of a dead chupacabras had been hidden there and that military officers had threatened him to stay silent.[53]

Allegations of conspiracies abounded. At a minimum, the federal government was charged with knowing more about the attacks than it acknowledged. But many suspected worse. The chupacabras itself could well be the product of experiments in genetic engineering conducted secretly on the island, or the result of successful attempts to contact alien life in space, as evidenced by the sighting of unidentified crafts. Although the Puerto Rican government was thought to have a hand in the cover-up, their involvement was said to be in a subaltern capacity.

Such charges were not new, nor were they as far-fetched as they might appear. The vampiro's depredations coincided with a dramatic rise in UFO sightings and with a renewal of miracles in Sabana Grande, where the Virgin Mary had appeared in 1953. Some took this for evidence that all the phenomena were interconnected. In 1975, witnesses reported seeing UFOs flying low over an area in Moca's barrio Mamey, where twelve goats were found dead. Similar reports came in from El Yunque and Ceiba, not far from the Roosevelt Roads naval base, one of the largest installations of its kind outside of the United States.[54] Rather than viewing these narratives as tall tales fabricated out of whole cloth, such rumors may be interpreted as meditations on dreadful and laughable possibilities. If reasons of state could permit the manipulation of women's reproductive systems without much apparent regard for Puerto Ricans' rights, why could not the state be supposed to engage secretly in other experimental monstrosities?[55] If a protected zone like El Yunque could be used to test defoliating chemicals like Agent Orange, could the rainforest offer cover for other depredations? If scientists at Arecibo's Radio Observatory were engaged in efforts to contact other life forms in space, could not they have succeeded in inviting a monstrous visitation? If the U.S. military pursued might without restraint, could not something like the chupacabras have gotten away from its walled compounds?[56]

Robin Derby's work on the chupacabras offers a provocative analysis of rumors involving the federal government. Rather than portraying Puerto Rico as a site of recent capitalist penetration, Derby has argued that Puerto Rico's neocolonial relationship with the United States may have insulated the island from the impact of the latest rounds of globalization. The chupacabras, she notes, speaks not of unfamiliarity with new political and economic structures but of an intimate acquaintance with them. Derby contends that under the commonwealth system, "the very concealment of federal authorities and their motivations produces a particular kind of 'state fantasy' or 'state effect' as people wonder and talk about what transpires behind the mask of power." This, in turn, accounts for Puerto Ricans' tendency to engage in spectacular "rites of exposure," such as the public unmasking of federal involvement in the attacks perpetrated by the chupacabras.[57]

Rather than challenge Derby's contentions, which I find persuasive, I want to offer a few qualifiers. I want to recall that the chupacabras discourses and social actions were not always aimed at federal agents. I also want to note that the rumors in question were not always proposed as matters of fact. Instead, they were asserted as inferences and defensible charges that took what was known already to its most laughable consequences. The bloodsuckers hinted and provoked, but they could not settle the veracity of all claims once and for all; with so many officials operating in secret, controlling access to evidence, pressuring witnesses, and engaging in disinformation campaigns, it could scarcely be otherwise.[58] UFO researchers, for example, charged that at first officials refused to collect the dead animals, study samples, or interview witnesses. Government personnel told callers that they were understaffed, that the tissue had not been preserved adequately, or that the Department of Natural Resources (DNR) rather than this or that agency was responsible for collecting materials. For its part, DNR officials claimed that they had no jurisdiction over matters involving domesticated animals. But once witnesses and others took the gathering of evidence into their own hands, deputizing their own experts (see below), officials from the Department of Agriculture, the Civil Defense, and police formed a "task force," and paramilitary organizations associated with the federal government allegedly turned up at killing sites, collecting evidence that was never seen again.

State officials also proposed unsatisfactory explanations, blaming the attacks on criminals, packs of feral dogs, and even Rhesus monkeys. But these explanations failed to assuage suspicions. In a telling instance, a police officer fired his service revolver and killed what he thought was the chupacabras; the victim turned out to be a monkey. But far from confirming official accounts and bringing rumors to an end, the episode had little effect. If anything, the incident tended to fuel speculation. If the officer had killed a monkey in an island that had no such indigenous fauna, it was precisely because these animals had escaped from an experimental reserve in Cayo Punta Santiago, as state officials themselves acknowledged. If this much was true, couldn't more ominous creatures have followed similar routes?[59]

Given these signs, some understood the chupacabras and the vampiro as manifesting political discontents aimed squarely at incompetent Puerto Rican agencies and duplicitous, all-powerful federal authorities. The predator, it would seem, inflamed a repressed and perhaps unrealizable desire to assert the rights of citizens and end the uncertainties surrounding Puerto Rico's political status. For Farhan Haq, a writer for the Inter Press Service, the infamous sounds of the chupacabras were groans (if not quite cries) for Puerto Rican independence. Haq found little cause for surprise in the goatsucker's depredations. As he put it, "At a time when Puerto Ricans still cling to autonomy from the United States, and when the island's mountain[-]based, proindependence forces have been largely quiet, the rise of a mythical national beast like the chupacabra may not be so odd, after all."[60]

Tempting as it is to follow Haq, his was a rather facile interpretation of the denunciation of colonialism and federal power implicit in many of the accounts above. Closer examination should have revealed difficulties in rendering the parodies into equations compatible with the formulae of Puerto Rico's partisan politics. In 1975, the Socialist organ *Claridad* looked at the vampiro's depredations and found no auspicious sentiments for independence, in spite of the fact that the most radical sectors of the proindependence movement were then very active. Instead, *Claridad* charged that Puerto Rico's government, faced with an economic crisis and official unemployment rates above 17 percent, was "desperately looking for topics to entertain the masses." The "colonial state," which is to say, the commonwealth government itself, had seized upon the vampire to distract the populace.

In 1996, Manuel García Passalaqua, a well-known, proindependence political commentator, proposed a similar argument. Although he did not argue that the chupacabras was the result of a ploy sponsored by the pro-statehood administration, he averred that supernaturalism surfaced whenever there was a crisis involving the island's political status. In support of this assertion, García Passalaqua adduced the turmoil of the elections of 1996 and the contentious plebiscite on Puerto Rico's political status of 1998.[61]

Neither Haq nor García Passalaqua recognized the profusion of satirical interventions, nor did they perceive that these satires contested the dominant modes of political dialogue at a moment when the conversation became most predictable. The denunciation of the ploys of the federal government did not imply a pronouncement in favor of independence. Mayor Soto, the most notorious chupacabras chaser, was a member of the pro-statehood party, as were Representatives Sánchez and Núñez González. Moreover, the statehood party was in control of the commonwealth government, an irony that was not lost on those who saw Soto asking for the governor's assistance to a very tepid response. One could suggest, as some scholars have, that the pro-statehooders' interest in the chupacabras expressed that political sector's anxieties over their own role in the destabilization of Puerto Rico's boundaries, but here, too, the evidence is inconclusive.[62] Statehooders were not alone in making claims on Puerto Rico's bloodsuckers. In the days of the Vampiro de Moca, it was Popular Democratic Party (PPD) politicians, those in favor of the commonwealth system, who called for investigations and fueled the rumor mill. Rather than argue that the procommonwealth sector suffered from misgivings about its hand in Puerto Ricans' alleged identity crisis, one might note the bloodsuckers' tendency to ensnare politicians in power regardless of the agendas they espoused.

A Wilderness Fit for Experts

Alongside politicians and law enforcement officers, the bloodsuckers called forth historians who sought to discipline revelers and demagogues so as to quell any panic that persisted. In a typical instance, a retired university professor wrote a letter to the editor of *El Nuevo Día* in which he cited Luis Díaz Soler's histories to explain the depredations of the chupacabras. He noted that Díaz Soler had found evidence of large vampire bats that attacked cattle and human beings, much to the consternation of Puerto Rico's nineteenth-century peasants. Other scholars saw the chupacabras as a contemporary updating of familiar Caribbean folklore, with its vampires, werewolves, and specters. In either case, the killers were either revenants from a forgotten past or harbingers of "the folklore of the future."[63]

While these analyses aimed to silence the rumors and halt the social actions they set in motion, experts that one might classify as "disrespectful" sought to keep the dialogue and the vacilón going. The likes of UFO investigators and latter-day jíbaros, Puerto Rico's exalted rural folk, often lionized as the truest national types, revealed the obfuscations of the state and the ferocity of the countryside.[64] The two groups shared a mordant wit, a talent for yarns, and a deep suspicion of the government. They also had a hand in digging the pit that captured politicians and experts who wanted nothing to do with bloodsuckers.

In 1975, there were numerous interpretations of the vampiro in circulation. Some credited a fifty-pound black bird that went so far as to attack a construction worker as he walked home. Others associated the killings with bats said to live in caves near Moca.[65] And yet others suspected exotic predators, including a "flock" of bloodsucking snakes, which appeared to be hiding in fields and caves in the northwest. But the most notable advocates of this vision of a feral country were don Luis Aldarondo, a seventy-eight-year-old "peasant," and his twenty-five-year-old son, José Daniel. The two were reported to be expert snake hunters from Aguadilla, a town adjacent to Moca and home to Ramey Air Force Base.

Drawing on their experience in the snake oil business, father and son organized several expeditions in search of the creatures responsible for the deaths in Moca and its environs. And on 16 March 1975 they succeeded; they captured two snakes that they found wrapped around the leg and neck of a calf. *El Vocero* appeared ready to dispose of the vampiro then and there. It ran the story under the headline "Vampires Discovered: They Are Enormous Serpents." This news attracted hundreds, who gathered at the police station in Moca. Lt. Enrique González, the district's highest-ranking police officer, took the opportunity to reassure the public that there were no vampires. Taking his cue from the hunters, González insisted that snakes were responsible for the killings. This did little to assuage concerns that a "maniac" could be responsible for the killings, the interpretation that the police had favored for months.[66]

News of the demise of the vampiro proved premature. No one ensured that the vacilón would go on better than the hunters. If don Luis and José Daniel were jíbaros, they belonged in an unfamiliar country and they were engaged in more than one hunt. José Daniel, known as "Danny el fakir," had a varied resume. He had worked as a magician in Puerto Rico and the United States. He had been crucified in public spectacles. And he had tended elephants in a circus in Aguadilla, from which he claimed several boas escaped. He reasoned that the drought affecting the region had caused reptiles to abandon their hideouts for the open, where they wrought havoc.[67] He also made public his suspicion that someone had taken advantage of the situation to play pranks in a vampire costume. But then, as if to advertise a sideshow, Danny and don Luis announced that they intended to conduct another expedition. They hoped to capture "the mother of all serpents," whom they called "the Seven Heads."[68]

The failures of the authorities, in this case Puerto Rico's law enforcement agents, were laid bare following the capture of the snakes. *El Vocero's* editorials and other media that claimed to speak for the public issued calls for "decisive [government] intervention." Senator Miguel A. Deynés Soto (PPD), who represented Aguadilla and Mayagüez, asked police to redouble their efforts to find the culprits, whom he was certain were human beings. Days later, the police announced that they were about to arrest several "two-legged vampires." The unidentified parties were suspected of staging the killings, which began on Héctor Vega's livestock farm in Moca, in an effort to bring down the value of his property before making him an offer.[69] It appears that shortly before the attacks, Vega had revealed his desire to urbanize one-fifth of his land. But nothing came of these rumors; in the end, no arrests were made. Instead, the issue disappeared from the news, but not before Vega had reported a visit from a government official who tried to buy his land. If there were bloodsuckers ready to profit from his misfortunes, they seemed to be on the state payroll. The characterization of the state as vampire—already implicit in the rumors—found its clearest expression in "la vampirita," the popular name given to an unpopular tax introduced in 1976.[70]

Disrespectful Remarks, Invitations to Dialogue

The vampiro and the chupacabras exposed afflictions plaguing Puerto Ricans in their dealings with federal and commonwealth government officials. The attacks spoke of a rural world that reasserted its ferocity, and of politicians who sought to mask their opportunism. The handling of the killings betrayed the state's blood-sucking machinations and more than one conspiracy. But these narratives of occult depredations were the stuff of spectacle-making and satire, too. Crowds gathered at killing sites to steal a glimpse of the monsters, make demands of officials, and participate in the vacilón. The vampiro and the chupacabras set the stage for exchanges that highlighted the laughable absurdities of the state in action and inaction and poked fun at prescribed modes of communication. Still, these discourses and social actions did more than reiterate Puerto Ricans' historical grievances; they articulated those grievances in a manner that resisted translation into the partisan formulae that the island's political parties promoted. Instead, chupacabras discourses authorized allegedly credulous citizens to speak for themselves.

Readers familiar with Puerto Rico's politics might recall that the citizenry's frustration with politicking was plain even before the plebiscite of 1998. After a year of vociferous disputes regarding the future of the commonwealth's relationship to the United States, historical and legal definitions of Puerto Rican identity, and the rights of island-born residents, after protests and counterprotests, massive street marches, and too many speeches, the plebiscite ended with a repudiation of all the options on the ballot. A clause reading "none of the above" earned more votes than the pro-statehood, procommonwealth, and proindependence proposals combined. One might characterize this impasse as evidence of a crisis of identity. Or one might describe the failure as evidence of a growing consensus over the sterility of the debate. If voters conveyed anything, it was their dissatisfaction with the millennial claims advanced by politicians in spite of an evident stalemate. As in earlier plebiscites—there have been three since the 1960s—politicians failed to offer detailed descriptions of what each status formula would entail, and they were unable to specify how the transition from the present system would be conducted. Final determination of such things rests with the Congress of the United States, which refused to lay out exact terms.

It is tempting to cast the vampiro and the chupacabras, bloodsuckers both, as manifesting vernacular forms of analysis that challenge the political rationality of the government and the disciplines of citizenship. But the vacilón points at other possibilities, too. The narratives of killings and conspiracies were in the fashion of inappropriate, disrespectful remarks in the course of exchanges that should have been serious (and often pointless) if the ordinary norms had prevailed. If these satirical performances deserve attention, it is because they offer one way of viewing the hidden works of the governing rationality, and because they point at ongoing efforts to open dialogues whose outcomes are not preordained.

Viewed in this light, the chupacabras attacks offered a rare opportunity; through the circulation of stories of ravages and the safaris those rumors inspired, it became possible to divorce the talk of citizenship from mere partisanship. The vacilón steered the public conversation away from propriety and predictability, allowing a profusion of criticisms to be voiced that could not be uttered in well-regulated venues without inviting canned responses. Rather than speaking through political representatives, those Fernando Picó has called *los irrespetuosos* took positions behind makeshift podiums throughout the island to the delight of sympathizers and the annoyance of those who regarded the chupacabras as an embarrassment.[71] Instead of explaining the rise of ill-understood phenomena, the chupacabras marked a detour. The predator denaturalized history and the norms of public speech. As the stories circulated, quotidian exchanges became noteworthy. They appeared at once gruesome and laughable, showing the relationships between citizens, the government, and the federal authorities in all their stagnation. In this regard, one might say that to speak of bloodsuckers was akin to the voodoo practice of working *wanga*. As Karen McCarthy Brown has shown, wanga, or so-called charms, are both "representations of troubled relationships" and ways of "solving the problem they represent."[72]

NOTES

Abbreviations

AGPR	Archivo General de Puerto Rico, San Juan
AH	Audiencia de la Habana
AHD	Archivo Histórico Diocesano, San Juan
ANC	Archivo Nacional de Cuba, Havana
APS	Archivo Provincial de Santiago de Cuba
AS	Audiencia de Santiago de Cuba
Fondo GP	Fondo Gobierno Provincial
leg.	Legajo
USNA	National Archives, Washington, DC

Introduction

1. *El Vocero*, 3 March 1906; 9 April 1975; *Claridad*, 1 April 1975; 2 April 1975.

2. *San Juan Star*, 19 November 1906; *San Juan Star* (Venue), 27 November 1995.

3. *El Vocero*, 25, 26, and 30 October 1995.

4. *El Vocero*, 2 November 1995.

5. *San Juan Star*, 6 May 1996; Corrales, *Chupacabras and Other Mysteries*; J. Martín, *La conspiración Chupacabras*.

6. Comaroff and Comaroff, "Occult Economies and the Violence of Abstraction," 281.

7. Robin Derby has linked the spread of chupacabras attacks in Latin America's "gray zones" to a shared history of imperial domination and capitalist penetration. She argues that the chupacabras preyed on Puerto Rico and northern Mexico because colonialism and globalization blurred boundaries in those locales, fostering the sense that the body politic was vulnerable. See Derby, "Vampiros del Imperio," 317–45.

8. See, among others, Cooper, Holt, and Scott, *Beyond Slavery*.

9. Bermúdez, "Notas para la historia del espiritismo en Cuba," 5–22; Koss, "Religion and Science Divinely Related," 22–43.

10. Ferrer, *Insurgent Cuba*, chap. 7.

11. De la Fuente, *A Nation for All*, 50.

12. Pérez, *Cuba between Empires*, 279.

13. Trías Monge, *Puerto Rico*, 43, 69; Santiago-Valles, *"Subject People" and Colonial Discourses*, 64–65.

14. Helg, *Our Rightful Share*, chap. 3; Helg, "Black Men, Racial Stereotyping, and Violence," 576–604.

15. Bronfman, *Measures of Equality*, 42.

16. Ibid., 45–46; Palmié, *Wizards and Scientists*, chap. 3.

17. Bronfman, *Measures of Equality*, 34.

18. David Brown, *The Light Inside*, 134.

19. Santaella Rivera, *Historia de los Hermanos Cheos*, 61.

20. Silva Gotay has rejected the view that the Cheos espoused anti-American or pro-independence sentiments, but he notes the dearth of information regarding Cheo politics. See Silva Gotay, *Catolicismo y política en Puerto Rico*, 455–57.

21. Pedro Puras to Bishop William A. Jones, 6 September 1911, AHD, Sección Gobierno, Serie Correspondencia, Sub-serie San Lorenzo, Obispo, caja G27, leg. s/n 1820–1928.

22. The translation of the Cuban text is Bronfman's; see *Measures of Equality*, 3; Office of the Commonwealth of Puerto Rico, *Documents on the Constitutional History of Puerto Rico*.

23. Howard, *Changing History*, chap. 7.

24. Yáñez Vda. de Otero, *El espiritismo en Puerto Rico*; Rodríguez Escudero, *Historia del espiritismo en Puerto Rico*. Note that Puerto Rico's judicial archives have not been explored systematically.

25. Picó, "Religiosidad institucional y religiosidad popular," 36–37.

26. For the history of the anti-witchcraft campaigns, see Roche Monteagudo, *La policía y sus misterios en Cuba*; Chávez Alvarez, *El crimen de la niña Cecilia*; Helg, *Our Rightful Share*; Palmié, *Wizards and Scientists*; and Bronfman, *Measures of Equality*.

27. *Gaceta de la Habana*, 4 December 1900.

28. J. Scott, *Seeing Like a State*.

29. José Varela to Military Governor, 27 January 1902, USNA, RG 140, Military Government of Cuba, Letters Received 1902, Entry 3, Box 235, File 309 (1902).

30. Report of the Havana Detectives Bureau, 21 December 1900, USNA, RG 140, Military Government of Cuba, Letters Received, Entry 3, Box 105, File 4163 (1900).

31. See Chapter 1 and V. Turner, *Drums of Affliction*.

32. ANC, AS, leg. 13, no. 1, causa 466/1902.

33. *Carteles*, 15 July 1956; *Bohemia*, 10 June 1956.

34. De la Fuente, *A Nation for All*, 161–63.

35. *El Mundo*, 11, 25, 26 May 1953.

36. ANC, Registro de Asociaciones, leg. 1090, Exp. 22859; Márquez Sterling, "Nuestra Asociación de la Prensa," *El Fígaro*, 17 April 1904; "El periodismo," *El Fígaro*, 24 April 1904; "¡Pobrecita Zoila!," *El Fígaro*, 4 December 1904.

37. Fields, "Political Contingencies of Witchcraft in Colonial Central Africa," 578.

38. ANC, AH, leg. 471, no. 3.

39. See, among others, R. Moore, *Nationalizing Blackness*; Hagedorn, *Divine Utterances*; Ayorinde, *Afro-Cuban Religiosity, Revolution, and National Identity*; and Dávila, *Sponsored Identities*.

40. Fernando Picó, "On Sensationalism," *San Juan Star*, 11 April 1975, 21.

41. Chávez Alvarez, *El crimen de la niña Cecilia*, 33, 37; López, *La radio en Cuba*; Pino Santos, *Los años 50*, especially the prologue by Jorge Ibarra; Portuondo Zúñiga, *La Virgen de la Caridad del Cobre*, 270–71.

42. *Bohemia*, 12 September 1943; 27 May 1956.

43. See, for instance, Rolando R. Pérez, "Otra vez los 'brujos' y la muerte de un chofer," *Carteles*, 3 June 1956.

44. Pessar, *From Fanatics to Folks*, chap. 7.

45. Romberg, "From Charlatans to Saviors," 153–56.

46. Romberg, *Witchcraft and Welfare*, 94.

47. Romberg has noted the estrangement of these "saviors" in "From Charlatans to Saviors," 157.

Chapter One

1. Readers interested in man-gods in other locales may consult Gruzinski, *Man-gods in the Mexican Highlands*; Van Young, "The Messiah and the Masked Man"; and Levine, *Vale of Tears*.

2. Chávez Alvarez, *El crimen de la niña Cecilia*; Helg, *Our Rightful Share*; Palmié, *Wizards and Scientists*.

3. Some newspapers claimed that Manso was a veteran of the Cuban War of Independence (1895–98). According to *La Razón* (Remedios), Manso served in the Philippines in the Cazadores de la Habana battalion. Cited in *El Iris de Paz* (Mayagüez, Puerto Rico), 8 October 1904.

4. Foucault, *Power/Knowledge*, 81.

5. The author described the region as "doubly-superstitious" because it was populated by "Frenchified" (Haitian) blacks. See *El Fígaro*, 1 September 1901.

6. The article did not include biographical details. See *La Opinión*, 10 October 1887.

7. Spain allowed the expansion of the Cuban public sphere precisely to quell the anticolonial sentiments. See Sartorius, "Limits of Loyalty," chap. 3.

8. The preoccupation with the dangers of "Africanization" was a defining feature of political debate by the 1860s, when Spanish propagandists fostered the fear that independence would transform Cuba into another Haiti. The charge succeeded in dividing Cuban insurgents because it exploited internal cleavages in their coalition. In the late 1890s, with Cuba's victory over Spain increasingly likely, conservative patriots worried that "rus-

tic" black and mulatto army officers could take power in the nascent republic. See Ferrer, *Insurgent Cuba*.

9. Pérez, *Cuba between Empires*.

10. Personal communication, November 2000.

11. Bastide, *African Religions of Brazil*, 28, 77.

12. D. Scott, *Refashioning Futures*, 107.

13. Amselle, *Mestizo Logics*, 33.

14. D. Scott, *Refashioning Futures*, 34.

15. Fields, "Political Contingencies of Witchcraft in Colonial Central Africa," 578.

16. V. Turner, *Drums of Affliction*.

17. Ortiz, "La Virgen de Jiquiabo."

18. Reyes, *La Santa Montaña de San Lorenzo*; Santaella Rivera, *Historia de los Hermanos Cheos*; Lundius and Lundahl, *Peasants and Religion*.

19. Austin-Broos, *Jamaica Genesis*, 83, 87; Bastide, *African Civilizations in the New World*, 166; Hill, "Dread History," 49.

20. The conditions under which Mustelier and Manso emerged are described poignantly and succinctly in Pérez, *Lords of the Mountain*. De la Fuente notes that Alto Songo was among the municipalities most deeply affected by postwar land grabs; 70–90 percent of independent farms were lost in a few years. See de la Fuente, *A Nation for All*, 105–7.

21. For critiques of the crisis and response model, see Román, "Conjuring Progress and Divinity," 360–93, and Pessar, *From Fanatics to Folks*.

22. APS, Fondo GP, Materia: Espiritismo, leg. 576, no. 2.

23. Bermúdez ("Notas para la historia del espiritismo en Cuba," 8) has argued that although most Spiritist centers were not engaged in sedition, Spiritists were well represented among exiled Cuban separatists.

24. APS, Fondo GP, Materia: Espiritismo, leg. 576, no. 2.

25. Ibid.

26. Ibid.

27. Ibid.

28. Ibid.

29. APS, Fondo GP, Materia: Espiritismo, leg. 576, no. 7.

30. There is no monographic history of Cuban Spiritism. Bermúdez's articles remain the most useful accounts.

31. See *Encyclopedia of Religions*, s.v. "Kardecism."

32. In 1944, bookstore owners in Puerto Rico reported selling more than 20,000 copies of *L'évangile*. See *El Mundo* (San Juan, Puerto Rico), 30 July 1944.

33. Bermúdez, "Notas para la historia del espiritismo en Cuba," 12.

34. Carrillo and Rodríguez, *Pentecostalismo y espiritismo*, 8–9.

35. Ortiz, *La filosofía penal de los espiritistas*; Ortiz, *Historia de una pelea cubana contra los demonios*, 592.

36. Carrillo and Rodríguez, *Pentecostalismo y espiritismo*, 10.

37. Nandy and Visvanathan, "Modern Medicine and Its Non-modern Critics," 159.

38. APS, Fondo GP, Materia: Espiritismo, leg. 576, no. 2.

39. APS, Fondo GP, Materia: Sociedades Espiritistas, leg. 2490, no. 1. The list is not dated, but accompanying documents indicate that it was compiled between 1900 and 1906.

40. The listing does not mention Mustelier's "Fraternal San Hilarión," which was founded in October 1901 but which seems to have disbanded by the time of the inventory.

41. Bacardí y Moreau, *Crónicas de Santiago de Cuba*, 267–68.

42. *El Fígaro*, 1 September 1901.

43. APS, Fondo GP, Materia: Sociedades Espiritistas, leg. 2490, no. 2. See also the "Cuban Liberation Army 1895–1898 Database" online at <http://www.cubagenweb.org/mil/mambi/index.htm>. The information regarding Hilario Mustelier Garzón is drawn from a card found at the ANC in a catalog to the Fondo Ejército Libertador. The card does not offer the dates of service, but it notes correctly that Mustelier was born in Santiago de Cuba, the son of Antonio and Escolástica, and that he was sixty-seven years of age. Mustelier claimed to have served in the First Corps of the Liberation Army. I am grateful to Marial Iglesias for providing this source.

44. APS, Fondo GP, Materia: Espiritismo, leg. 576, no. 5.

45. Several clarifications of the procedures to be followed in cases of insanity were issued around this time. See APS, Fondo GP, Materia: Dementes, leg. 449, no. 2.

46. On 27 June, the governor had already instructed Arias to ascertain whether the patient had any relatives who might take responsibility for him. See APS, Fondo GP, Materia: Sociedades Espiritistas, leg. 2490, no. 2.

47. *El Fígaro*, 8 September 1901.

48. If true, this practice had long been known in Cuba, where Catholic priests resorted to similar measures when conducting exorcisms. See Ortiz, *Historia de una pelea cubana contra los demonios*, 158.

49. I do not mean to propose that the press and the state were indistinguishable. Rather, I want to suggest that the two operated dialectically to produce knowledge about "superstition" and the "primitive."

50. San Hilarión's temple was unusual, but it was not unique. An October 1903 telegram mentions a healer named Juana Pérez, whose home compound in Arroyo Blanco (Bayamo) included fourteen "ranchos." See APS, Fondo GP, Materia: Espiritismo, leg. 576, no. 7.

51. For two penetrating accounts of the construction of *brujería*, see Palmié, *Wizards and Scientists*, and Bronfman, *Measures of Equality*.

52. APS, Fondo GP, Materia: Espiritismo, leg. 576, no. 9.

53. The fraternal's application for registration as an association was granted on 22 November 1901. Accompanying records identify Mustelier as director. See APS, Fondo GP, Materia: Sociedades Espiritistas, leg. 2490, no. 2.

54. ANC, AS, leg. 13, no. 1.

55. F. E. y C. appears to be an acronym for "Fe, Esperanza, y Caridad," or "Faith, Hope, and Charity," a Spiritist maxim.

56. See, for instance, *La Lucha*, 14 December 1904.

57. Bronfman, *Measures of Equality*, chap. 1.

58. The surviving records do not include any licensing documents. See ANC, AS, leg. 13, no. 1.

59. APS, Fondo GP, Materia: Sociedades Espiritistas, leg. 2490, no. 1.

60. ANC, AS, leg. 13, no. 1.

61. Pérez has argued that Protestantism offered Cubans "a way to cope in the new order of things." Protestantism "suggested modernity and progress" (Pérez, *Essays on Cuban History*, 54, 56).

62. The authorities identified a thirty-seven-year-old woman named Cristina Lao Marrero as a cure-seeker who had taken up residence in a room adjacent to the temple. See ANC, AS, leg. 13, no. 1.

63. *El Iris de Paz*, 8 October 1904 and 25 June 1905.

64. Ibid., 5 August 1905.

65. Ibid., 22 July and 19 August 1905; *La Lucha*, 2 July 1906.

66. *La Lucha*, 7 July 1905. I have been unable to ascertain the identity of Prophet Elias.

67. *El Iris de Paz*, 22 July 1905.

68. *La Lucha*, 8 July 1905; *El Mundo*, 5 July 1905.

69. *El Fígaro*, 30 July 1905.

70. *La Lucha*, 7 July 1905.

71. *El Iris de Paz*, 5 August 1905.

72. Ibid., 14 October 1905.

73. Ibid.

74. Manso is said to have seen as many as 200 patients every morning. Most were treated in Esteban Parodi's guesthouse on 87 Prado Street, where Manso resided. By the time the healer moved to La Loma de San Juan, his services were in such demand that only collective treatments were practicable. In December 1905, when the ministry was already losing strength, eight buses traveled to El Cerro each day to convey cure-seekers.

75. *El Iris de Paz*, 22 July 1905.

76. Quintero Rivera, ed., *Vírgenes, magos y escapularios*.

77. San Hilarión's prayer is sold in typed sheets in Santiago de Cuba.

78. San Hilarión is revered among practitioners of *espiritismo de cordón*. Over one

dozen Spiritist societies registered under the name "San Hilarión" between the 1900s and 1950s. When nearly fifty societies from the eastern provinces organized a federation in 1937, they took the name "Federación Espiritista de Oriente y Camagüey Cordón de San Hilarión." See APS, Fondo GP, Materia: Sociedades Espiritistas, leg. 2530, no. 2.

Chapter Two

1. The Puerto Rican Spiritists included Ramón Vega, Manuel Devis, principal correspondent for *El Iris de Paz*, and José Reyes Calderón, director of *El Racionalista Cristiano*. See *El Iris de Paz*, 16 September 1905.

2. Rosendo Matienzo Cintrón (1855–1913) was born in Luquillo, Puerto Rico, but spent most of his youth in Spain, where he attended law school. In the 1890s, Matienzo joined the Autonomist Party and was elected Provincial Representative. He was also a member of the commission that negotiated Puerto Rico's autonomy from Spain. After the U.S. occupation, he was elected president of Ponce's court. In 1900, he broke with the Autonomists, joined the Republicans, and was named to the governing executive council. In 1904 he cofounded the Unionist Party. He was president of the House of Delegates from 1904 to 1906. In 1912 he founded the Independence Party. He was also a noted essayist. See Díaz Soler, *Rosendo Matienzo Cintrón*, and Bernabé, *Repuestas al colonialismo*.

3. *El Iris de Paz*, 2 September 1905.

4. Martínez-Fernández, *Protestantism and Political Conflict in the Nineteenth-Century*; Silva Gotay, *Protestantismo y política*, 7–8, 113; Rodríguez, *La primera evangelización norteamericana en Puerto Rico*, 122.

5. Silva Gotay, *Catolicismo y política en Puerto Rico*, chap. 3.

6. Dohen, *Two Studies of Puerto Rico*, 42; Picó, "El catolicismo popular en el Puerto Rico," 157.

7. *Boletín Eclesiástico*, 20 January 1899.

8. Ibid., 1 January 1899 and 30 January 1900.

9. Elenita established her base in barrio Espino, between San Lorenzo and Patillas, but her preaching covered the southwestern and central regions. The Cheos concentrated in Utuado's coffee country, which then included Jayuya and Ponce's environs.

10. *Guía Eclesiástica*, 1 January 1898; Santaella Rivera, *Historia de los Hermanos Cheos*, 35–41.

11. Picó, "Religiosidad institucional y religiosidad popular," 36–37.

12. Agosto Cintrón (*Religión y cambio social en Puerto Rico*, 83) discounts the possibility of mediations. She argues that the rise of the Cheos revealed the existence of two religions: orthodox and peasant Catholicism.

13. In 1864, the Jesuits preached missions in twenty-four towns, promoting devotion to the Sacred Heart and the Virgin. See Picó, "El catolicismo popular en el Puerto Rico," 158.

14. According to Reyes, Elenita never called herself a *misionera*. Others used that title, however, as can be seen in Puras's letter to Bishop William A. Jones (6 September 1911, AHD, Sección Gobierno, Serie Correspondencia, Sub-serie San Lorenzo, Obispo, caja G27, leg. s/n 1820–1928). See Reyes, *La Santa Montaña de San Lorenzo*, 52.

15. Santaella Rivera, *Historia de los Hermanos Cheos*, 208.

16. AHD, Sección Gobierno, Serie Correspondencia Parroquias, Sub-serie Cayey Parroquia-Obispo, caja G23, leg. 1, 1820–1931.

17. Santaella Rivera, *Historia de los Hermanos Cheos*, 65.

18. Picó, "El catolicismo popular en el Puerto Rico," 158–59.

19. Reyes, *La Santa Montaña de San Lorenzo*, 72–73.

20. Christian, *Local Religion in Sixteenth-Century Spain*, 83–88.

21. The men shared the nickname "Cheo." They joined forces in 1904 in what is known as the "Cheo Pact." See Santaella Rivera, *Historia de los Hermanos Cheos*, 70, 105–6.

22. Ibid., 246.

23. *El Ideal Católico*, 30 March 1901.

24. A transcript appears in Santaella Rivera, *Historia de los Hermanos Cheos*, 181–84.

25. Puras to Bishop William A. Jones, 6 September 1911, AHD, Sección Gobierno, Serie Correspondencia, Sub-serie San Lorenzo, Obispo, caja G27, leg. s/n 1820–1928.

26. Reyes, *La Santa Montaña de San Lorenzo*, 74.

27. Schwartz, "Hurricane of San Ciriaco," 304.

28. Centro de Investigación Social (Universidad de Puerto Rico), Microfilm no. 1389061, San Lorenzo, Matrimonios, Parroquia Nuestra Señora de las Mercedes, 1843–52, 1864–1910, 1925–27.

29. Reyes, *La Santa Montaña de San Lorenzo*, 109.

30. Santaella Rivera, *Historia de los Hermanos Cheos*, 65–67.

31. Ibid., 87–88.

32. Ibid., 12.

33. Entries from the annals of the Redemptorist order are quoted verbatim in Santaella Rivera, *Historia de los Hermanos Cheos*, 178–80.

34. Francisco Vicario, "El diablo predicador," *Anales de la Congregación de la Misión* (Madrid) 17 (1909): 623–25. Quoted verbatim in Santaella Rivera, *Historia de los Hermanos Cheos*, 170–72, 202.

35. Agosto Cintrón, *Religión y cambio social en Puerto Rico*, 60–70; Rodríguez Pérez, "La obra de los hermanos Cheos," 154.

36. Baldrich, *Sembraron la no siembra*.

37. Zayas Micheli, *Catolicismo popular en Puerto Rico*, 75; Silva Gotay, *Catolicismo y política en Puerto Rico*, 454–57.

38. José Dimas Soberal, a historian and onetime spiritual director of the Cheos, echoes this judgment. He finds "inspiration" in keeping with church doctrine. See interview with the author, Bayamón, Puerto Rico, 4 December 1997.

39. *El Ideal Católico*, 4 August 1906.

40. Torres Oliver, "Datos sobre 'Nuestra Madre.'"

41. Reyes, *La Santa Montaña de San Lorenzo*, 80–82.

42. In 1997, I interviewed two elderly witnesses and the descendants of several others.

43. "Circular del 15 de junio de 1910," *Boletín Eclesiástico*, 20 June 1910.

44. Monsignor Byrne, bishop of Ponce, approved the founding of the "Asociación, Católica, Apostólica, y Romana de San Juan Evangelista" on 4 February 1927. See Santaella Rivera, *Historia de los Hermanos Cheos*, 189.

45. In 1899, when Father Puras was in charge of the parish in Caguas, Col. W. H. Hubbell wrote the bishop seeking his dismissal for "promoting disorder." In January 1901, Father Benito Puig wrote the bishop regarding 1,100 pesos from a trust that Father Puras admitted he had employed for private purposes. See AHD, Sección Gobierno, Serie Correspondencia, Sub-serie Obispo, caja G10, fecha 1893–99, leg. s/n 1900–1901; AHD, Sección Gobierno, Serie Correspondencia, Sub-serie Obispo, fecha 1893–99, caja G9, leg. 41, 1896–99; Sección Gobierno, Serie Correspondencia Parroquias, Sub-serie Caguas, Obispo, caja G22, leg. 3, 1890–99.

46. The article reportedly appeared on 2 September 1911 in *Heraldo Español* (San Juan).

47. A transcript of Bishop Jones's letter to Father Puras can be found in Reyes, *La Santa Montaña de San Lorenzo*, 215–16.

48. *El Iris de Paz*, 10 May 1902.

49. Ibid., 12 July 1902.

50. Ibid., 27 April 1901.

51. Santaella Rivera, *Historia de los Hermanos Cheos*, 79–85.

52. One leaflet was kept at the Cheos's center in Peñuelas; its content is discussed below. See Santaella Rivera, *Historia de los Hermanos Cheos*, 100 n. 28.

53. Ibid., 114.

54. The contributors to *La Conciencia Libre*, a free-thought journal, included well-known Spiritists and masons. Graciano Sánchez, the freethinker who denounced Hermano Pancho and Father Puras, published his article in the pages of this journal.

55. Reyes, *La Santa Montaña de San Lorenzo*, 60.

56. Zayas Micheli, *Catolicismo popular en Puerto Rico*, 13.

57. Reyes, *La Santa Montaña de San Lorenzo*, 74.

58. On 12 April 1901, *San Juan News* reported on the "angels'" early successes in the northeast as confirmation of the spread of Spiritism. The paper observed that on 8 April 1901 as many as 3,000 people had gathered in San Sebastián to listen to a María Generosa and a Mrs. Telesfora.

59. *El Ideal Católico*, 26 August 1906.

60. "Circular del 15 de junio de 1910," *Boletín Eclesiástico*, 20 June 1910.

61. Kardec, *El libro de los mediums*; Matienzo Cintrón, *Sobre espiritismo*.

62. Rodríguez Pérez ("La obra de los hermanos Cheos," 155) remarks that "the Spiritist flavor at the beginning of their mission was natural, since they [the Cheos] lacked any great theological knowledge or religious instruction." José Dimas Soberal has expressed a similar view in a personal communication.

63. *El Ideal Católico*, 26 August 1906.

64. The preacher is not identified in the document. Francis Arrighetto was born in Siena, Italy, ca. 1328. A priest of the Servite order, he was famed for his devotion to the Virgin Mary and for his ability to preach extemporaneously.

65. A transcript of this document is included in an appendix to Rodríguez Pérez, "La obra de los hermanos Cheos." Rodríguez Pérez identifies a Domingo Castro as the chronicler of the speech; he appears to be the man that Santaella Rivera identified as Domingo Quiñones.

66. Santaella Rivera, *Historia de los Hermanos Cheos*, 62–63; Reyes, *La Santa Montaña de San Lorenzo*, 74.

67. Reyes, *La Santa Montaña de San Lorenzo*, 27.

68. Ibid., 35–37.

69. *El Iris de Paz*, 13 December 1902.

70. Agosto Cintrón, *Religión y cambio social en Puerto Rico*, 70–81.

71. *El Ideal Católico*, 26 August 1906. The *partidas* were composed of small property owners, day laborers, and tenant farmers who took advantage of Spain's ouster to settle scores with landowners and shopkeepers. See Picó, *La guerra después de la guerra*.

72. *La Conciencia Libre*, 26 September 1909 and 5 November 1911.

73. *San Juan News*, 12 April 1901.

74. José Rodríguez Medina, "Historia de los Hermanos Cheos de Puerto Rico," quoted in Santaella Rivera, *Historia de los Hermanos Cheos*, 78.

75. Santaella Rivera, *Historia de los Hermanos Cheos*, 77–83; Rodríguez Pérez, "La obra de los hermanos Cheos," 72.

76. Reyes transcribed the letter in *La Santa Montaña de San Lorenzo*, 198–99.

77. The *inspirados* did not attempt to "camouflage" their ethnicities, but they conform to Quintero Rivera's notion that popular movements often opted for withdrawal. See Quintero Rivera, "Vueltita con mantilla, al primer piso: Sociología de los santos," in Quintero Rivera, ed., *Vírgenes, magos y escapularios*, 100.

78. Zayas Micheli (*Catolicismo popular en Puerto Rico*, 76–78) argues that "the Cheo Brothers Messianic Movement emerged in and was inspired by the environment of the *Partidas*." Beyond the temporal coincidence, he offers no evidence of links between the two.

79. *El Ideal Católico*, 30 March 1901.

80. San Lorenzo was growing at the time. In 1899, its population was approximately 13,500, but by 1910, there were 19,300 residents, mostly in rural areas. See John P. Augelli,

"San Lorenzo, a Case Study of Recent Migrations in Interior Puerto Rico," in Fernández Méndez, ed., *Puerto Rico*, 202.

81. "Puesto Policía Insular de San Lorenzo-Relación de los servicios prestados por la fuerza de este puesto," AGPR, Fondo Policía de Puerto Rico, Tarea 57 P, caja 3; Santiago-Valles, *"Subject People" and Colonial Discourses*, 100.

82. Santiago-Valles, *"Subject People" and Colonial Discourses*, 33, 46–47, 92–93; Silvestrini, *Violencia y criminalidad en Puerto Rico*, 48.

83. A son of Cheo leader Pedro Laboy has said that José Rodríguez Medina, cofounder of the brotherhood, was a Republican who favored Puerto Rico's annexation to the United States. See Rodríguez Pérez, "La obra de los hermanos Cheos," 106.

84. The invitation is reproduced in Reyes, *La Santa Montaña de San Lorenzo*, 206. A transcript of the letter, dated 17 April 1911, appears in ibid., 204.

85. Reyes, *La Santa Montaña de San Lorenzo*, 93–101.

86. Santaella Rivera, *Historia de los Hermanos Cheos*, 61.

87. For a discussion of this aspect of Spiritist doctrine, see Chapter 4.

88. In January and February 1901, *La Correspondencia* published a series of Matienzo's articles on Spiritism.

89. *El Iris de Paz*, 6 July 1901.

90. *El Ideal Católico*, 13 October 1906.

91. Ibid., 2 March 1901.

92. Dr. Manuel Quevedo Báez (1865–1955) founded the Medical Association of Puerto Rico, over which he presided from 1902 to 1909. He directed the association's official organ during its early years. Between 1912 and 1914, Quevedo Báez was president of the Ateneo Puertorriqueño. In his mature years, Quevedo Báez wrote the island's first history of medicine, *Historia de la medicina y cirugía en Puerto Rico* (vol. 1, 1946, and vol. 2, 1949). See *Boletín de la Asociación Médica de Puerto Rico*, July and October 1903; and Rosa-Nieves and Melón, *Biografías Puertorriqueñas*, 341–42.

93. The Italian school of criminology, which included Cesare Lombroso (1835–1909) and his students Enrico Ferri and Raffaele Garofalo, proposed that born-criminals—a distinct "type," according to Lombroso—bore physical markers that revealed them as evolutionary atavisms and betrayed their kinship with the "inferior peoples" of the modern world. Lombroso influenced Cuban and Puerto Rican criminologists and persuaded Spriritists that "positive science" was crucial for social regeneration. Lombroso's writings on mediums and related phenomena were well known to Spiritists. See Bronfman, *Measures of Equality*, 29–31, 62–63, and Cesare Lombroso, "Fenómenos Medianímicos," *El Buen Sentido*, 11 January 1908.

94. *El Ideal Católico*, 2 December 1905.

95. Herzig Shannon, *El Iris de Paz*, chap. 4.

96. *El Ideal Católico*, 11 September 1902.

97. Braude, *Radical Spirits*, 82–83.

98. *El Iris de Paz*, 14 February 1903.

99. Ibid., 10 October 1903.

100. Ibid., 16 May 1906.

101. AHD, Sección Gobierno, Serie Correspondencia, Sub-serie Obispo, caja G9, leg. s/n 1895–98; *Boletín Eclesiástico*, 30 May 1899.

102. Missionary priests measured the fruits of their labors partly in terms of number of marriages. See AHD, Sección Gobierno, Serie Correspondencia, Sub-serie Obispo, fecha 1893–1899, caja G10, leg. s/n 1910–11.

103. Santaella Rivera, *Historia de los Hermanos Cheos*, 49–50.

104. Rodríguez Pérez, "La obra de los hermanos Cheos," 68; Agosto Cintrón, "Género y discurso religioso en un movimiento carismático."

105. Santaella Rivera, *Historia de los Hermanos Cheos*, 159, 197.

106. Ibid., 151–60.

107. Reyes, *La Santa Montaña de San Lorenzo*, 121–25; author interview with Joaquina Galarza, the only surviving member of the entourage, November 1997.

108. Agosto Cintrón, "Género y discurso religioso en un movimiento carismático," 198.

109. For a brief account of the recent controversies, see *El Nuevo Día*, 9–12 August 1997.

Chapter Three

1. On the Partido Independiente de Color, see, among others, Helg, *Our Rightful Share*; Pérez, "Politics, Peasants, and People of Color"; and Fernández Robaina, *El negro en Cuba*.

2. Ferrer, *Insurgent Cuba*, 84; Chávez Alvarez, *El crimen de la niña Cecilia*, 26.

3. Primelles, *Crónica cubana*, 134.

4. For incisive analyses of how this category was constructed, see Palmié's *Wizards and Scientists*, chap. 3, and Bronfman, *Measures of Equality*, chap. 1.

5. The turn that "broke" the case varied according to the various accounts. Rafael Roche Monteagudo, at one time Havana's chief of police, argued that testimony from Reyes's eight-year-old nephew—reported by Pedro M. García of *El Heraldo de Cuba*—gave investigators their first break. Observers like León Primelles, however, note the use of terror tactics to secure the confession. See Roche Monteagudo, *La policía y sus misterios en Cuba*, 230, and Primelles, *Crónica cubana*, 135.

6. *El Heraldo de Cuba*, 4 July 1919.

7. Ibid., 7 and 10 July 1919.

8. According to Helg (*Our Rightful Share*, 115), few were arrested on brujería charges after Zoila's murder in 1904. In 1906, she notes, only 13 of over 7,000 arrests were connected to witchcraft.

9. Márquez Sterling, then vice president of the Cuban Press Association, wrote in regard to Zoila's murder that the use of a human heart in a healing ritual appeared to him to be a first. See *El Fígaro*, 4 December 1904. Moreover, Palmié has observed that while Ortiz claimed that the sacrifice of white children had not been seen since the days of slavery, the noted criminologist and ethnographer was hard-pressed to name a single precedent for these acts of savagery. See Palmié, *Wizards and Scientists*, 340 n. 14.

10. *La Lucha*, 26 November 1904.

11. Ibid., 9 December 1904.

12. Chávez Alvarez, *El crimen de la niña Cecilia*, 26.

13. The information available for each case varies considerably from no more than a passing remark to complete judicial records as long as several hundred pages.

14. In Oriente, bandits and brigands kidnapped the children of planters, most of whom were released after ransoms were paid. See Perez, *Lords of the Mountain*, 178.

15. Palmié notes that the term "daño" is associated "with unspeakable violations—such as rape or witchcraft—in Cuban popular speech" (Palmié, *Wizards and Scientists*, chap. 3).

16. Helg, "Políticas raciales en Cuba después de la independencia," 65.

17. Oral tradition maintains that brujos were particularly active during the Christmas season. See Chávez Alvarez, *El crimen de la niña Cecilia*, 2.

18. ANC, AH, leg. 471, no. 3.

19. Primelles, *Crónica cubana*, 593.

20. Chávez Alvarez (*El crimen de la niña Cecilia*, 52) reports that a hypothesis denying Cecilia's existence surfaced in Matanzas years after the murder. The proponents of this view argued that the girl's birth had been registered legally only after her supposed demise, and that she could not have been the victim of a ritual crime because she was mulatto.

21. ANC, AH, leg. 475, no. 3.

22. Castellanos, "Un diagnóstico criminológico," 203.

23. ANC, AH, leg. 475, no. 3. See especially p. 52 of the first bound volume.

24. "Conciliabulus" is a corruption of the Latin word "conciliabulum," or a place of assembly. See Espinosa, *El destino de una criatura o la víctima de la superstición*, 5.

25. ANC, AH, leg. 714, exp. 1.

26. *El Mundo*, 22 November 1904.

27. ANC, AH, leg. 459, no. 5.

28. McLeod, "Undesirable Aliens."

29. *El Heraldo*'s editorial justified the lynchings, arguing among other things that rapes were a greater threat now that "the bestial appetite had increased with the growth of Jamaican migration" (*El Heraldo de Cuba*, 1 July 1919).

30. Castellanos, "La brujería y el ñañiguismo desde el punto de vista médico legal," 120.

31. *El Heraldo de Cuba*, 9 July 1919.

32. De la Fuente, *A Nation for All*, 161–63.

33. ANC, Registro de Asociaciones, leg. 1090, exp. 22859, (hojas sueltas sin procesar); Márquez Sterling, "Nuestra Asociación de la Prensa," *El Fígaro*, 17 April 1904, 192; "El periodismo," *El Fígaro*, 24 April 1904.

34. *El Fígaro*, 24 April 1904.

35. See Márquez Sterling, *Alrededor de nuestra psicología*, 75–82.

36. *La Lucha*, 15 July 1905.

37. *El Fígaro*, 4 December 1904.

38. Eduardo Varela Zequeira (1860–1918) was born in Nuevitas, Camagüey. In 1895, he covered the anticolonial insurgency for *La Discusión*. Following the destruction of the newspaper's offices, he joined the Liberation Army in May of 1898, serving in the brigade headquarters for the provinces of Havana and Matanzas. Varela Zequeira published numerous reports about Zoila and similar crimes. For biographical details, see *El Mundo Ilustrado*, 11 December 1904, and <http: www.cubaliteraria.com/autor/ficha.php?Id=774>. For Varela Zequeira's reports, see *El Mundo*, 14 November to 18 December 1904, and *El Mundo Ilustrado*, 27 November and 11 December 1904 and 19 March 1905.

39. "La prensa fue la auxiliar / más poderosa del caso / y de todo dió traspaso / a Landa sin descansar." See Espinosa, *El destino de una criatura o la víctima de la superstición*, 7, 21–27.

40. ANC, AH, leg. 714, exp. 1.

41. ANC, AH, leg. 471, no. 3.

42. *El Fígaro*, 21 June 1908.

43. Roche Monteagudo, *La policía y sus misterios en Cuba*, 186–87.

44. Ibid., 230.

45. Ibid., 233.

46. Quílez Vicente himself was responsible for publicizing the most notorious of these cases, known in the press as the "bohío de Mamá Coleta" affair. Here incest, murder, and insanity figured prominently in the story of a family torn apart by the belief that a brujo's spirit possessed some of them and that beatings were required as treatment. Quílez Vicente's account appeared in *Bohemia* in 1944; a radio version was broadcast on Radio Azul.

47. There had been similar efforts in the past. Fernando Ortiz was perhaps the most noted proponent of this view. In a speech before the Cuban legislature, Ortiz declared war on both black and white witchcraft and argued that backwardness and not blackness was the enemy of civilization. In spite of the occasional arrest of white brujos, brujería continued to be imagined as a black phenomenon. See *El Heraldo de Cuba*, 3 July 1919.

48. José Quílez Vicente, "¿Brujos ladrones de niños en las tierras pinareñas?" *Bohemia*, 12 September 1943.

49. *El Mundo*, 18 November 1904.

50. *La Lucha*, 2 and 12 December 1904.

51. Ibid., 28 November 1904; *El Mundo*, 7 December 1904.

52. *El Heraldo de Cuba*, 9 July 1919.

53. *El Mundo*, 13 December 1904.

54. *La Lucha*, 2 July 1919.

55. *El Heraldo de Cuba*, 2 July 1919.

56. Ibid., 3 July 1919.

57. Helg, *Our Rightful Share*, 135–36.

58. Ibid., 149.

59. *El Día*, 6 September 1918.

60. "Manifiesto relativo a los sucesos ocurridos en Regla y Matanzas a consecuencia de las prácticas de brujería y canibalismo. Julio 1919," ANC, Fondo Adquicisiones, caja 65, signatura 4201.

61. *El Heraldo de Cuba* (letter to the editor), 4 July 1919.

62. ANC, AH, leg. 215, exp. 10.

63. *El Mundo*, 6 January 1906.

64. *La Lucha*, 28 November 1904.

65. ANC, AH, leg. 722, exp. 5.

66. *La Lucha*, 3 December 1904.

Chapter Four

1. Pérez García argues that "Centro Unión" was founded in Mayagüez in 1875. Yáñez dates the founding of "Luz del Progreso" to 1879–89. Rodríguez Escudero argues that Spiritists began gathering before 1870 and opened the first center in Mayagüez in 1881, closing soon after because of official hostility. The center reopened in 1884, taking the names "Luz del Progreso," "Unión," and, finally, "Renacimiento." See Pérez García, "Spiritism," 74; Yáñez Vda. de Otero, *El espiritismo en Puerto Rico*, 5, 19–20; and Rodríguez Escudero, *Historia del espiritismo en Puerto Rico*, 35–37.

2. Alvarez-Curbelo, *Un país del porvenir*. See also Rama, *La ciudad letrada*.

3. Rosendo Matienzo Cintrón, Spiritism's leading ideologue in Puerto Rico, argued that political change was only a precondition for regeneration. He saw education and "will" as keys to the project. See Matienzo Cintrón, "Regeneración," *El Iris de Paz*, 28 May 1904.

4. For a discussion of Spiritist anticlericalism, see Herzig Shannon, *El Iris de Paz*, 51–74.

5. Ibid., 39, 60–72; *El Iris de Paz*, 6 July 1901.

6. Cited in Pérez García, "Spiritism," 75.

7. Hess, *Spirits and Scientists*.

8. Rodríguez Escudero, *Historia del espiritismo en Puerto Rico*, 80–83.

9. Ponte Jiménez, "Desarrollo del espiritismo en Puerto Rico," 890–94. See also *El Mundo*, 12 January 1934, and Andino, *El espiritismo en Puerto Rico y La Reforma*.

10. La Samaritana's niece argues that her aunt saw herself as a devout Catholic. See author interviews with Carmen Julia Vázquez, 5 December 1997 and 4 June 2002.

11. *La Correspondencia*, 29 July and 15 August 1922.

12. See, for example, Stevens-Arroyo and Díaz-Stevens, *Enduring Flame*; Agosto Cintrón, *Religión y cambio social en Puerto Rico*; Duany, "La religiosidad popular en Puerto Rico"; Picó, "El catolicismo popular en el Puerto Rico."

13. Vanderwood, *Power of God Against the Guns of Government*.

14. Tolezano García and Chávez Alvarez, *La leyenda de Antoñica Izquierdo*; Levine, *Vale of Tears*; Lundius and Lundahl, *Peasants and Religion*.

15. V. Turner, *Drums of Affliction*.

16. Díaz-Quiñones, "Fernando Ortiz and Allan Kardec," 9–27.

17. Koss, "El porqué de los cultos religiosos," 69.

18. *La Correspondencia*, 22 July 1922.

19. Vázquez, "La Samaritana de San Lorenzo," 1.

20. *La Democracia*, 22 July 1922.

21. Clara Vázquez was an agregado who lived with his wife, Carmen Torres, on land owned by Francisco Sánchez. Julia was their youngest child and only daughter. See author interview with Carmen Julia Vázquez, 10 January 1998.

22. *Puerto Rico Ilustrado*, 29 July 1922.

23. *La Correspondencia*, 11 May, 29 July, and 3 August 1922.

24. There are no indications that Vázquez met Elenita. But the two have been linked in popular memory. The blurring of identities is telling: many who sought aid in barrio Hato did so without distinguishing sharply between *inspirados* and other sorts of religious figures. See Agosto Cintrón, *Religión y cambio social en Puerto Rico*; Reyes, *La Santa Montaña de San Lorenzo*; and Santaella Rivera, *Historia de los Hermanos Cheos*.

25. For a critique of the crisis and response model, see Román, "Conjuring Progress and Divinity," 360–97.

26. Santiago-Valles, *"Subject Peoples" and Colonial Discourses*, 118; Paralitici, *No quiero mi cuerpo pa' tambor*, 21–49.

27. Cabo Rojo's Mallita la Médica was described as an "exact copy" of Vázquez, but she never acquired a mass following. See *La Correspondencia*, 15 August 1922.

28. *La Correspondencia*, 25 August 1992.

29. Suárez, *Nuestra réplica al artículo del Dr. don Manuel Guzmán Rodríguez*, 9.

30. Koss, "Religion and Science Divinely Related."

31. See, for instance, Silvestrini, "El impacto de la política de salud pública."

32. *La Democracia*, 10 June 1922. The relevant passage is John 4:16–19.

33. Curiously, advocates of La Samaritana did not refer explicitly to the parable of the good samaritan (Luke 10:25–37) in their defense of the healer.

34. Suárez-Findlay, *Imposing Decency*.

35. Trigo, "Anemia and Vampires."

36. See, for instance, *La Democracia*, 8 August 1992.

37. The 1920 census shows Vázquez residing with her parents, Clara Vázquez and Carmen Torres, in barrio Hato, San Lorenzo. She is listed as white and twenty years old; baptismal records suggest that she was in fact twenty-six. The 1930 census shows Vázquez residing in the town of San Lorenzo. She is married to Rafael Fernández, a cigar factory worker, and has two children, who are also classified as "de color." See Clara Vázquez household, San Lorenzo, Bario Hato, 1920 U.S. Census, p. 115, enumeration district 880, sheet 7, dwelling 53, family 53; and Rafael Fernández household, San Lorenzo, Pueblo, 1930 U.S. Census, p. 33, enumeration district 75-1-A, sheet 33, dwelling 125, family 169.

38. Bayron Toro, *Estadísticas de las elecciones municipales de Puerto Rico*, 138, and *Elecciones y partidos políticos de Puerto Rico*, 159–63.

39. *La Correspondencia*, 29 July 1922.

40. *La Democracia*, 10 June 1922. The critic's assertion is misleading. Although Spiritists supported Socialist causes, there were Spiritists of all persuasions. Matienzo Cintrón was a Unionist leader and the founder of a proindependence party. José Tous Soto headed the Republican Party and the Spiritist Federation. See Rodríguez Escudero, *Historia del espiritismo en Puerto Rico*, 291.

41. *El Mundo*, 11 August 1922; *La Democracia*, 25 May 1922.

42. *La Democracia*, 27 August 1922.

43. Rodríguez Escudero, *Historia del espiritismo en Puerto Rico*, 80; Acosta, *Santa Juana y Mano Manca*, 56–58.

44. *La Correspondencia*, 28 June and 1 August 1922.

45. Ibid., 8 June and 9 August 1922.

46. Ibid., 7 August 1922; *El Mundo*, 11 August 1922.

47. See Chapter 2.

48. The club was founded in Aguadilla in March 1921 to promote the "experimental study of Spiritist science" and assist the needy. See AGPR, Fondo Departamento de Estado, Serie Corporaciones Sin Fines de Lucro, caja 17A, exp. 235.

49. In 1904 the Spiritist press published a series of communiqués from a spirit identified as Francisco Alvarado, Arroyo's parish priest. See *El Iris de Paz*, March and April 1904. Matías Usero Torrente renounced the priesthood and became a practitioner of Spiritism. He then toured the island, lecturing in favor of the new doctrine. See Rodolfo López Soto, "El espiritismo en Puerto Rico y sus instituciones," in Yáñez Vda. de Otero, *El espiritismo en Puerto Rico*, 108. Joaquín Saras, born in Jaca Huesca, Spain, in 1834, headed San Lorenzo's parish in the 1890s and early 1900s. He baptized Vázquez on 10 February 1893. See *Boletín Eclesiástico*, 15 January 1897, and Centro de Investigaciones Sociales, Libro de Bautismos 20 (1891–94), Parroquia de San Lorenzo, Microfilm 13889053.

50. *El Mundo*, 25 July 1922.

51. Ibid., 25, 28 July and 16 August 1922; *La Correspondencia*, 27 July and 5 August 1922.

52. *La Correspondencia*, 13 July 1922.

53. *El Mundo*, 28 August and 5 September 1922. Rosario Bellber was president of the Liga Social Sufragista. See Rodríguez Escudero, *Historia del espiritismo en Puerto Rico*, 78–80.

54. *El Mundo*, 27 July 1922.

55. An investigation by the federation cleared the club of any wrongdoing. See *La Democracia*, 29 July 1922, and *El Tiempo*, 2 August 1922.

56. The original, printed in *La Correspondencia* on 20 June 1922, reads: "¿Qué va a ser de la ciencia si a esta se sobrepone la superchería de una negra cualquiera?"

57. Kardec, *El génesis*, 22–23.

58. *El Buen Sentido*, July 1908.

59. Kardec, *El libro de los espíritus*, 307.

60. Herzig Shannon, *El Iris de Paz*, 83, 101–3.

61. *El Iris de Paz*, 19 July 1902.

62. Kardec, *El génesis*, 95.

63. *La Correspondencia*, 13 July 1922.

64. Vázquez, "La Samaritana de San Lorenzo," 5; *El Mundo*, 21 May 1953.

65. *El Mundo*, 21 May 1953.

66. *La Correspondencia*, 14 July 1922; *El Mundo*, 25 July and 3 August 1922.

67. *La Correspondencia*, 3 and 8 August 1922.

68. Ibid., 27 July 1922.

69. *La Democracia*, 7 July 1922; *La Correspondencia*, 26 and 27 August and 5 and 13 September 1922.

70. The exact dates remain uncertain. La Samaritana moved to town in San Lorenzo before marrying sometime in the 1920s. See author interview with Carmen Julia Vázquez, 4 June 2002.

71. *El Mundo*, 21 May 1953.

72. *La Correspondencia*, 29 July and 25 August 1922.

73. *El Mundo*, 10 November 1944.

74. Herzig Shannon, *El Iris de Paz*, 30–39.

75. In 1928 the medical association urged physicians to "raze the legendary magnetism of the illiterate," citing "the little jíbara who comes down from the mountains wearing the cloak of a new Samaritan." See *Boletín de la Asociación Médica de Puerto Rico* 21 (June 1928). See also ibid., 44 (June 1944).

Chapter Five

1. Other stigmatics also suffered their trials during Lent and Easter. See note 9, below.

2. *Carteles*, 27 May 1956.

3. *Bohemia*, 20 May 1956. *Carteles*, 27 May 1956, gave a different version of the message, which foregrounded Izquierdo as agent.

4. *Carteles*, 27 May 1956.

5. Wilson, *Stigmata*, 50.

6. Christian, *Apparitions in Late Medieval and Renaissance Spain*, 31, 73.

7. The article appeared in *Bohemia* in early March. *Carteles* published similar reports on 25 March and 27 May 1956.

8. *Carteles*, 15 July 1956.

9. Therese Neuman (1898–1962) was born in Konnersreuth, Bavaria. She suffered numerous afflictions in her youth, including blindness and paralysis. She recovered her vision in 1923 on the day that St. Therese of Lisieux was beatified and recovered her mobility when the saint was canonized. Like Izquierdo, she bled during Lent, especially on Fridays. Her wounds appeared in March 1926 after a vision of Christ's passion. It was said that she spoke Aramaic during her visions. It was also said that she consumed no food or drink. See Wilson, *Stigmata*, 145, and Christian, *Visionaries*, 283–87.

10. According to Monsignor Raúl del Valle, orthodox hagiographies included only fifty cases of saints who had suffered stigmata. The larger figure of 321, which appeared in *Carteles*, derived from René Biot's findings. See *Carteles*, 27 May and 3 June 1956.

11. *Bohemia*, 8 July 1956.

12. Father Pio (1887–1968), a Capuchin monk born in the Italian village of Pietralcina, rose to international prominence after World War II. Besides the stigmata, which appeared in 1918 and lasted his entire life, he was credited with miraculous powers of bilocation, perfect knowledge, mind reading, and extraordinary healing talents. Father Pio was also said to exude a perfume that could manifest itself at great distances. See McCaffery, *Friar of San Giovanni*, and Wilson, *Stigmata*, 6–10, 63–70, 144.

13. For an account of political violence during this period, see Pérez, *Cuba*, 288–95.

14. *Carteles*, 3 June 1956.

15. Ibid., 10 June and 1 July 1956.

16. Pérez, *Cuba*, 290.

17. *Carteles*, 10 June 1956.

18. Ibid., 1 July 1956.

19. Ibid., 10 June 1956.

20. Father Pio and Neumann fasted strictly. Many claimed that the German stigmatic consumed neither food nor drink between 1926 and 1962. See Wilson, *Stigmata*, 114–15.

21. *Carteles*, 15 July 1956.

22. Ibid., 1 July 1956.

23. Ibid., 15 July 1956.

24. *El Imparcial*, 31 May 1953.

25. *Bohemia*, 20 May 1956.

26. *Carteles*, 15 July 1956.

27. Pérez, *Cuba*, 303.

28. The procession and masses, which took place in May 1952, received widespread

coverage. *Bohemia* published photographs of the crowds and, significantly, of Batista and his wife as they greeted Cardinal Manuel Arteaga and other church dignitaries.

29. On 17 May 1956, the *Diario de la Marina* reported that hundreds of pilgrims were gathering in Assolo, Italy, where four children claimed to have witnessed an apparition of the Virgin.

30. *Diario de la Marina*, 16 and 17 May 1956.

31. M. Carroll, *Cult of the Virgin Mary*, 136.

32. Ibid., 138.

33. Pérez, *Cuba*, 288.

34. Ibarra, *Prologue to Revolution*, 103, 170.

35. Pérez-Stable, *Cuban Revolution*, 47–48, 54–58.

36. Pérez, *Cuba*, 277, 311.

37. *Diario de la Marina*, 6 June 1956.

38. Ibid., 1 June 1956.

39. *Carteles*, 27 May 1956.

40. Ibid., 10 June 1956.

41. *Bohemia*, 20 May 1956.

42. *Carteles*, 15 July 1956.

43. The reporter's assessment was incorrect. Izquierdo wondered how she would perform on an opinion poll and posed the question to a journalist. See *Carteles*, 2 June and 15 July 1956.

44. Ibid., 1 July 1956.

45. See, among others, Ortiz, *Historia de una pelea cubana contra los demonios*, 71–72.

46. *Carteles*, 1 July 1956.

47. Ibid., 3 June 1956.

48. Ibid., 10 June 1956.

49. López, *La radio en Cuba*, 146.

50. According to a survey published in *Bohemia* on 6 July 1952, Radio Unión's weekday rating was 1.19 points, Radio Progreso's 2.46, RHC's 3.28, and CMQ's 11.09.

51. López, *La radio en Cuba*, 145; *Bohemia*, 3 August 1952.

52. An actor with CMQ claimed that Clavelito hosted a similar show there in 1950. See *Bohemia*, 10 August 1952.

53. According to Clavelito, these were the words of Miguel Gabriel, a manager at CMQ. See *Bohemia*, 31 August 1952.

54. Ibid., 2 March 1952.

55. "Pon tu pensamiento en mi / y harás que en este momento / mi fuerza de pensamiento / ejerza el bien sobre ti" (ibid., 3 August 1952).

56. Ibid., 31 August 1952.

57. Ibid., 3 August 1952.

58. Ibid., 3 March 1952.

59. Personal communication from José Moya Sr., July 1999.

60. López, *La radio en Cuba*, 145.

61. *Bohemia*, 10 August 1952.

62. Ibid.

63. Clavelito's titles included *Mis puntos cubanos, Rincón campesino, Los guajiros de la radio, Décimas de Clavelito*, and *Controversias de Clavelito y Clarivel: Novela de amor y dolor*. In addition, the Biblioteca Nacional José Martí, Havana, holds *Hacia la felicidad: Un viaje a través de los astros*, the third of three esoteric works published in Havana after the author's failed run for office. See Fidelzait and Pérez de la Riva, *San José de Sumidero*, 69.

64. The first of the relevant stanzas reads: "Yo no sé por qué será / nada el pueblo nunca alcanza / para mayor acechanza / hemos podido palpar / que ya ní le dejan dar / un poquito de esperanza" (*Bohemia*, 10 August 1952).

65. Clavelito claimed that his father, Belén Alfonso Benítez, was an insurgent in the Cuban War of Independence. Other sources identify his maternal grandfather as a *mambí*. Clavelito owed his stage name to his grandparents, too. Among his mother's family, the Clavelos, the grandchildren were known as "Clavelitos." See *Bohemia*, 17 August 1952.

66. Ibid., 24 August 1952.

67. Ibid., 10 August 1952.

68. Ibid., 3 August 1952.

69. Ibid.

70. Ibid., 17 August 1952.

71. Ibid., 10 August 1952.

72. Priests of Ifá are called *babalawos*, hence Mañach's sardonic neologism.

73. *Bohemia*, 24 August 1952.

74. Ibid.

75. The full stanza reads: "Reunirse es delito grave; hablar, un grave delito / y lo demás Clavelito, ya todo el mundo lo sabe / Piensas que Batista es suave / porque te ha dejado actuar, / mas si quisieras hablar / como al pueblo hablar debieras, / seguro que entonces vieras que otro gallo iba a cantar." Cited in López, *La radio en Cuba*, 147.

76. Pozo, *Hacia la felicidad*, 122. The stanza reads: "Clavelito prometió, / darle su sueldo a hospitales; / y a los que sufrieran males / y eso lo crucificó. / Clavelito prometió / que se sabrá quién es quien / Y así le pasó también / a Jesús el Nazareno / se crucificó por bueno / y por predicar el bien."

Chapter Six

1. *El Mundo*, 23 May 1953.

2. Ibid., 30 May 1953.

3. Certeau, *Practice of Everyday Life*, introduction.

4. Díaz-Quiñones, *La memoria rota*, 44–46.

5. *El Imparcial*, 6 May 1953. The only published devotional account highlights three of the dozen or so seers known from contemporary reports. The seers named there are Juan Angel Collado and Ramonita and Isidra Belén. See Méndez de Guzmán, *La verdadera historia*, 33–50.

6. *El Imparcial*, 8 May 1953.

7. Christian, *Apparitions in Late Medieval and Renaissance Spain*, 14–15.

8. *El Mundo*, 29 May 1953.

9. Ibid., 18 May 1953.

10. Ibid., 5 May 1953; *El Imparcial*, 17 May 1953.

11. Méndez de Guzmán, *La verdadera historia*, 56.

12. *El Imparcial*, 20 May 1953.

13. Ibid., 18 May 1953.

14. *El Mundo*, 9 and 21 May 1953.

15. For a provocative if debatable account of the miracle of Hormigueros, see Zayas Micheli, *Catolicismo popular en Puerto Rico*, 13–43.

16. *El Mundo*, 20 May 1953.

17. *El Imparcial*, 27 May 1953.

18. *El Mundo*, 26, 27, and 29 May 1953; *El Imparcial*, 27 and 28 May 1953.

19. *El Mundo*, 27 May 1953.

20. Ibid., 29 May 1953.

21. Ibid., 23 May 1953.

22. *El Imparcial*, 23 May 1953.

23. Ibid., 23 and 25 May 1953.

24. Tumin and Feldman, "Miracle at Sabana Grande," 359.

25. *El Mundo*, 11 and 25 May 1953.

26. According to Angel Nazario, his father had a first glimpse of the grotto in a dream. He completed the picture by looking at photographs of Lourdes and carried out the project with the assistance of a man known only as don Manuelito. See Méndez de Guzmán, *La verdadera historia*, 115.

27. *El Mundo*, 11 May 1953.

28. Ibid., 2 February 1950.

29. Following the visions in Sabana Grande, there were reports of similar events in Santurce, Ponce, Vega Baja, and Isabela. See *El Mundo*, 1 and 27 May, 13 June, and 2 July 1953; *El Imparcial*, 28 May, 5 and 6 June 1953.

30. Bishop Jaime P. Davis had petitioned the Vatican to grant the lady this honor in 1950. See *El Mundo*, 2 February 1950 and 4 May 1953.

31. *El Imparcial*, 18 May and 6 June 1953.

32. *El Mundo*, 28 May 1953.

33. Ibid., 1 May 1953; *El Imparcial*, 18 June 1953.

34. *El Mundo*, 14 May 1953.

35. *El Imparcial*, 6 May 1953.

36. *El Mundo*, 30 April 1953.

37. Ibid., 18 May 1953.

38. The existence of these messages was first publicized in a radio program in 1975. See *El Vocero*, 4 March 1975. For transcriptions, see Méndez de Guzmán, *La verdadera historia*, 163–99.

39. *El Mundo*, 6 May 1953.

40. Ibid., 12 May 1953.

41. Ibid., 25 May 1953.

42. Ibid., 11 May 1953.

43. Ibid., 21 and 25 May 1953.

44. Ibid., 23 May 1953.

45. Tumin and Feldman, "Miracle at Sabana Grande," 357.

46. *El Imparcial*, 23 May 1953.

47. Ibid., 15 and 28 May 1953.

48. Ibid., 15 and 28 May and 14 June 1953.

49. *El Mundo*, 7 and 23 May 1953; *El Imparcial*, 14 May 1953.

50. *El Mundo*, 25 May 1953; *El Imparcial*, 14 June 1953.

51. *El Imparcial*, 19 May 1953.

52. When lightning struck near the Virgin's well, some pilgrims proposed that this was a sign of heaven's displeasure with the cancellation of San Isidro's procession on 15 May. See ibid., 20 May 1953.

53. *El Mundo*, 26 May 1953.

54. María Milagros Borreli, one of the first girls to see the Virgin, spent her days seeing to visitors at her home. According to the papers, some pilgrims believed that the seer had divine faculties. Unlike the others, Milagros Borreli did not lead processions; she stayed home to see supplicants and bless relics. See ibid., 25 May 1953.

55. *El Imparcial*, 29 May 1953.

56. Alvarez-Curbelo and Rodríguez Castro, eds., *Del nacionalismo al populismo*.

57. *El Mundo*, 18, 21, and 25 May 1953.

58. *El Imparcial* was designated the official organ for the committee's public statements and announcements. See *El Imparcial*, 29 May and 17 June 1953.

59. *El Mundo*, 25 May 1953.

60. For a description of Puerto Rico in U.S. foreign policy, see Mayra Rosario Urrutia, "Detrás de la vitrina: Expectativas del Partido Popular Democrático y política exterior norteamericana, 1942–1954," in Alvarez-Curbelo and Rodríguez Castro, eds., *Del nacionalismo al populismo*, 147–78.

61. *El Mundo*, 31 August 1954.

62. Ibid., 23 October 1949.

63. Ibid., 23 August 1951.

64. For additional information on this conflict, see Silva Gotay, "El Partido Acción Cristiana," and Zayas Micheli, *Catolicismo popular en Puerto Rico*, 124–30.

65. *El Mundo*, 29 May 1953.

66. Ibid., 16 and 26 May 1953.

67. *El Imparcial*, 26 May 1953.

68. From 4 May to 28 May, WKAQ broadcast from barrio Rincón in two half-hour blocks daily. See Tumin and Feldman, "Miracle at Sabana Grande," 359.

69. *El Mundo*, 7 May 1953.

70. *El Imparcial*, 15 May 1953.

71. *El Mundo*, 27 May 1953.

72. *El Imparcial*, 26 May 1953.

73. Christian, *Visionaries*, 347–48.

74. *El Mundo*, 20 and 26 May 1953.

75. *El Imparcial*, 13 May 1953.

76. Ibid., 12 June 1953.

77. Ibid., 3 May 1953.

78. *El Mundo*, 21 May 1953.

79. Ibid.

80. *El Imparcial*, 5 June 1953.

81. *El Mundo*, 20 May 1953.

82. Ibid., 26 May 1955.

83. *El Imparcial*, 15 May 1953.

84. *El Mundo*, 12 May 1953.

85. *El Imparcial*, 5 June 1953.

86. Ibid., 7 May 1953.

87. *El Mundo*, 11 and 18 May 1953.

88. Ibid., 21 May 1953.

89. *El Imparcial*, 14 June 1953.

90. *El Mundo*, 27 April 1953.

91. Pinto was president of the barrio's Catholic association. See ibid., 30 April 1953.

92. Ibid., 27 April and 1 May 1953.

93. Ibid., 30 April 1953.

94. Ibid., 27 April 1953.

95. Ibid., 1 and 8 May 1953; *El Imparcial*, 1, 2, and 4 May 1953.

96. Tumin and Feldman, "Miracle at Sabana Grande," 361–62.

97. *El Mundo*, 27 May 1953.

98. Ibid., 26 May 1953.

99. Díaz-Quiñones, *La memoria rota*, 45.

100. Zayas Micheli, *Catolicismo popular en Puerto Rico*, 140–41.

Epilogue

1. Comaroff and Comaroff, "Occult Economies and the Violence of Abstraction," 280.

2. Ibid., 279.

3. Robin Derby's first account of the chupacabras in Mexico and Puerto Rico applied the Comaroffs' model. In "Vampiros del Imperio," Derby argued that if the chupacabras opted for locales like Canóvanas and northern Mexico, it was because these were areas in which capital penetration had blurred the boundaries between Latin America and the United States, fostering a sense that the body politic was vulnerable. In "Imperial Secrets," Derby proposes an interpretation that points at Puerto Rico's unsettled relationship with the United States; see below.

4. Niehaus, "Witches and Zombies of the South African Lowveld," 191.

5. Ibid., 200.

6. White (*Speaking with Vampires*) makes a similar assertion regarding vampire rumors in East Africa.

7. Studies of rumors among African Americans constitute an exception to the general trend. Jackson puts humor at the center of his analysis of rumors of racist conspiracies and describes the events in which such accounts circulate as "story telling potlach" ("Soles of Black Folk," 176–90). Although the matter is not central to her analysis, P. Turner notes the playfulness of rumors in *I Heard It through the Grapevine*.

8. Niehaus, "Witches and Zombies of the South African Lowveld," 196; Comaroff and Comaroff, "Occult Economies and the Violence of Abstraction," 281.

9. Scheper-Hughes, "Global Traffic in Human Organs," 191–224; Palmié, *Wizards and Scientists*, 20, 64–69; White, "Traffic in Heads," 334.

10. On the Puerto Rican economy, see Dietz, *Economic History of Puerto Rico*. On the modernization of the Caribbean, see Mintz, "Caribbean as a Socio-Cultural Area."

11. Asad, *Formations of the Secular*, 3.

12. Stoler, "'In Cold Blood,'" 151–89.

13. Niehaus, "Witches and Zombies of the South African Lowveld," 203–6.

14. See Lauria, "'Respeto,' 'Relajo' and Inter-personal Relations in Puerto Rico," 53–67.

15. Pérez proposed the moniker in March of 1995 following attacks on goats in an area known appropriately as Saltos Cabra. See J. Martín, *La conspiración Chupacabras*, 28–29.

16. Derby, "Vampiros del Imperio," 327, 341.

17. On 9 November 1995, López and Núñez González sponsored House Resolution 5012, ordering the Agriculture Commission to initiate a "deep investigation to clarify the unknown phenomenon and to quantify the damages caused by the so-called 'chupacabras.'" A facsimile appears in J. Martín, *La conspiración Chupacabras*, 211–14.

18. *Evidencia Ovni* 6, 30–40; *Ocurrió Así*, broadcast 26 April 1996; and NotiUno's *Evidencia Ovni*, radio broadcast 16 November 1996.

19. Mayor Soto included a photocopy of *El Vocero*'s cartoon in a package he distributed to journalists and researchers. See author interview with José R. Soto, 22 January 1998.

20. *El Vocero*, 31 October and 2 November 1995.

21. *El Nuevo Día*, 21 January 1996.

22. Stoler, "'In Cold Blood,'" 151–89.

23. *El Vocero*, 25, 27, 30, and 31 October 1975; 7, 10, and 13 November 1995.

24. According to some analysts indebted to Richard Hofstaders's essay "The Paranoid Style in American Politics" (1952), conspiracy rumors are monological; they resist disconfirmation and integrate information on overdetermined terms. For a review of this literature, see Marcus, introduction to *Paranoia within Reason*, 1–12; and Parish and Parker, *Age of Anxiety*. There are also scholars who emphasize contestation between official accounts and rumors; see the works by White, Brown, and Palmié cited below.

25. Known popularly as "diablitos," or little devils, *íremes* are high-ranking officials in Abakuá lodges. During Havana's Epiphany (January 6), processions of African "nations," troupes known as *comparsas*, were led by masked *íremes*. See David Brown, *The Light Inside*, 133–40.

26. My assertions echo White's analysis of rumors involving the traffic in children's heads in southern Africa. See White, "Traffic in Heads," 325–38.

27. Neither predator resembled vampires in the literary tradition; they were not human nor did they consort with human beings. Derby has noted, however, that some described the chupacabras as mechanical while the vampiro remained organic. See Auerbach, *Our Vampires, Ourselves*, and Derby, "Imperial Secrets," 5.

28. Misty Bastian ("'Diabolic Realities,'" 65–90) has used this elegant phrase to characterize the Nigerian government's account of events leading to a riot in Owerri, where it was rumored that evidence of traffic in human body parts had been uncovered in 1996. Although Bastian highlights the dialogue between rumors and reports, she relates the circulation of stories about body parts to the impact of capitalism.

29. My efforts to obtain these documents were unsuccessful.

30. In February of 1996, Marc Davenport and Bob Buck led a group of U.S.-based UFOlogists in a research trip to the island. They interviewed residents of Canóvanas, Mayor Soto, and Dr. Carlos Soto, whose necropsies they recorded. The footage was available for sale from Buck Productions in the late 1990s. An edited version billed as a documentary by Joseph Palermo is available under the title *Chupacabras! The True Story of the 1996 Expedition*.

31. J. Martín, *La conspiración Chupacabras*, 60–62.

32. *El Vocero*, 1, 2, and 9 April 1975; *Claridad*, 15 February and 19 April 1975.

33. *El Vocero*, 20 March 1975.

34. Wiltenburg ("True Crime," 1377–1404) has shown that sensationalism in European letters harks back to early days of the printing press. Rather than marking the rise of immoral commercialism, graphic accounts of heinous crimes were thought to be edifying.

35. *Washington Post*, 26 December 1995.

36. Ibid.

37. The *Boston Globe* reported that a Puerto Rican government office in Massachusetts received an anonymous note addressed to the governor. The letter called the chupacabras a threat to Puerto Rico's "national security" but directed the governor to look for the predator near an Argentine restaurant in Cambridge. See the *Boston Globe*, 13 April 1996.

38. A *coquí* is a small frog regarded as a symbol of Puerto Rico. "Chupaquí" is a compound word formed by adding "chupar" to "aquí," or here. Translated literally, it means "suck here."

39. In Canóvanas, for example, police officer Collazo Vázquez confronted the chupacabras as it attacked his dog. He fired a shot and hit the predator, but the chupacabras escaped unharmed. See *Ocurrió Así*, broadcast 26 April 1996.

40. J. Martín, *La conspiración Chupacabras*, 19, 31; *Evidencia Ovni Especial* (1997), 32–37.

41. Witness Margie Rivera claimed that chupacabras males were "grotesque." Females were "delicate" and had no visible sexual organs. See J. Martín, *La conspiración Chupacabras*, 94.

42. Corrales, *Chupacabras and Other Mysteries*, 43–48.

43. White's review of abduction stories in the United States suggests that abductees' reports of alien interest in human sexuality have to do with a preoccupation with race and reproduction. Derby argues that the chupacabras' concern with reproduction recalls Puerto Ricans' experience with modern medicine in the context of U.S. imperialism. See White, "Alien Nation," 24–33, and Derby, "Vampiros del Imperio," 336–37.

44. *El Vocero*, 20, 28 March 1975, and 6 November 1995.

45. Comandancia de la Policía, Hato Rey, Puerto Rico, Informe de Delito Tipo II, No. de Informe 35, No. de Querella 5-12-00432.

46. P. Turner, *I Heard It through the Grapevine*, 190, and Jackson, "The Soles of Black Folk," 187, have both made similar observations.

47. *Ocurrió Así*, broadcast 26 April 1996.

48. J. Martín, *La conspiración Chupacabras*, 42.

49. *El Vocero*, 17 March and 29 May 1975.

50. García Muñiz, "U.S. Military Installations in Puerto Rico."

51. At 28,000 acres, the Caribbean National Forest is the largest holding of public lands in Puerto Rico. Roosevelt Roads Naval Base covered 31,000 acres, most of which were

located in the island of Vieques. For a discussion of El Yunque in Puerto Rico's imaginary, see Derby, "Imperial Secrets," 10.

52. Mike Davis makes a similar claim in "Monsters and Messiahs."

53. J. Martín, *La conspiración Chupacabras*, 154.

54. *Evidencia Ovni* dedicated a special issue in 1997 to the rainforest and U.S. military bases. The subject was discussed on Martín's radio show and in Corrales, *Chupacabras and Other Mysteries.* See also Redacción Noticiosa, *La verdadera historia del chupacabras*, 45–47; McMahon, "Goatsucker Sighted, Details to Follow," 92–100; and *El Vocero*, 25 March and 27 May 1975.

55. Briggs (*Reproducing Empire*, 110–11) has shown that memories circulating in Puerto Rico regarding the state's involvement in population control are selective and often discount the popularity of these programs among their alleged victims.

56. *Evidencia Ovni*, no. 6 (1995): 14, 27; and no. 8 (1995): 24.

57. Derby, "Imperial Secrets," 3, 11, 14.

58. Martín alleges that a group posing as UFOlogists has spread disinformation at the behest of the U.S. federal government. See J. Martín, *La conspiración Chupacabras*, 34, 74–76, 89, 110.

59. Ibid., 34, 54–56, 60; *Evidencia Ovni, no.* 8 (1995): 8; Méndez de Guzmán, *La verdadera historia*, 82.

60. *Inter Press Service*, 23 January 1996.

61. *San Juan Star*, 19 November 1995.

62. Derby has suggested that statehooders were prone to conjuring beasts associated with "the predatory designs of the United States" ("Imperial Secrets," 8).

63. *El Nuevo Día*, 24 March and 5 September 1996.

64. For a discussion of the deployment of jíbaro images in Puerto Rico, see Scarano, "*Jíbaro* Masquerade," and Duany, *Puerto Rican Nation on the Move.*

65. *El Vocero*, 27 March 1975.

66. Ibid., 2 April 1975.

67. Moca's drought-related losses were estimated at 1 million dollars. The vampiro's first victims belonged to Héctor Vega, whose losses were substantial. See *El Vocero*, 7 and 16 May 1975.

68. *El Mundo* and *El Vocero*, 17 March 1975.

69. *El Vocero* reported abnormal radiation levels on Vega's property. *El Mundo*'s tests reflected nothing unusual. Senator Deynés Soto joined personnel from the Department of Agriculture, who found no abnormalities. See *El Vocero*, 31 March and 22 May 1975; and *El Mundo*, 24 and 25 March 1975.

70. *El Vocero*, 20, 21, and 31 March, and 7 May 1975. The records show that in 1972 Héctor Vega and his wife bought 195 *cuerdas* in Moca's barrio Cruz for $125,000. In April 1975, when vampiro sightings were at their peak, Vega registered an easement allowing access from a farm to a public road and another for the state-owned power company. It

is unclear whether the offer made to Vega had anything to do with these transactions. See Departamento de Justicia, Registro de la Propiedad, San Sebastián, Ayuntamiento de Moca, Tomo 71, Folio 74.

71. Picó, *Los irrespetuosos*. Feelings of embarrassment were common; see *Associated Press*, 20 November 1995.

72. Wanga demand work. One aiming to control an errant lover might represent the offender as a doll bound to a chair with wire. The montage, however, will require care if it is to be of use. An oil lamp, for example, may be kept burning next to the object. Brown argues that Haitian immigrants in New York worked wanga to reclaim objects that symbolized their abuse at the hands of the police. When protesting the crimes against Abner Louima, Haitians took to the streets with toilet plungers—the object reported as the instrument of his rape. Words and names were also used as wanga. See K. Brown, "Making *Wanga*," 236–37 and 252.

BIBLIOGRAPHY

Archival Sources

CUBA

Archivo Nacional de Cuba, Havana
  Audiencia de la Habana
  Audiencia de Santiago de Cuba
  Registro de Asociaciones
Archivo Provincial de Santiago de Cuba
  Fondo Gobierno Provincial

Biblioteca Nacional José Martí, Havana
  Hemeroteca
Instituto de Literatura y Lingüística,
  Havana
  Hemeroteca

PUERTO RICO

Archivo General de Puerto Rico, San Juan
  Fondo Departamento de Estado
  Fondo Policía de Puerto Rico
Archivo Histórico Diocesano, San Juan
  Sección de Gobierno
Asociación Médica de Puerto Rico,
  San Juan
Centro de Investigaciones Sociales,
  Río Piedras
  Libros de Parroquias

Comandancia de la Policía, San Juan
Departamento de Justicia, San Sebastián
  Registro de la Propiedad
Universidad de Puerto Rico, Río Piedras
  Colección Puertorriqueña, Sistema
    de Bibliotecas
  Proyecto de Digitalización de la
    Colección de Fotos del

UNITED STATES

Library of Congress, Washington,
  DC
  Periodicals

National Archives, Washington, DC
  Record Group 140
  Record Group 350

Periodicals and Newspapers

CUBA

Bohemia	El Fígaro	El Mundo
Carteles	Gaceta de la Habana	El Mundo Ilustrado
El Día	Havana Post	La Opinión
Diario de la Marina	El Heraldo de Cuba	La Política Cómica
La Discusión	La Lucha	

PUERTO RICO

Boletín de la Asociación	La Democracia	El Mundo
Médica de Puerto Rico	Evidencia Ovni	El Nuevo Día
Boletín Eclesiástico	Evidencia Ovni Especial	Puerto Rico Ilustrado
El Buen Sentido	Guía Eclesiástica	San Juan News
Claridad	El Ideal Católico	San Juan Star
La Conciencia Libre	El Imparcial	El Tiempo
La Correspondencia	El Iris de Paz	El Vocero

UNITED STATES

Boston Globe	New York Times	Washington Post

Books, Articles, Pamphlets

Acosta, Ivonne. *Santa Juana y Mano Manca*. San Juan: Editorial Cultural, 1995.

Adas, Michael. *Prophets of Rebellion: Millenarian Protest Movements against the European Colonial Order*. Chapel Hill: University of North Carolina Press, 1979.

Agosto Cintrón, Nélida. "Género y discurso religioso en un movimiento carismático en Puerto Rico: La Madre Elenita de la Montaña Santa." In *Los arcos de la memoria: El '98 de los pueblos puertorriqueños*, edited by Silvia Alvarez-Curbelo, Mary Frances Gallart, and Carmen I. Raffucci de García, 193–207. San Juan: Postdata, 1998.

———. *Religión y cambio social en Puerto Rico, 1898–1940*. Río Piedras, PR: Ediciones Huracán, 1996.

Alvarez-Curbelo, Silvia. *Un país del porvenir: El afán de modernidad en Puerto Rico, siglo XIX*. San Juan: Ediciones Callejón, 2001.

Alvarez-Curbelo, Silvia, and María Elena Rodríguez Castro, eds. *Del nacionalismo al populismo: Cultura y política en Puerto Rico*. Río Piedras, PR: Ediciones Huracán, 1993.

Amselle, Jean-Loup. *Mestizo Logics: Anthropology of Identity in Africa and Elsewhere*. Translated by Claudia Royal. Stanford: Stanford University Press, 1998.

Anderson, Benedict. *Imagined Communities*. New York: Verson, 1993.

Anderson, David M., and Douglas Johnson, eds. *Revealing Prophets: Prophecy in Eastern African History*. London: James Currey, Ltd., 1995.

Andino, Telesforo. *El espiritismo en Puerto Rico y La Reforma*. San Juan: Tipografía San Juan, 1937.

Argüelles Mederos, Aníbal, and Ileana Hodge Limonta. *Los llamados cultos sincréticos y el espiritismo*. Havana: Editorial Academia, 1991.

Asad, Talal. *Formations of the Secular: Christianity, Islam, Modernity*. Stanford: Stanford University Press, 2003.

Auerbach, Nina. *Our Vampires, Ourselves*. Chicago: University of Chicago Press, 1995.

Austin-Broos, Diane. *Jamaica Genesis: Religion and the Politics of Moral Orders*. Chicago: University of Chicago Press, 1997.

Ayorinde, Christine. *Afro-Cuban Religiosity, Revolution, and National Identity*. Gainesville: University Press of Florida, 2004.

Bacardí y Moreau, Emilio. *Crónicas de Santiago de Cuba*. Vol. 10. Santiago de Cuba: Tipografía Arroyo Hermanos, 1924.

Baldrich, Juan José. *Sembraron la no siembra: Los cosecheros del tabaco puertorriqueños frente a las corporaciones tabacaleras, 1920–1934*. Río Piedras, PR: Huracán, 1988.

Barkun, Michael. *Disaster and the Millennium*. New Haven: Yale University Press, 1974.

Barreras y Martínez Malo, Antonio. *Textos de las constituciones de Cuba, 1812–1940*. Havana: Editorial Minerva, 1940.

Bastian, Misty L. "'Diabolic Realities': Conspiracy, Transparency and 'Ritual Murder' in the Nigerian Popular Print and Electronic Media." In *Transparency and Conspiracy*, edited by Harry G. West and Todd Sanders, 65–90. Durham: Duke University Press, 2003.

Bastide, Roger. *African Civilizations in the New World*. Translated by Peter Green. New York: Harper and Row, 1971.

———. *The African Religions of Brazil: Toward a Sociology of the Interpenetration of Civilizations*. Translated by Helen Sebba. Baltimore: Johns Hopkins University Press, 1978.

Bayron Toro, Fernando. *Elecciones y partidos políticos de Puerto Rico, 1809–1976*. Mayagüez, PR: Editorial Isla, 1977.

———. *Estadísticas de las elecciones municipales de Puerto Rico, 1900–1988*. Mayagüez, PR: Comisión Estatal de Elecciones, 1992.

Benítez-Rojo, Antonio. *The Repeating Island: The Caribbean and the Postmodern Perspective*. Translated by James E. Maraniss. Durham: Duke University Press, 1992.

Berenguer, Antonio, *Tradiciones villaclareñas*. Havana: n.p., 1929.

Bermúdez, Armando Andrés. "La expansión del espiritismo de cordón." *Revista de Etnología y Folklore* 5 (1968): 5–32.

———. "Notas para la historia del espiritismo en Cuba." *Revista de Etnología y Folklore* 4 (1967): 5–22.

Bernabé, Rafael. *Repuestas al colonialismo, 1899–1929*. Río Piedras, PR: Ediciones Huracán, 1996.

Borges, Dain. "Healing and Mischief: Witchcraft in Brazilian Law and Literature, 1890–1922." In *Crime and Punishment in Latin America*, edited by Carlos Aguirre, Gilbert Joseph, and Ricardo Salvatore, 181–210. Durham: Duke University Press, 2001.

Boyer, Paul, and Stephen Nissenbaum. *Salem Possessed: The Social Origins of Witchcraft*. Cambridge, MA: Harvard University Press, 1974.

Brandon, George. "African Influences in Cuba, Puerto Rico, and Hispaniola." *Journal of Caribbean Studies* 7, no. 2–3 (1989): 201–31.

Braude, Ann. *Radical Spirits: Spiritualism and Women's Rights in Nineteenth-Century America*. Boston: Beacon Press, 1989.

Briggs, Laura. *Reproducing Empire: Race, Sex, Science, and U.S. Imperialism in Puerto Rico*. Berkeley: University of California Press, 2002.

Bronfman, Alejandra. *Measures of Equality: Social Science, Citizenship, and Race in Cuba, 1902–1940*. Chapel Hill: University of North Carolina Press, 2004.

Brooke, John. *Civil Report of Major-General John R. Brooke, U.S. Army, Military Governor of Cuba*. Washington, DC: Government Printing Office, 1900.

Brown, David H. *The Light Inside*. Chicago: University of Chicago Press, 2003.

———. *Santería Enthroned*. Washington, DC: Smithsonian Books, 2003.

Brown, Diana De G. *Religion and Politics in Urban Brazil*. New York: Columbia University Press, 1986.

Brown, Karen McCarthy. "Making *Wanga*: Reality Constructions and the Magical Manipulation of Power." In *Transparency and Conspiracy*, edited by Harry G. West and Todd Sanders, 233–57. Durham: Duke University Press, 2003.

Burchell, Graham, Colin Gordon, and Peter Miller. *The Foucault Effect: Studies in Governmentality: With Two Lectures by and an Interview with Michel Foucault*. Chicago: University of Chicago Press, 1991.

Burton, Richard D. E. *Afro-Creole: Power, Opposition, and Play in the Caribbean*. Ithaca: Cornell University Press, 1997.

Butler, Jon. "The Dark Ages of American Occultism, 1760–1848." In *The Occult in America: New Historical Perspectives*, edited by Howard Kerr and Charles L. Crow, 59–75. Urbana: University of Illinois Press, 1983.

Cabrera, Lydia. *La medicina popular de Cuba: Médicos de antaño, curanderos, santeros y paleros de hogaño*. Miami: n.p., 1984.

Carrillo, Elizabeth, and Minerva Rodríguez. *Pentecostalismo y espiritismo*. Havana: Editorial Academia, 1997.

Carroll, Bret E. *Spiritualism in Antebellum America*. Bloomington: Indiana University Press, 1997.

Carroll, Michael P. *The Cult of the Virgin Mary: Psychological Origins*. Princeton, NJ: Princeton University Press, 1986.

Castellanos, Israel. "La brujería y el ñañiguismo desde el punto de vista médico legal." *Revista de Técnica Policial y Penitenciaria* 4 (1936): 83–186.

———. "Un diagnóstico criminológico." *Revista de Técnica Policial y Penitenciaria* 4 (1936): 203.

Centro de Investigaciones Psicológicas y Sociológicas. *La religión en la cultura*. Havana: Editorial Academia, 1990.

Certeau, Michel de. *The Practice of Everyday Life*. Translated by Steven Rendall. Los Angeles: University of California Press, 1988.

Chávez Alvarez, Ernesto. *El crimen de la niña Cecilia: La brujería como fenómeno social, 1902–1925*. Havana: Editorial de Ciencias Sociales, 1991.

Christian, William A., Jr. *Apparitions in Late Medieval and Renaissance Spain*. Princeton, NJ: Princeton University Press, 1981.

———. *Local Religion in Sixteenth-Century Spain*. Princeton, NJ: Princeton University Press, 1981.

———. *Moving Crucifixes in Modern Spain*. Princeton, NJ: Princeton University Press, 1992.

———. *Visionaries: The Spanish Republic and the Reign of Christ*. Berkeley: University of California Press, 1996.

Cohn, Norman. *The Pursuit of the Millennium*. Oxford: Oxford University Press, 1957.

Comaroff, Jean, and John L. Comaroff. "Alien Nation: Zombies, Immigrants, and Millennial Capitalism." *Codesria Bulletin* 3–4 (1999): 17–26.

———. "Occult Economies and the Violence of Abstraction: Notes from the South African Postcolony." *American Ethnologist* 26, no. 2 (1999): 279–303.

Cooper, Frederick, Thomas C. Holt, and Rebecca Scott. *Beyond Slavery: Explorations of Race, Labor, and Citizenship in Postemancipation Societies*. Chapel Hill: University of North Carolina Press, 2000.

Córdova Martínez, Carlos, and Oscar Barzaga Sablón. *El espiritismo de Cordón*. Havana: Fundación Fernando Ortiz, 2000.

Corrales, Scott. *Chupacabras and Other Mysteries*. Murfreesboro, TN: Greenleaf Publications, 1996.

Cuba. *The Penal Code in Force in Cuba and Porto Rico*. Washington, DC: Government Printing Office, 1901.

Cuéllar Vizcaíno, Manuel. *Doce muertes famosas*. Havana: Editorial Sánchez, 1957.

Dávila, Arlene M. *Sponsored Identities: Cultural Politics in Puerto Rico*. Philadelphia: Temple University Press, 1997.

Davis, Mike. "Monsters and Messiahs." *Grand Street Magazine*, no. 61. Also online at
<http://www.grandstreet.com/gsissues/gs61/gs61a.html>.

de la Fuente, Alejandro. "Myths of Racial Democracy: Cuba, 1900–1912." *Latin
American Research Review* 34, no. 3 (1999): 39–73.

———. *A Nation for All: Race, Inequality, and Politics in Twentieth-Century Cuba*.
Chapel Hill: University of North Carolina Press, 2001.

———. "Race, National Discourse, and Politics in Cuba: An Overview." *Latin American
Perspectives* 25, no. 3 (1998): 43–69.

Derby, Robin L. H. "Imperial Secrets: Vampires and Nationhood in Puerto Rico." In
Superstition in Historical and Comparative Perspective, edited by Steven Smith.
London: Past and Present, forthcoming.

———. "Vampiros del Imperio, o por qué el Chupacabras acecha a las Américas." In
Culturas imperiales, edited by Ricardo Salvatore, 300–345. Rosario, Argentina: Beatriz
Viterbo Editora, 2005.

Diacon, Todd A. *Millenarian Vision, Capitalist Reality: Brazil's Contestado Rebellion,
1912–1916*. Durham: Duke University Press, 1991.

Díaz-Quiñones, Arcadio. "Fernando Ortiz and Allan Kardec: Transmigration and Transculturation." In *The Cultures of the Hispanic Caribbean*, edited by Conrad James and
John Perivolaris, 9–27. Gainesville: University Press of Florida, 2000.

———. *La memoria rota: Ensayos sobre cultura y política*. 2nd ed. San Juan: Ediciones
Huracán, 1996.

Díaz Soler, Manuel. *Rosendo Matienzo Cintrón: Guardián de una cultura*. Río Piedras,
PR: Editorial de la Universidad de Puerto Rico, 1967.

Dietz, James L. *Economic History of Puerto Rico: Institutional Change and Capitalist
Development*. Princeton, NJ: Princeton University Press, 1986.

DIVEDCO. *La ciencia contra la superstición*. San Juan: División de Educación de la
Comunidad, 1951.

Dohen, Dorothy. *Two Studies of Puerto Rico: Religion Data and the Background of
Consensual Union*. Sondeos no. 3. Cuernavaca, Mexico: CIDOC, 1966.

Domínguez García, Julio. *Noticias de la república: Apuntes cronológicos, 1900–1929*.
Vol. 1. La Habana: Editorial de Ciencias Sociales, 2003.

Douglas, Mary. *Purity and Danger: An Analysis of the Concepts of Pollution and Taboo*.
London: Ark Paperbacks, 1985.

Duany, Jorge. "Making Indians Out of Blacks." In *Taino Revival*, edited by Gabriel
Haslip-Viera, 31–55. New York: Centro de Estudios Puertorriqueños, 1999.

———. *The Puerto Rican Nation on the Move: Identities on the Island and in the United
States*. Chapel Hill: University of North Carolina Press, 2002.

———. "La religiosidad popular en Puerto Rico: Reseña de la literatura desde la perspec-
tiva antropológica." In *Vírgenes, magos y escapularios*, edited by Angel G. Quintero
Rivera, 163–86. San Juan: Centro de Investigaciones Sociales, 1998.

Espinosa, Angel. *El destino de una criatura o la víctima de la superstición: Horrible asesinato perpetrado por los brujos del Gabriel en la infeliz niña Zoila Díaz*. Havana: Imprenta de M. Marrero, 1905.

Fenton, Jerry. *Understanding the Religious Background of the Puerto Rican*. Sondeos no. 52. Cuernavaca, Mexico: CIDOC, 1969.

Fernández Méndez, Eugenio, ed. *Portrait of a Society: Readings on Puerto Rican Sociology*. Río Piedras, PR: University of Puerto Rico Press, 1972.

Fernández Robaina, Tomás. *El negro en Cuba, 1902–1958*. Havana: Editorial de Ciencias Sociales, 1994.

Ferree, William, Ivan Illich, and Joseph P. Fitzpatrick, eds. *Spiritual Care of Puerto Rican Migrants*. Sondeos no. 74. Cuernavaca, Mexico: CIDOC, 1970.

Ferrer, Ada. *Insurgent Cuba: Race, Nation, and Revolution, 1868–1898*. Chapel Hill: University of North Carolina Press, 1999.

Fidelzait, Sarah, and Juan Pérez de la Riva. *San José de Sumidero: Demografía social en el campo cubano*. Havana: Editorial de Ciencias Sociales, 1987.

Fiedler, Leslie. *Freaks: Myths and Images of the Secret Self*. New York: Simon and Schuster, 1978.

Fields, Karen E. "Political Contingencies of Witchcraft in Colonial Central Africa: Culture and the State in Marxist Theory." *Revue canadienne des études africaines/Canadian Journal of African Studies* 16, no. 3 (1982): 567–93.

Fornet, Ambrosio. *El libro en Cuba: Siglos XVIII y XIX*. Havana: Editorial Letras Cubanas, 1994.

Foucault, Michel. *Power/Knowledge: Selected Interviews and Other Writings, 1972–1977*. Edited by Colin Gordon. New York: Pantheon Books, 1980.

García Muñiz, Humberto. "U.S. Military Installations in Puerto Rico: Controlling the Caribbean." In *Colonial Dilemma: Critical Perspectives on Contemporary Puerto Rico*, edited by Edgardo Meléndez, 53–66. Boston: South End Press, 1993.

Garrido Puello, Emigdio Osvaldo. *Olivorio, ensayo histórico*. Santo Domingo: Librera Dominicana, 1963.

Gerschiere, Peter. *The Modernity of Witchcraft: Politics and the Occult in Postcolonial Africa*. Translated by Peter Gerschiere and Janet Roitman. Charlottesville: University Press of Virginia, 1997.

Ginzburg, Carlo. *The Cheese and the Worms: The Cosmos of a Sixteenth-Century Miller*. Translated by John Tedeschi and Anne Tedeschi. New York: Penguin Books, 1982.

Glucklich, Ariel. *The End of Magic*. Oxford: Oxford University Press, 1997.

Gruzinski, Serge. *The Conquest of Mexico: The Incorporation of Indian Societies into the Western World, 16th–18th Centuries*. Translated by Eileen Corrigan. Cambridge, UK: Polity Press, 1993.

———. *Man-gods in the Mexican Highlands: Indian Power and Colonial Society, 1550–1800*. Translated by Eileen Corrigan. Stanford: Stanford University Press, 1989.

Habermas, Jürgen. *The Structural Transformation of the Public Sphere: An Inquiry into a Category of Bourgeois Society*. Translated by Thomas Burger with Frederick Lawrence. London: Polity Press, 1989.

Hagedorn, Katherine. *Divine Utterances: The Performance of Afro-Cuban Santería*. Washington, DC: Smithsonian Institution Press, 2001.

Harley, David. "Explaining Salem: Calvinist Psychology and the Diagnosis of Possession." *American Historical Review* 101, no. 2 (1996): 307–30.

Harris, W. W. *Puerto Rico's Fighting 65th U.S. Infantry: From San Juan to Chorwan*. San Rafael, CA: Presidio Press, 1980.

Helg, Aline. "Black Men, Racial Stereotyping, and Violence in the U.S. South and Cuba at the Turn of the Century." *Comparative Studies in Society and History* 42 (2000): 576–604.

———. *Our Rightful Share: The Afro-Cuban Struggle for Equality, 1886–1912*. Chapel Hill: University of North Carolina Press, 1995.

———. "Políticas raciales en Cuba después de la independencia: Represión de la cultura negra y el mito de la igualdad racial." *América Negra* 11 (1996): 65

Herzig Shannon, Nancy. *El Iris de Paz: El espiritismo y la mujer en Puerto Rico, 1900–1905*. Río Piedras, PR: Ediciones Huracán, 2001.

Hess, David. *Spirits and Scientists: Ideology, Spiritism, and Brazilian Culture*. University Park, PA: Pennsylvania State University Press, 1991.

Hill, Robert A. "Dread History: Leonard P. Howell and Millenarian Visions in Early Rastafari Religions in Jamaica." *Epoche* 9 (1981): 30–71.

Hobsbawm, Eric J. *Primitive Rebels: Studies in Archaic Forms of Social Movement in the 19th and 20th Centuries*. New York: W. W. Norton & Co., 1965.

Hobsbawm, Eric, and Terence Ranger. *The Invention of Tradition*. New York: Cambridge University Press, 1983.

Hodge Limonta, Ileana, and Minerva Rodríguez. *El espiritismo en Cuba: Percepción y exteriorización*. Havana: Editorial Academia, 1997.

Hostos, Adolfo de. *Tesauro de datos históricos*. Río Piedras, PR: Editorial de la Universidad de Puerto Rico, 1990.

Howard, Philip A. *Changing History: Afro-Cuban Cabildos and Societies of Color in the Nineteenth Century*. Baton Rouge: Louisiana State University Press, 1998.

Hurbon, Laënnec. *El bárbaro imaginario*. Translated by Jorge Padín Videla. Mexico City: Fondo de Cultura Económica, 1993.

———. "New Religious Movements in the Caribbean." In *New Religious Movements and Rapid Social Change*, edited by James A. Beckford, 146–76. Beverly Hills, CA: Sage Publications, 1986.

Ibarra, Jorge. *Prologue to Revolution: Cuba, 1898–1958*. Translated by Marjorie Moore. Boulder, Colo.: Lynne Rienner Publishers, 1998.

Iglesias Utset, Marial. *Las metáforas del cambio en la vida cotidiana: Cuba 1898–1902*. Havana: Ediciones Unión, 2003.

Ileto, Reynaldo Clemeña. *Pasyon and Revolution: Popular Movements in the Philippines, 1840–1910*. 4th ed. Manila: Ateneo de Manila University Press, 1997.

Instituto de Historia de Cuba. *La neocolonia: Organización y crisis desde 1899 hasta 1940*. Havana: Editora Política, 1998.

Jackson, John L., Jr. "The Soles of Black Folk: These Reeboks Were Made for Runnin' (From the White Man). In *Race and Race Consciousness*, edited by Judith J. Fossett and Jeffrey A. Tucker, 176–90. New York: New York University Press, 1997.

Kardec, Allan. *El génesis: Los milagros y las predicciones según el espiritismo*. Buenos Aires: Editorial Kier, 1994.

———. *El libro de los espíritus*. Mexico City: Editorial Diana, 1958.

———. *El libro de los mediums*. Mexico City: Editorial Orion, 1962.

Koss, Joan D. "El porqué de los cultos religiosos: El caso del espiritismo en Puerto Rico." *Revista de Ciencias Sociales* 16, no. 1 (1972): 61–72.

———. "Religion and Science Divinely Related: A Case History of Spiritism in Puerto Rico." *Caribbean Studies* 16, no. 1 (1976): 22–43.

Koss-Chioino, Joan D. *Women as Healers, Women as Patients: Mental Health Care and Traditional Healing in Puerto Rico*. Boulder, CO: Westview Press, 1992.

Lachatañeré, Rómulo. "Las creencias religiosas de los afrocubanos y la falsa aparición del término brujería." *Estudios Afrocubanos* 3, no. 1–4 (1939): 28–85.

Lago Vieito, Angel. "El espiritismo en la región oriental de Cuba en el siglo XIX." *Del Caribe* 35 (2001): 72–79.

———. *Fernando Ortiz y sus estudios acerca del Espiritismo en Cuba*. Havana: Centro de Investigación y Desarrollo de la Cultura Cubana Juan Marinello, 2002.

Lauria, Anthony, Jr. "'Respeto,' 'Relajo' and Inter-personal Relations in Puerto Rico." *Anthropological Quarterly* 37 (1964): 53–67.

Levine, Robert M. *Vale of Tears: Revisiting the Canudos Massacre in Northeastern Brazil, 1893–1897*. Berkeley: University of California Press, 1992.

López, Oscar Luis. *La radio en Cuba*. Havana: Editorial de Letras Cubanas, 1998.

López Cantos, Angel. *La religiosidad popular en Puerto Rico, siglo XVIII*. San Juan: Centro de Estudios Avanzados de Puerto Rico y el Caribe, 1993.

López Pulido, Alberto. "Sacred Expressions of the Popular: An Examination of Los Hermanos Penitentes of New Mexico and Los Hermanos Cheos of Puerto Rico." *Centro Journal* 16, no. 2 (2000): 57–69.

Lundius, Jan, and Mats Lundahl. *Peasants and Religion: A Socioeconomic Study of Dios Olivorio and the Palma Sola Movement in the Dominican Republic*. London: Routledge, 2000.

Marcus, George E., ed. *Paranoia within Reason: A Casebook on Conspiracy as Explanation*. Chicago: University of Chicago Press, 1999.

Marín y Pedraza, Raúl, and Ana Mercedes Aponte. *La Historia de San Lorenzo*. San Juan: n.p., 1986.

Márquez Sterling, Manuel. *Alrededor de nuestra psicología*. Havana: Imprenta Avisador Comercial, 1906.

Martín, Jorge. *La conspiración Chupacabras*. San Juan: CEDICOP, 1998.

Martín, Juan Luis. *Ecué, Changó y Yemayá: Ensayos sobre la sub-religión de los afro-cubanos*. Havana: Cultural S.A., 1930.

Martínez-Fernández, Luis. *Protestantism and Political Conflict in the Nineteenth-Century Hispanic Caribbean*. New Brunswick, NJ: Rutgers University Press, 2002.

Martínez Heredia, Fernando, Rebecca J. Scott, and Orlando F. García Martínez. *Espacios, silencios, y sentidos de la libertad: Cuba entre 1878 y 1912*. Havana: Ediciones Unión, 2001.

Matibag, Eugenio. *Afro-Cuban Religious Experience: Cultural Reflections in Narrative*. Gainesville: University Press of Florida, 1996.

Matienzo Cintrón, Rosendo. *Sobre espiritismo: Colección de artículos*. Ponce, PR: Tipografía Siglo XX, 1901.

McCaffery, John. *The Friar of San Giovanni: Tales of Padre Pio*. London: Darton, Longman & Todd, 1978.

McLeod, Marc. "Undesirable Aliens: Haitian and British West Indian Immigrant Workers in Cuba, 1898 to 1940." Ph.D. diss., University of Texas, Austin, 2000.

McMahon, Bucky. "Goatsucker Sighted, Details to Follow." *Outside Magazine* 21, no. 9 (1996): 92–100.

Méndez de Guzmán, Noelle. *La verdadera historia: Aparición de la Virgen del Rosario*. 3rd ed. San Juan: First Book Publishing Co., 1996.

Millet, José. *El espiritismo: Variantes cubanas*. Santiago de Cuba: Editorial Oriente, 1996.

———. "Sustrato cultural de la santería santiaguera." *Catauro: Revista Cubana de Antropología* 3, no. 2 (2001): 128–47.

Mintz, Sidney W. "The Caribbean as a Socio-Cultural Area." In *Peoples and Cultures of the Caribbean*, edited by Michael Horowitz, 17–46. Garden City, NY: Natural History Press, 1971.

Moore, R. Laurence. *In Search of White Crows: Spiritualism, Parapsychology, and American Culture*. New York: Oxford University Press, 1977.

Moore, Robin. *Nationalizing Blackness: Afrocubanismo and Artistic Revolution in Havana, 1920–1940*. Pittsburgh: University of Pittsburgh Press, 1997.

Moore, Sally Falk. "Reflections on the Comaroff Lecture." *American Ethnologist* 26, no. 2 (1999): 303–6.

Moreno Vega, Marta. "Espiritismo in the Puerto Rican Community: A New World

Recreation with the Elements of Kongo Ancestor Worship." *Journal of Black Studies* 29, no. 3 (1999): 325–53.

Murga, Vicente. *Historia documental de Puerto Rico*. Vol. 1. Río Piedras, PR: Editorial Plus Ultra, 1973.

Nandy, Ashis, and Shiv Visvanathan. "Modern Medicine and Its Non-modern Critics: A Study in Discourse." In *The Savage Freud and Other Essays on Possible and Retrievable Selves*, edited by Ashis Nandy, 145–95. Princeton, NJ: Princeton University Press, 1995.

Niehaus, Isak. "Witches and Zombies of the South African Lowveld: Discourse, Accusations and Subjective Reality." *Journal of the Royal Anthropological Institute* 11 (2005): 191–210.

Office of the Commonwealth of Puerto Rico. *Documents on the Constitutional History of Puerto Rico*. 1948. Reprint, Washington, DC: n.p., 1964.

Ortiz, Fernando. "Buscando Luz en Monte Oscuro." *Bohemia* 42, no. 17 (23 April 1950): 20–23, 113–15, 121.

———. *Contrapunteo cubano del tabaco y del azúcar*. Havana: Consejo Nacional de la Cultura, 1963.

———. "En el Solar de la Prieta." *Bohemia* 41, no. 20 (15 May 1949): 20–22, 88–89.

———. "Los espirituales cordoneros del orilé." *Bohemia* 42, no. 5 (29 April 1950): 20–22, 118–19, 122–23.

———. *Las fases de la evolución religiosa*. Havana: Tipografía Moderna, 1919.

———. *La filosofía penal de los espiritistas*. 4th ed. Madrid: Editorial Reus, 1924.

———. *La hampa afrocubana: Los negros brujos*. 1906. Reprint, Havana: Editorial de Ciencias Sociales, 1995.

———. *Historia de una pelea cubana contra los demonios*. Havana: Editorial de Ciencias Sociales, 1975.

———. "Los muertos sacaos." *Bohemia* 42, no. 11 (12 March 1950): 28–31, 112–15, 140.

———. "Orígenes de los cordoneros del orilé." *Bohemia* 42, no. 23 (9 July 1950): 34–36, 105–7.

———. "La Paz del Mundo en Bayamo, o el Caney de los Espíritus." *Bohemia* 41, no. 12 (March 1949): 28–30, 97–99.

———. "Lo que no hay en Guantánamo." *Bohemia* 41, no. 8 (February 1949): 4–6, 106–7, 109–12.

———. "Tata Mbumba, mi colega en Songo." *Bohemia* 41, no. 26 (26 June 1949): 28–30, 98–100.

———. "Una moderna secta espiritista de Cuba." *Bohemia* 42, no. 3 (15 January 1950): 8–9, 137–39.

———. "Una cubana danza de los muertos." *Bohemia*, 42, no. 7 (12 February 1950): 28–31, 107, 110–11.

———. "La Virgen de Jiquiabo." *Archivos del Folklore Cubano* 1 (1930): 34–39.

Palmié, Stephan. "Ethnogenetic Processes and Cultural Transfer in Afro-American Slave Populations." In *Slavery in the Americas*, edited by W. Binder, 337–63. Würtzburg: Königshausen u. Neumann, 1993.

———. *Wizards and Scientists: Explorations in Afro-Cuban Modernity and Tradition.* Durham: Duke University Press, 2001.

Paralitici, Che. *No quiero mi cuerpo pa' tambor: El servicio militar obligatorio en Puerto Rico.* San Juan: Ediciones Puerto, 1998.

Parish, Jane, and Martin Parker. *The Age of Anxiety: Conspiracy Theory and the Human Sciences.* Oxford: Blackwell/Sociological Review, 2001.

Pedreira, Antonio S. *El periodismo en Puerto Rico.* Río Piedras, PR: Editorial Edil, 1969.

Pérez, Louis A., Jr. *Cuba: Between Reform and Revolution.* New York: Oxford University Press, 1988.

———. *Cuba between Empires, 1878–1902.* Pittsburgh: University of Pittsburgh Press, 1982.

———. *Essays on Cuban History: Historiography and Research.* Gainesville: University Press of Florida, 1995.

———. *Lords of the Mountain: Social Banditry and Peasant Protest in Cuba, 1878–1918.* Pittsburgh: University of Pittsburgh Press, 1989.

———. "Politics, Peasants, and People of Color: The 1912 'Race War' in Cuba Reconsidered." *Hispanic American Historical Review* 66 (1986): 509–39.

Pérez García, Marvette. "Spiritism: Historical Development in France and Puerto Rico." *Revista/Review Interamericana* 16, no. 1–4 (1986): 67–76.

Pérez-Stable, Marifeli. *The Cuban Revolution: Origins, Course, and Legacy.* New York: Oxford University Press, 1993.

Pérez y Mena, Andrés Isidoro. *Speaking with the Dead: Development of Afro-Latin Religion among Puerto Ricans in the United States: A Study into the Interpenetration of Civilizations in the New World.* New York: AMS Press, 1991.

Pessar, Patricia. *From Fanatics to Folks: Brazilian Millenarianism and Popular Culture.* Durham: Duke University Press, 2004.

Picó, Fernando. "El catolicismo popular en el Puerto Rico del siglo 19." In *Vírgenes, magos y escapularios: Imaginería, etnicidad y religiosidad popular en Puerto Rico*, edited by Angel G. Quintero Rivera, 151–62. San Juan: Centro de Investigaciones Sociales, 1998.

———. *La guerra después de la guerra.* Río Piedras, PR: Ediciones Huracán, 1987.

———. *Historia general de Puerto Rico.* Río Piedras, PR: Ediciones Huracán, 1988.

———. *Los irrespetuosos.* Río Piedras, PR: Ediciones Huracán, 2000.

———. *Libertad y servidumbre en el Puerto Rico del siglo XIX: Los jornaleros utuadeños en vísperas del auge del café.* Río Piedras, PR: Ediciones Huracán, 1979.

———. "Religiosidad institucional y religiosidad popular en el siglo 19." *Revista Universidad de América* 6 (1994): 36–38.

Pino Santos, Oscar. *Los años 50: En una Cuba que algunos añoran, otros no quieren ni recordar y los más desconocen.* Havana: Instituto Cubano del Libro, 2001.

Ponte Jiménez, Francisco. "Desarrollo del espiritismo en Puerto Rico: Federación de los Espiritistas." In *El Libro de Puerto Rico*, edited by Eugenio Fernández García, 890–94. San Juan: El Libro Azul Publishing Co., 1923.

Portuondo Zúñiga, Olga. *La Virgen de la Caridad del Cobre: Símbolo de cubanía.* Santiago de Cuba: Editorial Oriente, 1995.

Pozo, Miguel Alfonso. *Hacia la felicidad: Un viaje a través de los astros.* Havana: n.p., n.d.

Primelles, León. *Crónica cubana, 1919–1922.* Vol. 2. Havana: Editorial Lex, 1957.

Quevedo Báez, Manuel. *Historia de la medicina y cirugía en Puerto Rico.* 2 vols. San Juan: Asociación Médica de Puerto Rico, 1946–49.

Quílez Vicente, José. *El bohío de Mamá Coleta: El crimen de santería más espeluzanante de todos los tiempos recogido en un reportaje.* Havana: Editorial La Habana, 1944.

Quintero Rivera, Angel G., ed. *Vírgenes, magos y escapularios: Imaginería, etnicidad y religiosidad popular en Puerto Rico.* San Juan: Centro de Investigaciones Sociales, 1998.

Raffucci de García, Carmen I. *El gobierno civil y la Ley Foraker: Antecedentes históricos.* Río Piedras, PR: Editorial Universitaria, 1981.

Rama, Angel. *La ciudad letrada.* Hanover, NH: Ediciones del Norte, 1984.

Redacción Noticiosa. *La verdadera historia del chupacabras.* San Juan: Redacción Noticiosa, 1996.

Reyes, Jaime M. F. *La Santa Montaña de San Lorenzo, Puerto Rico y el misterio de Elenita de Jesús, 1899–1909.* Mexico: n.p., 1992.

Ricardo, José G. *La imprenta en Cuba.* Havana: Editorial de Letras Cubanas, 1989.

Roche Monteagudo, Rafael. *La policía y sus misterios en Cuba.* 1908. Reprint, Havana: La Moderna Poesía, 1925.

Rodríguez, Daniel R. *La primera evangelización norteamericana en Puerto Rico, 1898–1930.* Rochester, NY: Ediciones Borinquen, 1986.

Rodríguez Escudero, Néstor. *Historia del espiritismo en Puerto Rico.* 2nd ed. Quebradillas, PR: Imprenta San Rafael, 1991.

Rodríguez Morales, Herminio R. *San Lorenzo: Notas para su historia.* San Juan: n.p., 1985.

Rodríguez Pérez, Liliam del Carmen. "La obra de los hermanos Cheos, 1902–1927." Master's thesis, Centro de Estudios Avanzados de Puerto Rico y el Caribe, 1994.

Román, Reinaldo L. "Conjuring Progress and Divinity: Religion and Conflict in Cuba and Puerto Rico, 1899–1956." Ph.D. diss., UCLA, Department of History, 2000.

———. "Spiritists versus Spirit-mongers: Julia Vázquez and the Struggle for Progress in 1920s Puerto Rico." *Centro Journal* 14, no. 2 (2002): 5–25.

Romberg, Raquel. "From Charlatans to Saviors: *Espiritistas, Curanderos,* and *Brujos* Inscribed in Discourses of Progress and Heritage." *Centro Journal* 15, no. 2 (2003): 146–73.

———. *Witchcraft and Welfare: Spiritual Capital and the Business of Magic in Modern Puerto Rico.* Austin: University of Texas Press, 2003.

Romeu, José A. *Panorama del periodismo puertorriqueño.* Río Piedras, PR: Editorial de la Universidad de Puerto Rico, 1985.

Rosa-Nieves, Cesáreo, and Esther M. Melón. *Biografías Puertorriqueñas: Perfil histórico de un pueblo.* Sharon, Conn.: Troutman Press, 1970.

Sánchez Lussón, José. "Los cordoneros de orilé: Presencia histórica y alcance cultural en Manzanillo." *Del Caribe* 25 (1996): 20–22.

San Lorenzo. Barrio Hato. 1920 U.S. Census, population schedule. Micropublication T625, roll 2066. Washington, DC: National Archives.

San Lorenzo. Pueblo. 1930 U.S. Census, population schedule. Micropublication T626, roll 2663. Washington, DC: National Archives.

Santaella Rivera, Esteban. *Historia de los Hermanos Cheos: Recopilación de escritos y relatos.* Ponce, PR: Editorial Alfa y Omega, 1979.

Santiago, Juan José. "Allan Kardec: Una lectura crítica de sus escritos." Paper delivered at the Museo Puertorriqueño de Antropología Religiosa, San Juan, 4 October 1994.

———. "The Spiritistic Doctrine of Allan Kardec: A Phenomenological Study." Ph.D. diss., Gregorian University, Rome, 1983.

Santiago-Valles, Kelvin A. *"Subject People" and Colonial Discourses: Economic Transformation and Social Disorder in Puerto Rico, 1989–1947.* Albany: SUNY Press, 1994.

Sartorius, David. "Limits of Loyalty: Race and the Public Sphere in Cienfuegos, Cuba, 1845–1898." Ph.D. diss., University of North Carolina, Chapel Hill, 2003.

Scarano, Francisco. "The *Jíbaro* Masquerade and the Subaltern Politics of Creole Identity Formation in Puerto Rico, 1745–1823." *American Historical Review* 101, no. 5: 1398–1431.

Scheper-Hughes, Nancy. "The Global Traffic in Human Organs." *Current Anthropology* 41, no. 2 (2000): 191–224.

Schwartz, Stuart B. "The Hurricane of San Ciriaco: Disaster, Politics, and Society in Puerto Rico, 1899–1901." *Hispanic American Historical Review* 72, no. 3 (1992): 303–34.

Scott, David. *Refashioning Futures: Criticism after Postcoloniality.* Princeton, NJ: Princeton University Press, 1999.

Scott, James. *Seeing Like a State: How Certain Schemes to Improve the Human Condition Have Failed.* New Haven: Yale University Press, 1998.

Scott, Rebecca J. *Slave Emancipation in Cuba: The Transition to Free Labor, 1860–1899.* Princeton, NJ: Princeton University Press, 1985.

Silva Gotay, Samuel. *Catolicismo y política en Puerto Rico bajo España y Estados Unidos: Siglos XIX y XX.* San Juan: Editorial de la Universidad de Puerto Rico, 2005.

———. "El Partido Acción Cristiana: Trasfondo histórico y significado sociológico del nacimiento y muerte de un partido político católico en Puerto Rico." *Cristianismo y Sociedad* 108 (1991): 95–116.

———. *Protestantismo y política, 1898–1930: Hacia una historia del protestantismo evangélico en Puerto Rico.* Río Piedras, PR: Editorial de la Universidad de Puerto Rico, 1997.

Silvestrini, Blanca. "El impacto de la política de salud pública de los Estados Unidos en Puerto Rico, 1898–1913." In *Politics, Society, and Culture in the Caribbean*, edited by Blanca G. Silvestrini, 69–83. San Juan: Editorial de la Universidad de Puerto Rico, 1983.

———. *Violencia y criminalidad en Puerto Rico, 1898–1973.* Río Piedras, PR: Editorial Universitaria, 1980.

Smorkaloff, Pamela Maria. *Readers and Writers in Cuba: A Social History of Print Culture, 1830s–1990s.* New York: Garland Publishing, 1997.

Stevens-Arroyo, Anthony M., and Ana María Díaz-Stevens. *An Enduring Flame: Studies on Latino Popular Religiosity.* New York: Bindner Center for Western Hemisphere Studies, 1994.

Steward, Julian H., and others. *The People of Puerto Rico: A Study in Social Anthropology.* Urbana: University of Illinois Press, 1956.

Stoler, Ann. "'In Cold Blood': Hierarchies of Credibility and the Politics of Colonial Narratives." *Representations* 37 (1992): 151–89.

Suárez, Francisca. *Nuestra réplica al artículo del Dr. don Manuel Guzmán Rodríguez titulado "La Religión del Porvenir" y publicado en el periódico "El Imparcial" de esta ciudad.* Mayagüez, PR: Tipografía Comercial, 1892.

Suárez-Findlay, Eileen J. *Imposing Decency: The Politics of Sexuality and Race in Puerto Rico, 1870–1920.* Durham: Duke University Press, 1999.

Taussig, Michael T. *The Devil and Commodity Fetishism in South America.* Chapel Hill: University of North Carolina, 1980.

———. *Shamanism, Colonialism, and the Wild Man: A Study in Terror and Healing.* Chicago: University of Chicago Press, 1987.

Tolezano García, Tania, and Ernesto Chávez Alvarez. "Estudio sobre un caso de movimiento mesiánico en Cuba." *Del Caribe* 5, no. 13 (1989): 30–37.

———. *La leyenda de Antoñica Izquierdo.* Havana: Editorial de Ciencias Sociales, 1987.

Torres Oliver, Rafael. "Datos sobre 'Nuestra Madre' obtenidos en los Barrios Espino y Jagual de San Lorenzo." Personal paper, April 1966. Photocopy.

Trías Monge, José. *Puerto Rico: The Trials of the Oldest Colony in the World.* New Haven: Yale University Press, 1997.

Trigo, Benigno. "Anemia and Vampires: Figures to Govern the Colony, Puerto Rico, 1880 to 1904." *Comparative Studies in Society and History* 41, no. 1 (1999): 104–23.

Tumin, Melvin M., and Arnold S. Feldman. "The Miracle at Sabana Grande." In *Portrait of a Society: Readings on Puerto Rican Sociology*, edited by Eugenio Fernández Méndez, 355–69. Río Piedras, PR: University of Puerto Rico Press, 1972.

Turner, Patricia. *I Heard It through the Grapevine: Rumor in African-American Culture*. Berkeley: University of California Press, 1993.

Turner, Victor. *The Drums of Affliction: A Study of Religious Processes among the Ndembu of Zambia*. Oxford, UK: Clarendon Press, 1968.

Tweed, Thomas A. *Our Lady of the Exile: Diasporic Religion at a Cuban Catholic Shrine*. New York: Oxford University Press, 1997.

United States War Department. *Civil Report of Brigadier General Leonard Wood, Military Governor of Cuba, for the period from January 1 to May 20, 1902*. 6 vols. Washington, DC: Government Printing Office, 1902.

Vanderwood, Paul. *The Power of God Against the Guns of Government: Religious Upheaval in Mexico at the Turn of the Nineteenth Century*. Stanford: Stanford University Press, 1998.

Van Young, Eric, "The Messiah and the Masked Man: Popular Ideology in Mexico, 1810–1821." In *Indigenous Responses to Western Christianity*, edited by Steven Kaplan, 144–73. New York: New York University Press, 1995.

Vázquez, Carmen Julia. "La Samaritana de San Lorenzo, doña Julia Vázquez." Personal paper, n.d. Photocopy.

Veer, Peter van der, and Lehman, Hartmut. *Nation and Religion: Perspectives on Europe and Asia*. Princeton, NJ: Princeton University Press, 1999.

Wallace, Anthony F. C. "Revitalization Movements." *American Anthropologist* 58 (1958): 264–81.

White, Luise. "Alien Nation." *Transition* 63 (1994): 24–33.

———. *Speaking with Vampires: Rumor and History in Colonial Africa*. Berkeley: University of California Press, 2000.

———. "The Traffic in Heads: Bodies, Borders and the Articulation of Regional Histories." *Journal of Southern African Studies* 23, no. 2 (1997): 325–38.

Wilson, Ian. *Stigmata: An Investigation into the Mysterious Appearance of Christ's Wounds in Hundreds of People from Medieval Italy to Modern America*. San Francisco: Harper & Row, 1989.

Wiltenburg, Joy. "True Crime: The Origins of Modern Sensationalism." *American Historical Review* 109, no. 5 (2004): 1377–1404.

XXX [pseudonym]. *La brujería y los brujos de Cuba*. Havana: Imprenta de "El Cubano," 1900.

Yáñez Vda. de Otero, Teresa. *El espiritismo en Puerto Rico: Relación Histórica de la Fundación en Mayagüez de la Federación de Espiritistas de Puerto Rico.* San Juan: n.p., 1963.

Zayas Micheli, Luis O. *Catolicismo popular en Puerto Rico: Una explicación sociológica.* Ponce, PR: n.p., 1990.

INDEX

Kardec, Allan (Hippolite Léon Denizard Rivail), 24, 32–34, 108, 111–12, 122. *See also* Spiritism
Knights of Columbus, 120
Korean War, 141, 169–70
Koss, Joan, 112

Landa, Manuel, 96, 99–100
Lay, Emilio, 30. *See also* Man-gods
Lázaro, Saint, 92
Leaflet war, 120
Ley de fugas, 13
Liberal Party, Cuba, 16–17, 94
Lola Rodríguez de Tió elementary school, 189–91
La Loma de San Juan, 44. *See also* El Cerro, Cuba
Lombroso, Cesare, 74, 225 (n. 93). *See also* Brujería: constitution of
López, José, 171, 189
López, María Faustina, 97
Lottery, 137, 139
Lugo-Viña, Ruy, 102
Lynchings: in Cuba, 7, 19, 82, 83, 99, 103; in South Africa, 196

Maceo, Antonio, 30, 96
Madero, Francisco, 109
Magnetic passes, 41, 43, 45 (ill.), 113, 145, 153. *See also* Spiritism: practices and tenets
Mañach, Jorge, 151, 155–56
Man-gods, 23, 24, 28–32, 49, 51–52, 80, 217 (n. 1); and disasters, 29; race relations, 24, 30, 47. *See also* Elenita; Manso Estévez, Juan; Morales, José de los Santos; Mustelier Garzón, Hilario
Manso Estévez, Juan, 23, 44–48; arrests of, 44–46; links to Hilario Mustelier, 48; practices of, 25–26, 37, 40, 45, 47–48, 220

(n. 74); press coverage of, 23–24, 44–48, 51; titles of, 23, 40, 45; trip to Puerto Rico, 51
María Inocencia, 163
Marooned ethnicity, 48, 68
Márquez Sterling, Manuel, 18, 46, 94–95. *See also* Press: governing functions of; Press: Press Association, Cuba
Marriage: in Cuba, 12; in Puerto Rico, 53, 55–57, 61, 63, 77
Martín, Jorge, 198, 204. *See also* Chupacabras: and conspiracy theories; EBAs; UFOs
Martínez Lugo, Santía, 162, 163. *See also* Virgen de Sabana Grande: seers of
Matanzas, Cuba, 19, 44, 45, 82–83, 94, 134

Mateo, Olivorio (Dios Olivorio), 29, 111
Matienzo Cintrón, Rosendo, 51, 67, 73, 108–9, 110, 221 (n. 2)
Mayagüez, Puerto Rico, 61, 107, 167
Mayarí, Cuba, 30
McManus, James Edward (bishop), 162–63, 171
Médica de Puerta de Tierra, 112
Medical Association, Puerto Rico, 165
Medina, Leocadio, 186
Méndez de Guzmán, Noelle, 172
Mesmerism, 32
Milagros, 160
Miles, Gen. Nelson, 9
Millenarianism, 28–29, 52, 54, 70–72, 115, 181, 184, 191
Millennial capitalism, 4. *See also* Occult economies
The Miracle of Our Lady of Fatima, 166–68
Miracles: making of, 29, 130–31, 158–59, 160–61, 162, 185
Misiones: church-led, 166, 169; and lay preachers, 9, 10, 12, 28–29, 52, 54–55,